Crime Science and Digital Forensics

A Holistic View

Editors

Anthony C. Ijeh

Founder and Director
DASCROSE Limited
England, United Kingdom

Kevin Curran

Professor of Cyber Security
Ulster University
Northern Ireland, United Kingdom

CRC Press
Taylor & Francis Group
Boca Raton London New York

CRC Press is an imprint of the
Taylor & Francis Group, an **informa** business

A SCIENCE PUBLISHERS BOOK

First edition published 2021
by CRC Press
6000 Broken Sound Parkway NW, Suite 300, Boca Raton, FL 33487-2742

and by CRC Press
2 Park Square, Milton Park, Abingdon, Oxon, OX14 4RN

© 2021 Taylor & Francis Group, LLC

CRC Press is an imprint of Taylor & Francis Group, LLC

Library of Congress Cataloging-in-Publication Data

Names: Ijeh, Anthony C., 1971- editor. | Curran, Kevin, 1969- editor.
Title: Crime science and digital forensics : a holistic view / editors,
    Anthony C. Ijeh, Kevin Curran.
Description: Boca Raton : CRC Press, 2021. | Includes bibliographical
    references and index. | Summary: "Crime science and digital forensics: A
    holistic view, is a collation of articles which contribute to the
    discourse on counter forensic practices and digital investigative
    methods from a crime science perspective. The book also shares
    alternative dialogue on information security techniques used to protect
    data from unauthorised access and manipulation. Scandals at OPCW and
    Gatwick Airport have reinforced the importance of Crime Science and the
    need to take proactive measures rather than a wait and see approach
    currently used by many organisations. The book is intended as a platform
    for showcasing a new approach to dealing with cybercrime and unsociable
    behaviour involving remote technologies"-- Provided by publisher.
Identifiers: LCCN 2021000944 | ISBN 9780367322557 (hardcover)
Subjects: LCSH: Criminal investigation. | Forensic sciences. | Digital
    forensic science. | Computer crimes--Investigation.
Classification: LCC HV8073 .C69365 2021 | DDC 363.250285--dc23
LC record available at https://lccn.loc.gov/2021000944

ISBN: 978-0-367-32255-7 (hbk)
ISBN: 978-0-367-77499-8 (pbk)
ISBN: 978-0-429-32287-7 (ebk)

Typeset in Times New Roman
by Radiant Productions

Preface

Crime science and digital forensics: A holistic view, is a collation of articles which contribute to the discourse on forensic practices and digital investigations from a crime science perspective. The book also shares alternative dialogue on cybersecurity and techniques used to protect data from unauthorised access and manipulation.

Scandals at OPCW and Gatwick Airport have reinforced the importance of crime science and the need to take proactive security measures rather than a wait and see approach, currently used by many organisations. This book is intended as a platform for showcasing new approaches to dealing with cybercrime and delivering digital investigations. It offers innovative approaches to crime analysis and prevention involving autonomous technology and a combination of evidence-based disciplines for digital forensic investigations, cybersecurity strategies, and policy frameworks.

The book is made up of a series of 12 chapters, structured in 3 areas on crime science, digital forensics, and cybersecurity. Each chapter features a literature review, implications for practice, policy, theory, and discussion of future directions. The essence of a holistic view is brought about by the challenge facing todays forensic and digital security professionals within industry were traditional practices are unable to provide satisfactory evidence or security. This book will be of much interest to students, academics and practitioners of digital security, forensics, and cybersecurity. It marks a new route in the study of combined disciplines to tackle and prevent crime using varied technologies and crime science.

Editors
Anthony C. Ijeh
Kevin Curran

Acknowledgement

The editors acknowledge and thank all authors and contributors for their effort and contributions.

As editors, we would also like to thank CRC Press Publications; especially the team that worked for the book to be completed.

Finally, the editors thank all readers of Crime Science and Digital Forensics: A Holistic View, for their interest in the book and encourage them to continue to send their invaluable feedback and ideas for further improvement of the book.

Contents

Part 1
Crime Science

1

Unraveling the Notre-Dame Cathedral Fire in Space and Time

An X-coherence Approach

Rafael Padilha, Fernanda A Andaló, Luís A M Pereira
and *Anderson Rocha**

1. Introduction

We live in a connected world, where events taking place across the globe often have the power to impact our daily lives. Such events reach us and are broadcasted by us in the form of visual and textual content, generating a massive unstructured pool of data. A paramount example is a recent blaze that struck the Notre-Dame Cathedral, an ancient Parisian architectural and religious symbol. In April 2019, a fire tore through the cathedral, devastating large parts of its structure and spire (Figure 1). People worldwide followed the tragic event through millions of images and videos that were shared by the media and everyday citizens, at the same time that part of the structure turned to dust.

The content generated from unprecedented events, such as the Notre-Dame fire, is potentially important to document our history and also as a source of information for investigations. This content, however, naturally comes from heterogeneous sources, often times lacking proper structure, as to where and when it was captured and how it is connected with other pieces of information. An effective way of understanding an event is to create a structure for this type of data by constructing a unified space where all pieces of related information can be coherently organized.

Institute of Computing, University of Campinas.
* Corresponding author: anderson.rocha@ic.unicamp.br

Figure 1: Notre-Dame Cathedral during a massive blaze that destroyed part of its structure and spire, in April 2019. Credit: Milliped [CC BY-SA 4.0] and Francois Guillot/AFP/Getty.

The process of synchronizing data by positioning its items in a common consistent system is called *X-coherence* (Ferreira et al. 2019). The idea is that by properly organizing an event's data, it is possible to navigate through it, understand how it unravels in time and space, and even observe the timeline for a specific person or object within the same context. *X-Coherence* could aid, for instance, fact-checking and the mining of suspects in forensic investigations.

Although achieving *X-coherence* for an event is beneficial, performing it manually might be an unfeasible task, given the large volume of data to be processed within a reasonable timeframe. Even worse is the possibility of a person interfering with the process by introducing unconscious bias, consequently invalidating the constructed space and any conclusions drawn from it. One such example is an unprecedented manhunt that followed the Boston Marathon Bombings, in April 2013. After two bombs exploded near the marathon finish line, several people tried to find the bombers by analyzing thousands of images and videos captured at the event, which turned into a major failure (Surowiecki 2013).

A way to overcome these problems is to automate the *X-coherence* process as much as possible, allowing the effective organization of all data generated from an event, while also mitigating possible biases. To this end, in this chapter, we show how state-of-the-art machine learning techniques can be used to achieve the *X-coherence*, by automatically sorting an unstructured collection of images, in space and time, while also providing a joint visualization system to understand the event as a whole.

We consider the Notre-Dame fire as the backdrop of our research and, for this, we gathered images and videos of the tragic event from social and mainstream media. For a given subset of annotated imagery from the same event, we train convolution neural networks (CNNs) to capture important visual clues to place each data item in space and time. The trained models can then be used to organize new images as well as placing them in a common coherent space for visualization.

Works in the literature focus on different tasks related to *X-coherence*. Considering the spatial ordering of images, Snavely et al. 2008 presented an interface to explore unstructured collections of photographs, by computing the viewpoint of each photograph as well as a sparse 3D model of the scene.

For temporal ordering, Schindler et al. 2007 described how to sort a collection of photos spanning many years, by extracting time-varying 3D models. Volokitin et al. 2016 studied the effectiveness of CNN features to predict the time of the year in an outdoor scene. For video sequences, Lameri et al. 2014 proposed a method to splice together sets of near-duplicate shots, thus aligning them temporally, in order to reconstruct a complete video sequence for an event.

Some works focus specifically on how to visualize data from events (Chung et al. 2005; Deligiannidis et al. 2008; Reinders et al. 2001), avoiding information overload and failure to indicate overall trends when analyzing events.

Different from these works, our goal is to explicitly and thoroughly tackle the problem of achieving the *X-coherence* for an event. For this, our main contributions are:

- A method for positioning images of an event in space, assigning them to different cardinal directions in relation to the event center;
- A method for placing images of an event to specific timeframes determined by important sub-events;
- A visualization approach to coherently represent images of an event in space and time.

Although we demonstrate these contributions on a specific event—the Notre-Dame Cathedral fire, we emphasize that the proposed methods and methodology can be applied to similar events, in which images are captured in different positions and angles around and throughout an event.

2. Proposed Solution

To solve the *X-coherence* for the Notre-Dame fire event, we divide the process into three steps: spatial classification, temporal classification, and visualization (Figure 2).

In the spatial and temporal classification steps, which can occur simultaneously, the input image is positioned in space and time by the analysis of its content. For spatial classification, a cardinal direction is assigned to the image depending on the location where the image was captured in relation to the cathedral. During temporal

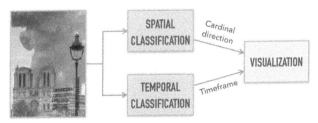

Figure 2: *X-coherence* solution for the Notre-Dame Fire event. For each available image, the method classifies it regarding its spatial position and temporal order. The spatial classification step assigns a cardinal direction to the image, depending on its position in relation to the cathedral. In temporal classification, the method defines a timeframe for the image with respect to important sub-events.

classification, our method detects when the image was taken in relation to important sub-events, such as the spire collapsing and the fire being extinguished.

Finally, the visualization step gathers the previously inferred information for all available images and represents them in a coherent space, allowing a better understanding of the event.

2.1 Spatial Classification

During a critical event, such as the fire that devastated the Notre-Dame Cathedral, people tend to capture images and videos from all possible locations overlooking the event. When this content is uploaded to social media or is made available by the press, metadata (such as time of capture and GPS coordinates) is generally lost. The only way to have this information is by inferring it from the content of the images.

In the spatial classification step, we aim at determining the cardinal direction of the cathedral's facade—*south, southwest, west, northwest, north, northeast, east,* or *southeast*—which was captured in an input image. Depending on the parts of the cathedral that appear on the image, it may not be possible to reliably infer spatial information due to the lack of spatial clues. In order to circumvent this problem, we train our method to classify this kind of input as having an *"unknown"* direction.

Figure 3a shows, on a map of the event's location, the possible positions from where an image could have been taken during the event and to which cathedral's facade each position is associated. Figure 3b depicts some examples of images capturing different facades of the cathedral during the event.

Our solution for this step consists in training a convolutional neural network (CNN) to associate image content (the cathedral's facade) to a cardinal direction, among the nine possibilities (including the *"unknown"* class). We rely upon the Inception-ResNetv2 architecture (Szegedy et al. 2017) and its pre-trained weights on the ImageNet dataset. This architecture mixes two state-of-the-art ideas—inception

(a) Possible camera positions and associated cardinal directions, in relation to the cathedral.

(b) Examples for each cardinal direction.

Figure 3: Cardinal directions for the spatial classification step: *south, southwest, west, northwest, north, northeast, east,* or *southeast.*

modules and residual connections, which allows a faster training process of much deeper networks, resulting in better results for classification tasks.

To adapt the network to our task, we add a dropout layer to the network output, with a rate of 0.7, in order to regularize the training process, and modify its fully-connected layer to the number of classes of this task. Then, we train the last convolutional layer and the modified fully-connected layer with the training data. It is known that the initial layers of networks optimized for distinct visual tasks learn to identify similar visual patterns, such as borders and edges (Yosinski et al. 2014). With this in mind, we fixed the weights of the other layers of the network with the original pre-trained weights and did not update them.

After the network is trained, the model can be used to infer a cardinal direction for new data. Finally, it is possible to sort all available images spatially.

2.2 Temporal Classification

The goal of the temporal classification step is to infer, for an input image, when it was taken during the time span of the event. Depending on the nature of the event being analyzed, it can be important to precisely define the time or timeframe an image or video was captured. In other occasions, it can be convenient to define if an image was captured before or after a specific time or if it corresponds to a major sub-event.

Our target event, the Notre-Dame fire, can be delineated by a series of important episodes that were captured live and shared as they took place. After the fire started, it spread to the cathedral's spire. A few minutes later, the spire collapsed and the fire continued burning until it was completed extinguished.

By analyzing the event's description, four main episodes can be highlighted: *spire on fire*, *spire collapsing*, *fire continues on roof*, and *fire extinguished* (Figure 4). We consider these events in order to place images temporally. For an input image, the method infers during which episode the image was captured. By doing this, we can tie a group of images to a specific sub-event, sorting the initial pool of images and videos in time.

Unlike the previous task, we now consider different training and inference strategies (Figure 5). The first strategy is to train the CNN with images of the four major subevents, considering each sub-event as a class. By doing so, we hypothesize that the CNN can learn how to correlate the images content with the visual clues for each sub-event. In fact, each sub-event has unique visual characteristics which are easily observable. For instance, for the first two classes (*fire on spire* and *fire collapsing*), the CNN can learn to model the appearance of the spire. For the last two classes (*fire continues on roof* and *fire extinguished*), besides from learning that the spire is no longer present, the CNN can focus on the fire.

In the second strategy, we apply a non-hierarchical approach similar to the one proposed by Martin et al. 2014. In this work, the authors postulate that it is often easier to answer the question "Was this image taken before or after this date?" rather than predicting the date directly. The idea is then to compare two contiguous groups of images in a binary fashion, in order to break the problem in smaller, ideally easier, problems. Because here we are dealing with sub-events rather than specific times, we need to break the multiclass problem into binary problems to answer questions

Spire on fire   Spire collapsing   Fire continues   Fire extinguished
                                                  on the roof

Figure 4: Major sub-events considered for the temporal classification step: *spire on fire*, *spire collapsing*, *fire continues on roof*, and *fire extinguished*.

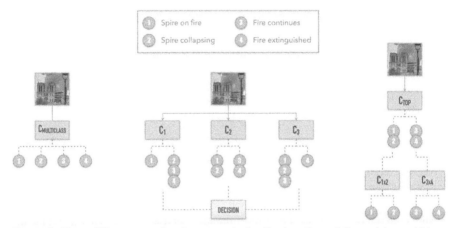

Figure 5: Three different strategies for temporal classification. From left to right: multiclass, non-hierarchical, and hierarchical approaches.

similar to "Was this image taken until this sub-event or after?" Considering this, we train three classifiers to answer the following question:

- C_1: "Was this image taken until the *spire on fire* sub-event or after?"
- C_2: "Was this image taken until the *spire collapsing* sub-event or after?"
- C_3: "Was this image taken until the *fire continues on roof* sub-event or after?"

Each classifier C_i gives us the probability p_i that an image was captured until a subevent. To finally decide during which sub-event an image was captured, we combine the predictions using a probabilistic model (Martin et al. 2014).

Considering possible sub-events $M = [$*spire on fire*, *spire collapsing*, *fire continues on roof*, *fire extinguished*$]$, indexed by $i \in [1,4]$, the probability that an image I was captured in a particular sub-event $m_i \in M$ is:

$$P(m_i|I) = \prod_{j=1}^{i-1}(1 - p_j)\prod_{j=i}^{|M|-1}(p_j). \qquad (1)$$

Finally, the predicted sub-event y is given by:

$$y = \arg\max_{m_i \in M} P(m_i|I). \qquad (2)$$

For the last strategy, we use a hierarchical approach. We have a top classifier (C_{top}) to first split the problem into "until and after the spire is collapsing". Depending on the decision, a different sub-classifier is considered. The first one ($C_{1 \times 2}$) decides between the first two classes (*spire on fire* and *spire is collapsing*) and the second one ($C_{3 \times 4}$) decides between the last two classes (*fire continues* and *fire extinguished*). The idea is that the spire collapsing is a major sub-event that heavily affects the appearance of the cathedral. It should be easier to firstly decide if an image was captured before/during this episode or after. Subsequently, specialized classifiers are used to decide between sub-events which are harder to differentiate.

In all described strategies for temporal classification, the classifiers are trained with images that have enough visual clues for predicting a sub-event. However, some images are zoom-ins of the cathedral or were taken from non-conventional angles. Because this could also happen in practice, we need to address it during training. In this vein, preceding the application of any of the strategies, we consider an *unknown classifier* which decides if an input image can be more easily classified as one of the sub-events. If the image sub-event is considered as *known*, the image follows to one of the described strategies.

For all classifiers, we also adopt the Inception-ResNet-v2 architecture (Szegedy et al. 2017) and its weights pre-trained on the ImageNet dataset. We perform the same modifications as before, including dropout and changing the fully-connected layer to the number of classes in each problem. Furthermore, only the last convolutional and the fully-connected layers are trained, while the rest of the weights are fixed.

2.3 Visualization

To enable the *X-coherence* for an event, the data needs to be structured in a joint coherence system for visualization and understanding. Considering the proposed methods for spatial and temporal classification, the goal is to classify each image in the initial pool of information, and sort them in space and time. Consequently, all the visual data of the target event can be analyzed in conjunction.

For this task, we consider a map of the Notre-Dame cathedral and its surroundings. For each facade cardinal direction (*south, southwest, west, northwest, north, northeast, east*, and *southeast*), there is a delimited area to group images that were captured from any of the contained positions.

After spatially sorting the images, the coherent system should allow the images to be accessed in temporal order. For each cardinal direction, the images that were captured from that viewpoint are sorted according to the order of the major sub-events: *spire on fire, spire collapsing, fire continues on roof*, and, finally, *fire extinguished*. Figure 6 shows same examples of the *X-coherence* space, and videos of the system in action can be seen in https://youtu.be/FeuIDK8xOI. Note that the images can be visited in the chronological order, using "back" and "next" buttons in the interface.

3. Dataset

In this section, we describe the created dataset and discuss some difficulties found on the process of creating it, related to filtering and annotating the data.

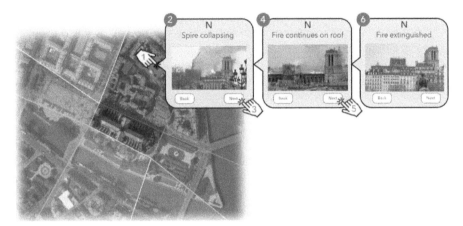

Figure 6: Snapshot of the *X-coherence* visualization. By selecting a region on the map, it shows an image captured in the correspondent intercardinal direction, allowing us to shuffle through different moments in time.

3.1 Description

During the tragic event, millions of images and videos were shared by users on social media and also by the press worldwide. To construct the initial dataset to train and test the proposed methods, we use a tool to scrape all these public content from the web. We considered images captured during and shortly after the event, when the fire was extinguished.

The dataset was manually curated to contain only valid and relevant data. We filtered the set of scrapped content, maintaining only images without overlays or elements added by users, and images captured only during the event and shortly after.

The second step was to annotate the data. For each image, we defined the cardinal direction of the cathedral's facade depicted on it, and also the sub-event during which it was captured. The description of the final curated set of images is presented in Table 1.

Table 1: Curated dataset for the Notre-Dame fire event.

	Spire on fire	Spire collapsing	Fire continues	Fire extinguished	Unknown	**Total**
N	68	14	19	3	2	106
NE	70	13	30	19	0	132
E	172	46	101	59	1	379
SE	161	5	177	118	4	465
S	23	1	21	34	1	80
SW	4	0	107	46	13	170
W	0	0	12	14	41	67
NW	10	0	3	0	7	20
Unknown	54	26	53	73	27	233
Total	562	105	523	366	96	1,657

After pre-processing, the dataset reaches a total of 1,657 images. The training set corresponds to 50% of the images. From the remaining images, we create two groups with roughly the same size, set_A and set_B, which are used for validation and testing interchangeably. To create the sets, the images were randomly distributed, trying to maintain the same proportion between classes as the whole dataset.

3.2 Manual vs. Automatic Data Pre-processing

Despite how well we perform *X-coherence*, achieving good accuracy on spatial and temporal classification tasks is dependent on the quality of the dataset. However, as we are using data from social media, there is no guarantee that the data is reliable. In the case of the Notre-Dame fire event, it was not. From the 23,683 initial images, only 5,206 depicted some content of the event. The remaining images—18,477, hereafter called *non-relevant* images—do not depict a content concerning the event—this includes memes, cartoons, compositions, random images, and also images from the cathedral before the fire, as illustrated in Figure 7. As we perform *X-coherence* in a supervised fashion, the lesser noisy and biased data, the higher the expected accuracy. Hence, it is necessary to discard, as much as possible, the non-relevant images.

Manually discarding non-relevant images is feasible on the scale of hundred or few thousands of images. However, this task may be impracticable on datasets with dozens or hundreds of thousands of images, even for experts on the event. Therefore, an automated solution could reduce the time of mining for relevant images on large scale datasets. Nonetheless, it is difficult to devise a supervised solution for this task, mainly because of the lack of annotation with respect to relevancy for a particular event. In an attempt to approach this problem, we experimented with two strategies: a semisupervised and a transfer learning-based one. In the following, we present how we performed both strategies.

A first idea is to ask an expert to select small sets of relevant and non-relevant images and then use semi-supervised methods to automatically annotate the images' relevancy. To illustrate the application of such approach on the Notre-Dame fire event, we experimented with a semi-supervised method based on the Optimum-path Forest theory (Amorim et al. 2016), employing a VGG16 (Simonyan and Zisserman 2014)

Figure 7: Examples of *non-relevant* images from the Notre-Dame fire event. They include cartoons, montages, memes, scenes from movies, artistic paintings, footage of distinct events involving fire or the cathedral prior to the event.

CNN pre-trained on scene classification (Zhou et al. 2017) as a feature extractor. First, we randomly selected some relevant images and some non-relevant ones to use as labeled data. To test the sensitivity to the size of the sets of labeled data, we ranged the number of labeled images from 5 to 50, with a step of 5, and performed 20 rounds for each setup.

The results for the semi-supervised approach are shown in Figure 8. We observed that increasing the number of labeled data also increased the accuracy but, on average, the method achieved around 58% of accuracy to spread the labels correctly to the unlabeled data. This poor performance may be due to a mismatch between the marginal probability distributions of the labeled and the unlabeled data (Pereira and Torres 2018). As the expert might not have access to every point of view of the event, it is not possible to select labeled image sets that cover all the distribution of the unlabeled data. This makes semi-supervised methods perform poorly (Oliver et al. 2018).

The second strategy relies upon the fact that we have some prior knowledge of the images of the Notre-Dame fire event: the relevant images must contain a building. The idea then is to exploit such knowledge to train a model in a transfer-learning fashion to identify if an image contains a building. To this end, we fine-tuned a VGG16 CNN using two datasets containing images of buildings, the Oxford and the Paris building datasets, and images from the Flickr 100k dataset depicting contents not related with buildings (Philbin et al. 2007, 2008). The results of this classifier on Notre-Dame imagery is shown in Figure 9. In terms of accuracy, the model achieved 14 percentual points above random guess (50%). However, we also observed a low precision rate, which means high rates of false-positive, including images of the cathedral before the fire and any other image depicting a building. Conversely, the high rates of recall imply that the majority of relevant images were correctly classified. Together these results suggest that if we have some prior knowledge on the event, we can use it as a first filter to mine a relevant set of images.

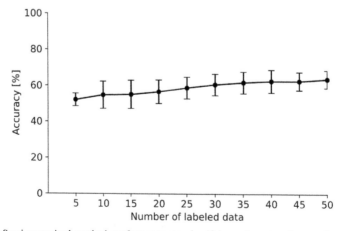

Figure 8: Semi-supervised method performance on classifying *relevant* and *non-relevant* images, considering different numbers of labeled images.

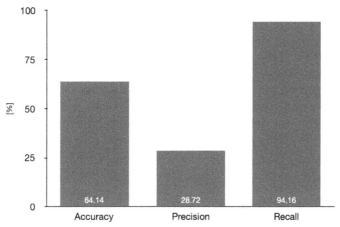

Figure 9: Transfer learning method performance on the Notre-Dame imagery to identify the presence of building in an image.

After mining the dataset and finding the set of relevant images, we also have to discard duplicates and near-duplicates. Duplicates are abundant in the type of dataset we are using because there is a high rate of sharing content on social media—probably more than original content. Near-duplicates (Dong et al. 2012), in turn, are also frequent as people manipulate the images before sharing. The most common manipulations are compression, cropping, and changing brightness and contrast. The task of finding duplicates and near-duplicates are well-studied, thus we can take advantage of existent solutions, especially image hashing methods such as Difference Hash, Perceptual Hash (Schneider and Chang 1996), and Wavelets Hash (Venkatesan et al. 2000). These methods are simple to implement and effective in finding duplicates and near duplicates.

As we are also interested in an automatic solution for this task, an issue that remains is: among the near-duplicates, which one we should keep in the set of relevant images? A simple idea is to keep the image that has the most density regarding its number of near-duplicates or the one with the highest pixel-density (high resolution). However, there is no guarantee that this image will be the best in terms of quality and content.

4. Experimental Evaluation

In this section, we present experimental results regarding the proposed methods to achieve the *X-coherence* for the Notre-Dame fire event. To train and test the methods, we utilize the curated dataset, considering the relevant groups of images for each classifier.

For the results in the next subsections, we trained the CNNs with the training set of the dataset, as described in Section 3.1. First, the best model was selected on set_A while testing was done in set_B. Then, the two sets were switched: validation was done in set_B while testing was done in set_A. We report the mean metric value with corresponding standard deviation.

The CNNs were fine-tuned with balanced batches (same quantity of samples per class) with *Adam* optimizer (Kingma and Ba 2014) and a starting learning rate of 0.0001. During training, some augmentation techniques were applied: rotation in range [−10°,10°], horizontal flip with 50% chance, and random scale and crop. For these last two techniques, the input image was resized so that its smaller dimension has size in the range of [340,520]—keeping the aspect ratio—and random crop was applied for the final size of 299 × 299 × 3 (expected input size).

During test, the input image was resized so that its smaller dimension has size of 340 pixels, and then a central crop was applied for the final size of 299 × 299 × 3. Besides that, some augmentation techniques were used during test. For each image, 10 versions were created with rotation and horizontal flip. These versions and the original input image were processed by the network, and the mean probability was computed to define the class.

4.1 Spatial Classification

To classify images spatially, we train and test our spatial classifier considering the images annotated with the corresponding cathedral's facade cardinal direction. We also utilize those images with uncertain cardinal direction to represent the "*unknown*" class. This class gathers the images that lack visual clues to precisely determine the facade of the cathedral that was photographed.

We conducted two experiments: one considering the eight cardinal directions (*south, southwest, west, northwest, north, northeast, east,* and *southeast*) and the "*unknown*" class; and other considering only the four main directions (*south, west, north,* and *east*) and the "*unknown*" class.

Table 2 presents the accuracy for each experiment. We also compute the 1-off accuracy, which considers as correct a prediction on a neighboring class. For example, if an image labeled as *North* is predicted as *Northwest* or *Northeast*, it is still considered as a correct prediction.

The classifier trained with four cardinal directions yields better accuracy, as expected. By merging the groups of images to construct the sets for the four directions, we obtain more images per class to train the classifier. Furthermore, the confusion between neighboring classes decreases, as there are fewer classes.

To understand what the CNN is learning to make predictions, we computed activation maps for each class (Selvaraju et al. 2017), highlighting informative image regions relevant to the prediction (more relevant regions in red and less relevant in blue). Figure 10 shows the activation maps for the four main cardinal directions.

By observing the maps, it is interesting to note that the CNN is making predictions manly based on the visible facades. There are also a few regions activated in the surroundings of the cathedral and in the smoke/fire regions. This means that

Table 2: Experimental results for the spatial classifier in the Notre-Dame fire event.

	ACC	*1-off ACC*
8 directions + unknown	72.2 ± 6.1	86.3 ± 1.2
4 directions + unknown	83.2 ± 1.2	91.3 ± 1.2

North   East

South   West

Figure 10: Activation maps for the main four cardinal directions. The maps show which regions in the images the CNN considers more important (red) and less important (blue) to make a prediction.

the CNN is often looking for the right visual clues (relevant characteristics on the facades), and is also considering how the smoke and fire evolve over time.

4.2 Temporal Classification

To classify images temporally, we train and test our temporal classifiers considering the images annotated with the sub-event in which they were photographed. We conducted two sets of experiments with all the proposed strategies: multiclass, non-hierarchical and hierarchical.

In the first set of experiments, we consider only images that have enough visual clues for predicting a sub-event. To model how *X-coherence* would be achieved in a real scenario, in a second set of experiments we first decide if an input image has enough visual clues for predicting a sub-event. To train this *unknown classifier*, we utilize images annotated with the "*unknown*" class. These are zoom-ins of the cathedral or pictures taken in non-conventional angles. For the multiclass strategy, we also consider training the CNN directly with five classes (four sub-events and a "*unknown*" class). Tables 3 and 4 present the results for each set of experiments.

It is clear that all strategies yield a better accuracy when considering only images that have enough visual clues for predicting a sub-event (Table 3). However, this assumption is not realistic, as it would not be reliable and efficient to filter images manually prior to image classification.

In a more realistic scenario (Table 4), we still achieve high accuracy, especially considering the multiclass setup (with five classes) and the hierarchical strategies. The hierarchical strategy benefits from the *unknown classifier*, as it has a considerable lower false positive rate (FPR) when compared to the multiclass strategy trained with an "*unknown*" class.

By comparing the non-hierarchical and hierarchical strategies, we can see that the latter provides a better accuracy in both sets of experiments. As the overall task is being solved hierarchically, the method can benefit from solving an easier sub-task

Table 3: Experimental results for the temporal classifier using three different strategies. Only images that have enough visual clues for predicting a sub-event are considered; i.e., zoom-ins and pictures taken in non-conventional angles are disregarded.

	ACC	*1-off ACC*
Multiclass	88.3 ± 2.2	96.3 ± 0.1
Non-hierarchical	86.5 ± 2.7	97.8 ± 0.1
Hierarchical	90.1 ± 2.0	97.0 ± 0.4

Table 4: Experimental results for the temporal classifier using three different strategies, considering an *unknown classifier*, which identifies if an image has enough visual clues for predicting a sub-event. FPR and FNR are the false positive and false negative rates for this *unknown classifier*, respectively.

	ACC	*1-off ACC*	FNR	FPR
Multiclass (5 classes)	84.0 ± 1.7	90.0 ± 0.7	1.8 ± 0.2	33.6 ± 4.5
Multiclass	81.7 ± 2.8	88.6 ± 0.7	7.5 ± 3.2	26.5 ± 2.7
Non-hierarchical	81.9 ± 1.9	89.7 ± 0.6	5.4 ± 1.3	26.5 ± 2.7
Hierarchical	84.2 ± 2.1	89.6 ± 0.7	5.6 ± 1.6	24.1 ± 5.1

first: deciding if a captured sub-event deals with the cathedral's spire or not, which is an important visual element. Indeed, the top classifier achieves 95.1% of accuracy compared to the overall 84.2%.

For this task, we also observed the activation maps for each class (Figure 11). The CNN activates the regions in the images that are more important to predict the subevents. For the *spire on fire* sub-event, the CNN appropriately activates the region representing the spire and the smoke around it. For the *spire collapsing* sub-event, the tip of the spire was activated, indicating that the CNN has learned the visual characteristics of the collapsing spire. For the *fire continues on roof* sub-event, the activated areas correspond precisely to the fire on the roof and

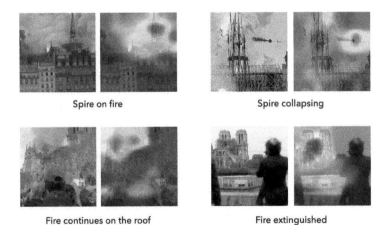

Spire on fire   Spire collapsing

Fire continues on the roof   Fire extinguished

Figure 11: Activation maps for the four major sub-events of interest. The maps show which regions in the images the CNN considers more important (red) and less important (blue) to make a prediction.

the smoke around it. In the last sub-event, *fire extinguished*, the CNN uses the facade to predict. We hypothesize that it is looking for clues that the fire or the spire is not present anymore.

5. Conclusions

From the heat of an event to the fact-checking phase, there is a gap that can be closed, or at least narrowed, by considering often disregarded information: the many images that are captured and shared by citizens and the press. In this chapter, we presented a machine learning approach to utilize this naturally unstructured source of information to unravel the event in space and time, i.e., to solve the *X-coherence*.

We resorted to the Notre-Dame Cathedral fire event to evaluate the methods proposed for spatially and temporally classifying images, and the final task of visualizing the event as a whole. During spatial classification, images related to the event are classified according to the facade of the cathedral they depict. In the temporal classification step, the goal is to classify images in accordance with the sub-event they were captured in. The final step enables the visualization of the data and the inferred information in a joint coherent system.

We postulated that data-driven methods, such as Convolutional Neural Networks (CNNs), can learn to correlate visual information with spatial cues, such as the different cathedral facades; and with temporal cues, such as the transformations occurring in the cathedral building and also the evolution of fire and smoke. For these two tasks, we showed that, in fact, the CNNs were able to utilize pertinent parts of the images to infer information.

Our method can spatially classify an image with 72.2% accuracy. The CNN mainly utilizes the cathedral facades to infer the cardinal direction from which an image was photographed. For temporal classification, our method is able to infer in which subevent an image was captured with 84.2% accuracy. The trained CNNs properly use different regions of the scene for each sub-event, such as the spire and smoke regions when predicting the *spire on fire* sub-event, and the roof and fire regions when predicting the *fire continues on roof* sub-event.

Although we demonstrated how to solve the *X-coherence* for a specific event, the proposed methods can be easily adapted to other similar events. The prerogative is to have plenty of visual data available, captured in different positions and moments throughout the event.

However, one of the main difficulties to achieve the *X-coherence* is the lack of proper data annotation. This fact implies that it is a challenge to mine from event imagery in a traditional supervised fashion. Besides, the subsequent steps on the *X-coherence* pipeline, the spatial and temporal classification, might also be unfeasible without properly annotated data—in the case of modeling them as supervised tasks. Therefore, it is imperative to propose solutions able to mine the data and perform *X-coherence* without the need for supervision. In a future exploration, we intend to study new methods to improve data pre-processing and annotation, to have a more automated and less error-prone process. As more data is gathered from an event, these tasks become even more critical. Instead of approaching the absence of annotated data in an unsupervised setting, it looks more reasonable first exploring transfer learning and weakly-labeled solutions (Arandjelović et al. 2018).

Acknowledgments

This research was supported by São Paulo Research Foundation (FAPESP), under the thematic project *DéjàVu*, grants 2017/12646-3, 2017/21957-2 and 2018/16548-9; by the Coordination for the Improvement of Higher Education Personnel (CAPES), DeepEyes grant; and by the National Council for Scientific and Technological Development (CNPq), grants #304472/2015-8 and #423797/2016-6.

References

Amorim, W. P., Falcão, A. X., Papa, J. P. and de Carvalho, M. H. 2016. Improving semi-supervised learning through optimum connectivity. Pattern Recognition 60: 72–85.

Arandjelović, R., Gronat, P., Torii, A., Pajdla, T. and Sivic, J. 2018. Netvlad: CNN architecture for weakly supervised place recognition. IEEE Transactions on Pattern Analysis and Machine Intelligence 40(6): 1437–1451.

Chung, W., Chen, H., Chaboya, L. G., O'Toole, C. D. and Atabakhsh, H. 2005. Evaluating event visualization: a usability study of coplink spatio-temporal visualizer. International Journal of Human-Computer Studies 62(1): 127–157.

Deligiannidis, L., Hakimpour, F. and Sheth, A. P. 2008. Event visualization in a 3D environment. In International Conference on Human System Interaction (HSI), pp. 158–164.

Dong, W., Wang, Z., Charikar, M. and Li, K. 2012. High-confidence near duplicate image detection. In ACM International Conference on Multimedia Retrieval (ACMMR), pp. 1.

Ferreira, A., Carvalho, T., Andaló, F. and Rocha, A. 2019. Counteracting the contemporaneous proliferation of digital forgeries and fake news. Anais da Academia Brasileira de Ciˆencias, 91.

Kingma, D. and Ba, J. 2014. Adam: A method for stochastic optimization. arXiv preprint, arXiv:1412.6980.

Lameri, S., Bestagini, P., Mellon, A., Milani, S., Rocha, A., Tagliasacchi, M. and Tubaro, S. 2014. Who is my parent? Reconstructing video sequences from partially matching shots. In IEEE International Conference on Image Processing (ICIP), pp. 5342–5346.

Martin, P., Doucet, A. and Jurie, F. 2014. Dating color images with ordinal classification. In ACM International Conference on Multimedia Retrieval (ACMMR), pp. 447.

Oliver, A., Odena, A., Raffel, C. A., Cubuk, E. D. and Goodfellow, I. 2018. Realistic evaluation of deep semi-supervised learning algorithms. In Advances in Neural Information Processing Systems (NIPS), pp. 3235–3246.

Pereira, L. A. M. and Torres, R. S. 2018. Semi-supervised transfer subspace for domain adaptation. Pattern Recognition 75: 235–249.

Philbin, J., Chum, O., Isard, M., Sivic, J. and Zisserman, A. 2007. Object retrieval with large vocabularies and fast spatial matching. In IEEE Conference on Computer Vision and Pattern Recognition (CVPR), pp. 63–71.

Philbin, J., Chum, O., Isard, M., Sivic, J. and Zisserman, A. 2008. Lost in quantization: Improving particular object retrieval in large scale image databases. In IEEE Conference on Computer Vision and Pattern Recognition (CVPR), pp. 1–8.

Reinders, F., Post, F. H. and Spoelder, H. J. 2001. Visualization of time-dependent data with feature tracking and event detection. The Visual Computer 17(1): 55–71.

Schindler, G., Dellaert, F. and Kang, S. B. 2007. Inferring temporal order of images from 3D structure. In IEEE Conference on Computer Vision and Pattern Recognition (CVPR), pp. 1–7.

Schneider, M. and Chang, S. -F. 1996. A robust content based digital signature for image authentication. In IEEE International Conference on Image Processing (ICIP) 3: 227–230.

Selvaraju, R. R., Cogswell, M., Das, A., Vedantam, R., Parikh, D. and Batra, D. 2017. Grad-cam: Visual explanations from deep networks via gradient-based localization. In IEEE International Conference on Computer Vision (ICCV), pp. 618–626.

Simonyan, K. and Zisserman, A. 2014. Very deep convolutional networks for large scale image recognition. arXiv preprint, arXiv: 1409.1556.

Snavely, N., Seitz, S. M. and Szeliski, R. 2008. Modeling the world from internet photo collections. International Journal of Computer Vision 80(2): 189–210.

Surowiecki, J. 2013. The wise way to crowdsource a manhunt. The New York Times, https://www.newyorker.com/news/daily-comment/the-wise-way-to-crowdsource-a-manhunt. Accessed: 2018-28-11.

Szegedy, C., Ioffe, S., Vanhoucke, V. and Alemi, A. A. 2017. Inception-v4, Inception ResNet and the impact of residual connections on learning. In AAAI Conference on Artificial Intelligence, pp. 4278–4284.

Venkatesan, R., Koon, S. -M., Jakubowski, M. H. and Moulin, P. 2000. Robust image hashing. In IEEE International Conference on Image Processing (ICIP) 3: 664–666.

Volokitin, A., Timofte, R. and Van Gool, L. 2016. Deep features or not: Temperature and time prediction in outdoor scenes. In IEEE Conference on Computer Vision and Pattern Recognition Workshops (CVPRW), pp. 63–71.

Yosinski, J., Clune, J., Bengio, Y. and Lipson, H. 2014. How transferable are features in deep neural networks? In Advances in Neural Information Processing Systems (NIPS), pp. 3320–3328.

Zhou, B., Lapedriza, A., Khosla, A., Oliva, A. and Torralba, A. 2017. Places: A 10 million image database for scene recognition. IEEE Transactions on Pattern Analysis and Machine Intelligence.

2

Using Gesture Recognition to Prevent Drowning
A Crime Science Perspective

Anthony C Ijeh[1,]* and *Ahmed Naufal AL Masri*[2]

1. Introduction

Every hour of every day more than 40 people lose their lives worldwide to drowning. Drowning is the third leading cause of unintentional injury death worldwide. Global estimates may significantly underestimate the actual public health problem related to drowning. Maritime police have reported that the cause of many adult drowning deaths is where a victim chooses not to wear a life jacket while wild swimming (Barakat 2015). The World Health Organization (WHO) says wearing a life jacket while boating and swimming is important for safety and can make a difference in drowning prevention (WHO 2014). At the research site, the target response time of maritime Police for drowning cases is six minutes, as also for boats and ships that are near the shore. However, the challenge is that it can take just three minutes to reach the last stage of drowning which is irreversible and causes death. The difference of three minutes in being able to reach a drowning person, calls for an intervention that can take less than three minutes to reach a person and save their life in a reliable, practical, and economical way. As a solution this chapter presents an invention which provides a drowning person a Portable Floating Device (PFD) delivered by a drone also known as Unmanned Aerial Vehicle (UAV) using gesture recognition and sensor technology in a defined area within one minute of the drowning cycle. A specification is modelled to fully automate the process of delivering a Portable Floating Device as done by lifeguards to a person who is drowning in the sea until a lifeguard or rescue boat arrives to save them.

[1] DASCROSE Limited, England, United Kingdom.
[2] American University in the Emirates.
* Corresponding author: enquiry@dascrose.com

Benefits of the invention are that it allows zoning of drones by specifying the area within which they operate, just as lifeguards are zoned at beaches. It ensures drones do not collide into each other whilst on search and rescue missions. It can deliver a portable life jacket to a drowning victim within one minute from its base station. It can provide continuous deployment of life jackets to drowning victims in multiple zones. The invention uses profiled behavioural gestures to detect Body Mass Index (BMI) and aerial alignment of BMI using Global Positioning System (GPS) and depth sensor. The invention can rescue of up to six BMI in one view, based on nearest distance and view. It also records data and has a manual intervention control for health, safety, and audit purposes.

The rest of the chapter is organised as follows, Section 2 presents a literature review of gesture recognition and drone technology. It also looks at existing patents and their prototype functionality, identifying the limitations of their capacity during search and rescue. Section 3 explains the research methodology used in the study and describes why alternative methods were not used. Section 4 presents the steps in the development of software and hardware used to build the prototype and a workflow. Section 5 presents the research findings. Section 6 describes the research benefits and limitations. Section 7 presents the conclusion and Section 8 suggests future work.

2. Literature Review

The literature search focused on frameworks which were key to the prototypes development. It reviewed existing interventions associated with drowning prevention and services provided by drones at the beach. Drowning is one of the hardest homicides to prove and by looking at its prevention this study aimed to mitigate its occurrence. The review therefore focuses on preventing drowning rather than its cause using scientific methodology. The stages of drowning and current prevention strategies show there is a need for a new initiative. The five stages of drowning are: Surprise, involuntary breath holding, unconsciousness, hypoxic convulsion, clinical death (Gilchrist et al. 2004; Armstrong et al. 2018). The first two stages (surprise and involuntary breath holding) are when a drowning victim makes any motion before going into unconsciousness.

The types of motion made by a drowning victim in the first two stages are rarely captured in wild swimming areas, e.g., sea and beach resorts but have been recorded at indoor swimming pools before lifeguards intervene to prevent drowning. It was necessary to understand the types of motion involved for an effective solution to be developed. These motions are also used by lifeguards to intervene in a swimmer's activity indoors or in a wild swimming area. Parenteau et al. (2018), presented a standardized framework to guide first responders in evaluating, diagnosing, and managing common water pathologies. Key steps recommended for first responders were for them to identify and locate the victim (ask if there are more than one) and rescue the drowning victim by the fastest means using methods like reach, throw, row, tow, go. Throwing an object like a rope or flotation devices was suggested as the safest option where the rescuers own safety may be at risk or compromised if they were to enter the water.

Any solution should be able to identify and recognize gestures made by swimmers and match them against datasets in its database. Ijeh (2011), presented a security strategy model which used geofencing to control the activities of a wireless device. The device functioned within a pre-defined geographical area and had an embedded system which was used to detect, observe, and record its movement. Whenever the device left the geographical area its connection to the wireless network was cut off. The approach ensured that the device was only able to communicate using the wireless network within the defined geographical area and acted as a security model.

2.1 Gesture Recognition Technology

Gesture recognition technology enables the capture and interpretation of human gestures as commands. Recognition of human gesture occurs when any physical movement, large or small, is successfully interpreted by a motion sensor as a command. Various frameworks, models and comparative studies have been presented on gesture recognition tools that capture and interpret human gestures. There is a plethora of literature on the application of gesture recognition tools and their improvement in capturing images for specific commands.

Wachs et al. (2008), presented a vision-based hand gesture capture and recognition system that interprets in real-time the user's gestures for navigation and manipulation of images in an electronic medical record database. Wipfli et al. (2016), compared different interaction modes for image manipulation that are usable for gesture control using Kinect. The study showcased oral instructions that manipulate images directly. Gillian and Paradiso (2014) presented an open-source gesture recognition toolkit designed to make real-time machine learning and gesture recognition more accessible for non-specialists. The toolkit has extensive support for building real-time systems which includes algorithms for signal processing, feature extraction and automatic gesture spotting. Nanivadekar and Kulkarni (2013) evaluated the various approaches deployed by gesture recognition systems and indicated areas where they will serve as a revolutionary tool. Rios Soria and Schaeffer (2012) developed a software tool for human-computer interaction based on hand gestures. The underlying algorithm utilized computer vision techniques and recognized in real-time six different hand gestures, captured using a web cam. Chen et al. (2014) presented a novel real-time method for hand gesture recognition. The study enabled the detection and recognition of hand palms and fingers using a rule classifier to predict labels of hand gestures. The data set of 1300 images showed the method performs well and is highly efficient. Khan and Ibraheem (2012), presented a comparative study on hand gesture recognition systems and explained their segmentation, modelling, analysis, and extraction features. Sharma et al. (2020), collated datasets of human hand images using standard American sign language under different environmental conditions. The study classified hand gestures according to the correctness of their commands using percentage accuracy. The pre-processed data used similar classifiers to draw effective results. Hoang (2020) presented the HGM-4 dataset built for hand gesture recognition showcasing its ability to capture 26 hand gestures on four cameras in different positions. The objective of the study was an improved training and testing set to create a benchmark framework for comparing experimental results.

Oudah et al. (2020), evaluated the literature on hand gesture techniques and discussed the merits and limitations of each under different circumstances. The paper tabulated the performance of different methods, focusing on computer vision techniques that deal with the similarity and difference points, technique of hand segmentation used, classification algorithms and drawbacks, number and types of gestures, dataset used, detection range (distance) and type of camera used. Wachs (2011), described the requirements of hand-gesture interfaces and the challenges in meeting the needs of various application types. The study concluded that system requirements vary depending on the scope of the application; for example, an entertainment system does not need the gesture-recognition accuracy required of a surgical system. Patel and He (2018), gave an up to date survey of different techniques in use for gesture recognition. The benefits and limitations of all methods surveyed were also covered. Mod Ma'asum et al. (2015), undertook a comparative study of several methods for hand gesture recognition using three main modules: camera and segmentation module, detection module and feature extraction module. Ambika and Chidananda (2014), undertook a comparative study between two tracking methods. The results justified a framework for real time hand gesture recognition in uncontrolled environment using a robust and efficient hand tracking algorithm by wearing a black glove on hand. The study also presented a separate tracking algorithm called free hand tracking which is based on skin pigments. Trigueiros et al. (2012), presented a comparative study of four classification algorithms for static hand gesture classification using two different hand feature data sets. The approach identified hand pixels in each frame, extract features and used them to recognize a specific hand pose. The results obtained proved that one method had an exceptionally good performance in feature selection and data preparation which is an important phase when using lower-resolution images like the ones obtained by cameras. Nigam et al. (2020), found that most respondents from a survey who applied the DTW (dynamic time wrapping) algorithm achieved 75% accuracy and 85% accuracy when using the LCS (Longest common subsequence) method in recognizing gestures. Al-qaness and Li (2016), developed a device-free Wi-Fi-based gesture recognition system (WiGeR) by leveraging the fluctuations in the channel state information (CSI) of Wi-Fi signals caused by hand motions. The study implemented and tested the system through experiments involving various scenarios. The results showed that WiGeR can classify gestures with high accuracy, even in scenarios where the signal passes through multiple walls which cause interference. Haker (2010), explained how computer vision using TOF cameras enabled human computer interaction. The study gave an overview of TOF cameras, algorithms and applications based on a specific type of image sensor. Ijeh (2018), evaluated the societal impact of a prototype solution for surveillance. The solution continuously monitored communication of a mobile device and intercommunication unit within a predefined space. Its use has become widely adopted for different applications. Ma'asum et al. (2017), presented a paper on input images which had been converted to a new model using threshold values. The values satisfied a predefined skin colour segmentation and the study concluded that using thresholds proved efficient in creating contour of hand images when compared to other types of segmentation techniques.

2.2 Drone Technology

A drone is a flying robot that can be remotely controlled or fly autonomously using software-controlled flight plans, onboard sensors, GPS, and an embedded system which a user to interact with it. Drones are also known as unmanned aerial vehicles (UAVs) or unmanned aircraft systems (UASes). Drones were initially used by the military for its operations but are now also used in a wide range of civilian roles such as search and rescue, surveillance, traffic and weather monitoring, firefighting, photography, videography, agriculture and even delivery services. There is a plethora of literature on drone technology and its application, more recently drone safety has become topical because of the disruption caused at Gatwick and Heathrow airports in England.

Euchi (2020), described the increase in use of drones in civil, commercial, and social applications due to their advancement. The widespread use of drones in the delivery of essential loads during the COVID-19 pandemic, subsequent lockdown, and fight against the coronavirus reduced the spread of coronavirus by removing human contact from the delivery process. Drones have also reduced the carbon footprint of individuals and businesses and reversed their negative impact on climate change. Estrada and Ndoma (2019), evaluated the crucial role of drones in an emergency response and how they could be used to help a casualty in various scenarios. Their paper concluded that drones could be used amongst other things for aerial monitoring and delivering loads for humanitarian relief. Kumar et al. (2020), developed a drone system which in real-time could be used for aerial thermal image collection and patient identification within a 2-kilometre range under 10 minutes. The study identified and discussed the limitations of having multiple drones working within a predefined area and proffered solutions. Whitelaw et al. (2020), described a framework for the application of digital technologies in pandemic planning, surveillance, testing, contact tracing, quarantine, and health care. The study described how big data and Artificial Intelligence (AI) helped combat the spread of coronavirus by tracking people. It also discussed the advantages and disadvantages of digital technologies in managing emergencies. Chamola et al. (2020), explored the use of Internet of Things (IoT), Unmanned Aerial Vehicles (UAVs), blockchain, Artificial Intelligence (AI), and 5G, amongst others, to help mitigate the impact of the coronavirus outbreak. The study drew on reliable sources to present a detailed review of contemporary technologies and how they can be used to combat emergencies such as the pandemic. Ruiz (2020) supported the use of drones for aerial monitoring of coronavirus and for logistic and cargo delivery. The paper described how the use of drones would enable a precise epidemic response and relief humanitarian aid framework. ITF OECD (2020) reported that while drones are proving to be versatile and effective tools their regulation is still in its infancy and their potential not fully exploited. The technical report highlighted the need for airspace regulations to be updated to facilitate their use beyond emergency responses.

Yang et al. (2020), supported the potential of robots such as drones in three broad areas were, they could be used to make a difference: telemedicine, logistics and reconnaissance. Skorup and Haaland (2020), agreed that drone technology reduced person-to-person contact. The paper however noted that the main obstacle in using drone delivery was a regulatory one.

2.3 Patents

There are patents on Unmanned Aerial Vehicles delivering drones to distressed persons in the sea but all of them have one thing in common and that is that they are not fully automated.

As described in an article titled "Rescue System" with patent number WO 2015144947 A1, the patent discloses that it uses a binocular for manual observation of Body Mass Index (BMI), the patent also discloses that the drone is remotely piloted by manual operation and the patent discloses that the distance between BMI and drone is calculated manually by observation through binoculars. Furthermore, the patent does not disclose that sensors are used to monitor the Body Mass Index. It also does not disclose anything about a designated area for serving local BMI population. In effect the invention is not fully automated, Marquez et al. (2015). As described in an art titled "Unmanned aerial device and system thereof" with patent number WO 2013123944 AI, the patent does not disclose that sensors are used to monitor the Body Mass Index. It also does not disclose anything about a designated area for serving local Body Mass Index population. The patent clearly states that the coupling mechanism is activated manually, that the inflating element is activated manually, that the heating source is activated manually, that the delivery of the life jacket is activated manually (Elkjær 2013). As described in an article titled Unmanned aerial vehicle life buoy dropping device—CN 105292479 A, the patent does not disclose that sensors are used to monitor the Body Mass Index. It also does not disclose anything about a designated area for serving local Body Mass Index population. The patent however talks about a flight directing mechanism and using a two-axis stabilization camera (Yukun 2015). As described in an article titled "Drone for Rescuing Drowning Person" with patent number WO2015167103 A1, the patent does not disclose that sensors are used to monitor the Body Mass Index. It also does not disclose anything about a designated area for serving local Body Mass Index population Jung-Cheol (2014). As described in an article titled "Motion capture and analysis system for assessing mammalian kinetics" with patent number WO 2015139145 A1 (Comeau et al. 2015), the patent does not make mention of Unmanned Aerial Vehicles. As described in an article titled "Systems and methods for initializing motion tracking of human hands" with patent number US 8615108 B1 equipment for recognizing captured gestures and storing them for recognition exists (Stoppa et al. 2013), the patent does not make mention of Unmanned Aerial Vehicles.

3. Methodology

The following research methodology was used in the study:

- Research Design: Literature review of interventions associated with drowning prevention and services provided by drones on the sea and beach.

- Patent search to ensure the idea is novel and can be commercialised without infringing on the rights of others.
- Design of prototype to obtain proof of concept using tested methods to collate and analyse the data with expected outcomes achieved.
- Testing and licensing of product to ensure that its use is reliable and safe for the public.
- Publication and demonstration of concept and prototype respectively to members of the public through book chapter, journal, and technology exhibition fairs.
- Creation of webpage on website to showcase product and market its features which are novel and unique.

3.1 Implementation

The study aims to provide an intervention for preventing drowning and essential maritime services needed at the sea. The fully automated prototype mitigates the 6-minute time lapse it takes maritime authorities to reach a drowning victim. The work to be done includes the development and testing of the prototype.

The expected results from actual testing of the prototype include:

- Zoning drones by specifying the area within which they operate, just as lifeguards are zoned at wild swimming areas.
- Geofencing the area in which the drone operates to avoid having drones colliding into each other.
- Delivery of a life jacket to a drowning person within 1 minute.
- Provide 24-hour drowning prevention protection.

The prototype uses specially programmed drone technology to locate swimmers and deliver life jackets. The objective is for the drone to be fully automated and function within a defined parameter. This is so that acts of the drone fall within the parameter. Currently drones are semi-automated, i.e., they are controlled manually by a drone pilot and are not Geofenced to specific zones. The novelty of the invention is that it is fully automated and is able to provides 24-hour coverage a day. The competitive edge of the prototype is that in addition to the fully automated service the drone covers a defined area and delivers a life jacket within 1-minute which the research sites maritime rescue team takes at least 6 minutes to achieve. This is proofed by a documented summary of the benefits and changes that occur through the adoption of the interventions offering, an assessment of the gravity such a change has and a perception of its value. The concept of the interventions applied development methodology, used a description of other methodologies not used and an appreciation of their non-suitability to the development situations. The implementation of the design, the development of an appropriate testing strategy, and the development of appropriate user documentation for the deliverables. Disclosed is the process automation method of an apparatus using integrated modelling of different software

Table 1: Invention description.

Step	Proposed prototype solution	Application mode
1	Multiple prototype solutions are present at beach station.	Fully Automated
2	Each prototype solution leaves its beach station and flies to the centre of its designated sea zone where it hovers and monitors Body Mass Index (BMI) activity.	Fully Automated
3	Onboard prototype solution makes a 360° turn whilst hovering in the centre of the designated zone whilst its sensors detect and monitor Body Mass Index (BMI) activity.	Fully Automated
4	Onboard prototype solution sensors detect and recognize gestures from Body Mass Index (BMI) using Artificial Intelligence and compares them with stored data collected by training from a distressed/drowning Body Mass Index (BMI) in the Sea.	Fully Automated
5	Prototype solution measures the distance between its position and up to six Body Mass Index (BMI) at the same time in one view.	Fully Automated
6	Prototype solution aligns directly above the Body Mass Index (BMI) of the nearest Body Mass Index (BMI).	Fully Automated
7	Prototype solution serves the closest Body Mass Index (BMI) using GPS coordinates under the same view.	Fully Automated
8	Prototype solution reallocates itself after serving a Body Mass Index (BMI) to the next nearest Body Mass Index (BMI) using GPS coordinates under the same view else it returns to and continues hovering in the centre of the designated zone.	Fully Automated
9	Prototype solution continues serving the next nearest Body Mass Index (BMI) using GPS coordinates until its load (six life jackets) are delivered.	Fully Automated
10	Prototype solution returns to its station once its load (six life jackets) is delivered or when its flight battery is critically low.	Fully Automated
11	Prototype solution provides constant monitoring of the zone by using two drones which alternate each other for reloading (six life jackets) and flight battery recharging.	Fully Automated
12	All Prototype solution data is recorded, and human intervention is optional from the base station for safety and audit purposes at any time.	Fully Automated
13	Prototype solution follows strict health and safety rules during flight service and has a failsafe mechanism which makes it hover above sea level or land smoothly and safely in the sea in case of critical system failure.	Fully Automated

platforms. The apparatus is a drone also widely known as an Unmanned Aerial Vehicle (UAV) or unmanned aircraft systems (UASes). The integrated software platform is modelled to fully automate the process of delivering a life jacket also known as a Portable Floating Device (PFD) as done by Lifeguards [1, 2] to a person who is drowning in the Sea until a lifeguard or rescue boat arrives to save them (Tables 1 and 2).

Table 2: Comparison with the manual process of a lifeguard rescuing a drowning victim.

Step	Lifeguard	Application mode	Proposed solution	Application mode
1	Present in designated zone	Manual	Multiple Prototype solutions are present at base station.	Automatic
2	Stand on ladder	Manual	Prototype solution makes a 360° turn whilst hovering in the centre of the designated zone.	Automatic
3	Use binoculars to watch the Sea	Manual	Onboard Prototype solution sensors detect and monitors Body Mass Index (BMI) activity.	Automatic
4	Assesses the victim's condition - Determine whether the victim is a distressed swimmer, is an active or passive drowning victim at the surface or submerged or has a possible head, neck, or back injury	Manual	Onboard Prototype solution sensors detect and recognize gestures from Body Mass Index (BMI) using Artificial Intelligence and compares them with stored data collected by training from a distressed/drowning Body Mass Index (BMI) in the Sea.	Automatic
5	Safely enter the water and use distance to determine speed of movement	Manual	Prototype solution measures the distance between its position and up to six Body Mass Index (BMI) at the same time in one view.	Automatic
6	Approach Victim with Portable Floating Device (PFD).	Manual	Prototype solution aligns directly above the Body Mass Index (BMI) of the nearest Body Mass Index (BMI).	Automatic
7	Repeat step 6	Manual	Prototype solution serves the closest Body Mass Index (BMI) using GPS coordinates under the same view.	Automatic
8	Repeat step 6	Manual	Prototype solution reallocates itself after serving a Body Mass Index (BMI) to the next nearest Body Mass Index (BMI) using GPS coordinates under the same view else it returns to and continues hovering in the centre of the designated zone.	Automatic
9	Repeat step 6	Manual	Prototype solution continues serving the next nearest Body Mass Index (BMI) using GPS coordinates until its load (six life jackets) are delivered.	Automatic
10	Repeat step 6		Prototype solution returns to its station once its load (six life jackets) is delivered or when its flight battery is critically low.	Automatic
11	Repeat step 6		Prototype solution provides constant monitoring of the zone by using two drones which alternate each other for reloading (six life jackets) and flight battery recharging.	Automatic

Table 2 Contd. ...

...Table 2 Contd.

Step	Lifeguard	Application mode	Proposed solution	Application mode
12	Repeat step 6		All Prototype solution data is recorded, and human intervention is optional from the base station for safety and audit purposes at any time.	Automatic
13	Deliver Portable Floating Device (PFD)		Prototype solution follows strict health and safety rules during flight service and has a failsafe mechanism which makes it hover above sea level or land smoothly and safely in the sea in case of critical system failure.	Automatic

4. Pseudocode

Pseudocode for Body Index-Gesture detector algorithm

Initialization (Kinect detection model, Motor, Gates, Onboard Embedded system, Drone Controller)
While Kinect = True (Kinect sensor is Activated)
For i in BodyIndex list:
    If 'help' Gesture for BodyIndex (i) is detected
        Drone GPS align with BodyIndex coordinates
        Check Confidence Percentage
        If Confidence in BodyIndex is more than 80%
            Release rescue equipment (i)
            Remove BodyIndex (i) from available BodyIndex list
            Close GateNumber (i)
            Save log status
        Else
            Save log status for detected bodies
    Else
        No Body is detected, detector is paused

Pseudocode for distance measurement and GPS

Kinect will provide the coordinates (x, y, z) of detected BodyIndex, therefore, this measurement will be used to re-locate the drone dramatically with associative gesture detector to bring the drone closer to the person who needs help.

    Function GPS = align
    If BodyIndex (i) is True and confidence level is more than 80%
        Determine the BodyIndex coordinates (x, y, z)
        Determine the GPS mapping for BodyIndex
        While GPS align with BodyIndex = True:
            Start the BodyIndex-Gesture detector
    Else
        Detect a new BodyIndex

Pseudocode for motor controller algorithm

Motor initialization (set the motor to zero angle degree)
While True (Data received from Embedded system)
    Try:
    If BodyIndex (i) is True and confidence level is more than 80%
        Gate (i) is initialized
        Gate (i) is opened
        Motor turn 30 degree
        Gate (i) is turned off
        Rescue equipment is successfully dropped
        Remove the BodyIndex (i) from available BodyIndex list
        Save motor angle for next move
    Else
        Save log 'Rescue equipment has not been loaded'
    Except:
        Save log 'Six rescue missions have been accomplished'
        Turn motor to zero angle degree

4.1 Prototype System and Components

The components used in building the prototype include an onboard Embedded System, Raspberry Pi 2, Portal Battery 5/12/19 Volts, Camera, Infra-Red Sensor, Servo Moto, Visual Studio 2015 Pro, Kinect SDK 2, Linux Debian 2, Python, Drone and Portable Floating Device. Figure 1 to Figure 15 are images and pictures collated during the study and development of the prototype system.

Figure 1: Imaging of body mass index.

Figure 2: Captured image in IDE.

Figure 3: Co-author setting up drone GPS coordinates.

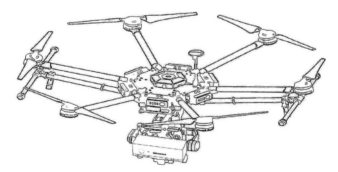

Figure 4: Aerial view of drone.

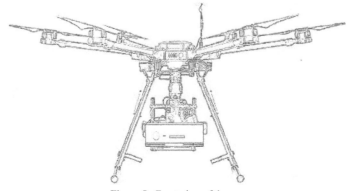

Figure 5: Front view of drone.

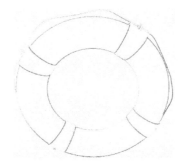

Figure 6: Portable floating device (Life buoy).

4.2 *Features of the Prototype System*

Step	Features of prototype system
1	Prototype fully automates the lifeguard's role on the beach
2	Prototype is Geofenced and will only work in predefined beach areas
3	Prototype monitors BMI by hovering in the middle of the beach areas circumference and rotating at 360°
4	Prototype recognizes the gesture of profiles of a BMI drowning with confidence value of 80%
5	Prototype measures the distance between itself and BMI
6	Prototype uses its coordinates to align with BMI drowning before delivering a portable floating device
7	Prototype serves the nearest BMI in ascending order using their distance to itself
8	Prototype will continue to serve BMI or return to the middle of the circumference and hover
9	Prototype has a payload of six life jackets
10	Prototype alternate duties by returning to the beach station to reload life jackets or recharge its battery
11	Prototype provides fully automated monitoring of BMI in the zone
12	N/A
13	N/A

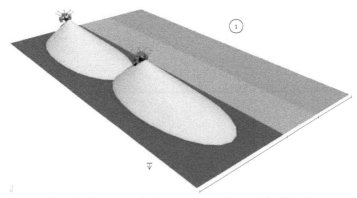

Figure 7: Prototype solutions are present at base station (Step 1).

Figure 8: Onboard prototype solution sensors detect and monitors BMI activity (Step 3).

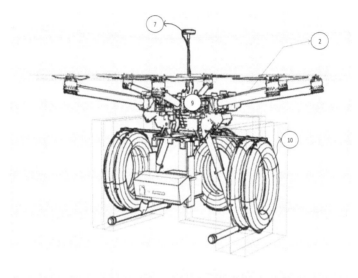

Figure 9: Makes a 360° turn whilst hovering in the centre of the designated zone (Steps 2, 7, 9, 10).

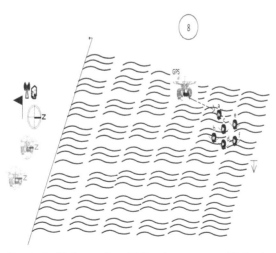

Figure 10: Reallocates itself after serving a BMI to the next nearest BMI using GPS (Step 8).

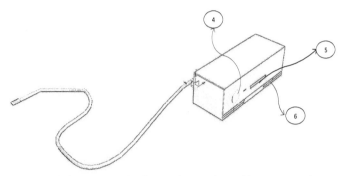

Figure 11: Prototype solution measures the distance between its position and up to six BMI at the same time in one view (Steps 4, 5, 6).

4.3 Prototype System Workflow

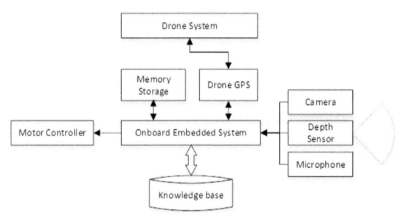

Figure 12: System block diagram.

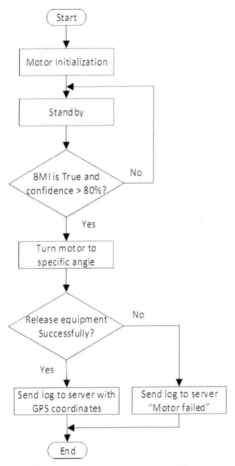

Figure 13: Motor controller algorithm.

5. Results

Testing of the prototype showed that the proposed intervention can carry and deliver at least six life jackets within a predefined area in under three minutes. The demonstration results showed that the invention can successfully follow programmed policies used to control flight path and delivery within the testbed parameters. This is of commercial value because it provides an answer to the existing drowning prevention challenge faced by lifeguards and maritime police which is their inability to reach a drowning person in less than three minutes. The prototype presents a novel intervention which can save a BMI from drowning within one minute. The limitations identified during testing can be overcome using imagery and geomatics.

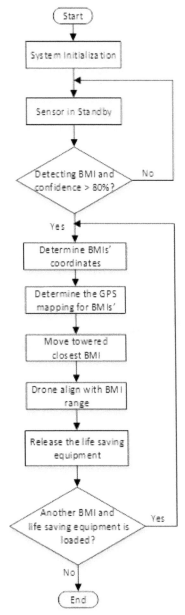

Figure 14: Distance measurements and GPS re-location.

6. Benefits and Limitations

Benefits include the zoning of drones by specifying the area within which they operate, just as lifeguards are zoned on beaches to control a designated area. The drones are Geofenced within their designated areas to prevent them colliding with each and can deliver a life jacket to a drowning person within 1 minute in the

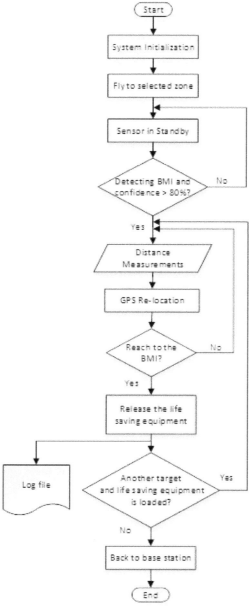

Figure 15: System operation overview.

designated area that they monitor. The drones can continuously deploy life jackets to swimmers in multiple zones. The drones to use behavioural gestures to detect BMI. The drones align with BMI using GPS and depth sensor to measure the distance before adjustment and can rescue up to six BMI in one view, based on nearest distance and view. There is also a manual intervention in the drone's flight for health, safety, and audit purposes.

Limitations: The radius of covered zone area is limited to 5 meters due to hardware functionality. The sensor can only recognize 6 BMI in one view at 45°. The flight battery has a short life span of 30 minutes. Results from testing the prototype are based on normal calm weather with temperature in the range of 20–40 degrees Celsius and not testing in extreme weather conditions.

7. Conclusion

The study developed a working prototype which uses gesture recognition technology for search and rescue to prevent drowning. The initial scope of the study raised the following questions which needed to be addressed: What are the causes of drowning at beach resorts and methods used in saving wild swimmers? What are the stages of drowning and how long does it take to complete the drowning cycle up until the point of death?

A feasibility study showed drone technology could be used to deliver life jackets and the resulting prototype was able to mitigate the time lag of 6 minutes which it takes maritime authorities at the base location to reach a drowning victim. A literature review was undertaken to understand the causes of drowning and existing lifeguard techniques in saving drowning victims. The resulting information was used to develop a framework for delivering a life jacket to a drowning person within the time a person is conscious, and motion occurs which is in the first 2 stages of drowning.

The literature review enabled the development of a testbed and framework for the prototype solution which met criteria for mitigation of drowning prevention at the base location. Towards achieving this, the existing traditional methods and patents filed were evaluated to ensure the development had originality and was commercially viable. The prototype solution recognises a drowning person and provides a life jacket within 1 minute from its base station. The fully automated prototype is based on machine learning that recognises behavioural gesture of a victim. Using Kinect sensors (IR and depth sensors) gesture recognition relays signals to raspberry pi which releases the life jacket. During earlier simulations, the drone flew to a drowning person having recognised the gestures and delivered a portable floating device.

8. Future Work

Future improvements can be made by testing the prototype in extreme conditions like under heavy rain. Improvements can also be made by testing for minimal interference from signals. Sensors with a wider range and better detection ability should be used in future, whilst computer vision for imagery and measurement of BMI can be improved.

References

Al-qaness, M. and Li, F. 2016. WiGeR: WiFi-based gesture recognition system. ISPRS International Journal of Geo-Information 5(6): 92.

Ambika, L. A. and Chidananda, H. 2014. A Comparative Analysis of Hand Tracking Algorithms for Gesture Recognition. [online] undefined. Available at: https://www.semanticscholar.

org/paper/A-Comparative-Analysis-of-Hand-Tracking-Algorithms-AmbikaL.-Chidananda/ d4aaf8fcc1f1dd31f4b713b84be7228cbde9e53b [Accessed 10 Sep. 2020].

Armstrong, E. J. and Erskine, K. L. 2018. Investigation of drowning deaths: a practical review. Academic Forensic Pathology 8(1): 8–43.

Barakat, N. 2015. Fewer cases of drowning at sea in Dubai in 2014. [online] Available at: http://gulfnews. com/news/uae/government/fewer-cases-of-drowning-at-sea-in-dubai-in-2014-1.1451466 [Accessed 12 Sep. 2020].

Chamola, V., Hassija, V., Gupta, V. and Guizani, M. 2020. A comprehensive review of the COVID-19 pandemic and the role of IoT, drones, AI, blockchain and 5G in managing its impact. IEEE Access, pp. 1–1.

Chen, Z., Kim, J. -T., Liang, J., Zhang, J. and Yuan, Y. -B. 2014. Real-time hand gesture recognition using finger segmentation. [online] The Scientific World Journal. Available at: https://www.hindawi. com/journals/tswj/2014/267872/ [Accessed 9 Sep. 2020].

Comeau, R., Pterneas, E. and Schnare, D. 2015. Motion capture and analysis system for assessing mammalian kinetics. [online] Available at: https://patents.google.com/patent/WO2015139145A1/ en?oq=WO+2015139145+A1+ [Accessed 13 Sep. 2020].

Elkjær, C. 2013. Unmanned aerial device and system thereof. [online] Available at: https://patents.google. com/patent/WO2013123944A1/en?oq=WO+2013123944+AI [Accessed 13 Sep. 2020].

Estrada, M. A. R. and Ndoma, A. 2019. The uses of unmanned aerial vehicles –UAV's- (or drones) in social logistic: Natural disasters response and humanitarian relief aid. Procedia Computer Science 149: 375–383.

Euchi, J. 2020. Do drones have a realistic place in a pandemic fight for delivering medical supplies in healthcare systems problems? Chinese Journal of Aeronautics.

Gilchrist, J. Gotsch, K. and Ryan, G. 2004. Nonfatal and fatal drownings in recreational water settings - United States, 2001–2002 (Reprinted from MMWR, 53: 447–452, 2004). JAMA The Journal of the American Medical Association 292: 164–166.

Gillian, N. and Paradiso, J. 2014. The gesture recognition toolkit. Journal of Machine Learning Research, [online] 15: 3483–3487. Available at: https://www.jmlr.org/papers/volume15/gillian14a/ gillian14a.pdf [Accessed 9 Sep. 2020].

Haker, M. 2010. Gesture-Based Interaction with Time-of-Flight Cameras. [online] Available at: https:// www.zhb.uni-luebeck.de/epubs/ediss901.pdf [Accessed 9 Sep. 2020].

Hoang, V. T. 2020. HGM-4: A new multi-cameras dataset for hand gesture recognition. Data in Brief 30: 105676.

Ijeh, A. C. 2011. Geofencing as a Security Strategy Model. [Thesis] pp. 1–140. Available at: https:// repository.uel.ac.uk/item/8608q [Accessed 2 Sep. 2020].

Ijeh, A. C. 2018. Annotated bibliography on the impact of geofencing as a security strategy model. Handbook of Cyber-Development, Cyber-Democracy, and Cyber-Defense. [online] pp. 1057–1075. Available at: https://link.springer.com/referenceworkentry/10.1007%2F978-3-319-09069-6_63 [Accessed 2 Sep. 2020].

ITF-OECD. 2020. Transport Brief: Drones in the Era of Coronavirus | Global Maritime Hub. [online] Available at: https://globalmaritimehub.com/articles/transport-brief-drones-in-the-era-of-coronavirus [Accessed 2 Sep. 2020].

Jung-Cheol, A. 2014. Drone for rescuing drowning person. [online] Available at: https://patents.google. com/patent/WO2015167103A1/en?oq=WO2015167103+A1 [Accessed 13 Sep. 2020].

Khan, R. Z. and Ibraheem, N. A. 2012. Comparative study of hand gesture recognition system. Computer Science & Information Technology (CS & IT). [online] Available at: https://airccj.org/CSCP/vol2/ csit2320.pdf [Accessed 9 Sep. 2020].

Kumar, A., Sharma, K., Singh, H., Naugriya, S. G., Gill, S. S. and Buyya, R. 2020. A Drone-based Networked System and Methods for Combating Coronavirus Disease (COVID-19) Pandemic. arXiv: 2006.06943 [cs, eess]. [online] Available at: https://arxiv.org/abs/2006.06943 [Accessed 2 Sep. 2020].

Ma'asum, F. F. M., Sulaiman, S. and Saparon, A. 2017. Comparative study of segmentation technique for hand gesture recognition system. Journal of Telecommunication, Electronic and Computer Engineering (JTEC), [online] 9(2–2): 7–10. Available at: https://journal.utem.edu.my/index.php/ jtec/article/view/2211 [Accessed 9 Sep. 2020].

Marquez, J. M. A., Sanchez, M. A. M. and Herrera, M. R. S. 2015. Rescue system. [online] Available at: https://patents.google.com/patent/WO2015144947A1/en?inventor=Jos%C3%A9+Manuel+ANDUJAR+MARQUEZ [Accessed 13 Sep. 2020].

Mod Ma'asum, F. F., Sulaiman, S. and Saparon, A. 2015. An overview of hand gestures recognition system techniques. IOP Conference Series: Materials Science and Engineering 99: 012012.

Nanivadekar, P. A. and Kulkarni, V. 2013. Gesture recognition: a revolutionary tool. International Journal of Technological Advancement and Research, Volume 3 Issue 3, ISSN: 2249–8141. Available at: https://www.academia.edu/6699796/Gesture_Recognition_A_RevolutionaryTool [Accessed 9 Sep. 2020].

Nigam, M., Richhariya, P. and Meena, A. 2020. Analysis of prediction based algorithm for hand gesture recognition. SSRN Electronic Journal.

Oudah, M., Al-Naji, A. and Chahl, J. 2020. Hand gesture recognition based on computer vision: a review of techniques. Journal of Imaging 6(8): 73.

Parenteau, M., Stockinger, Z., Hughes, S., Hickey, B., Mucciarone, J., Manganello, C. and Beeghly, A. 2018. Drowning Management. Military Medicine, [online] 183(suppl_2): 172–179. Available at: https://academic.oup.com/milmed/article/183/suppl_2/172/5091146 [Accessed 27 Oct. 2019].

Patel, N. and He, J. 2018. A survey on hand gesture recognition techniques, methods and tools. International Journal of Research in Advent Technology, [online] 6(6). Available at: http://www.ijrat.org/downloads/Vol-6/june-2018/paper%20ID-66201807.pdf [Accessed 9 Sep. 2020].

Rios Soria, D. J. and Schaeffer, S. E. 2012. A tool for hand-sign recognition. Lecture Notes in Computer Science, pp. 137–146.

Ruiz Estrada, M. A. 2020. The uses of drones in case of massive epidemics contagious diseases relief humanitarian aid: Wuhan-COVID-19 crisis. SSRN Electronic Journal.

Sharma, A., Mittal, A., Singh, S. and Awatramani, V. 2020. Hand gesture recognition using image processing and feature extraction techniques. Procedia Computer Science 173: 181–190.

Skorup, B. and Haaland, C. 2020. How drones can help fight the coronavirus. SSRN Electronic Journal.

Stoppa, M., Hummel, B., Mutto, C. D. and Pasgualotto, G. 2013. Systems and methods for initializing motion tracking of human hands. [online] Available at: https://patents.google.com/patent/US8615108B1/en?oq=US+8615108+B1+ [Accessed 13 Sep. 2020].

Trigueiros, P., Ribeiro, F. and Reis, L. P. 2012. A comparison of machine learning algorithms applied to hand gesture recognition. [online] IEEE Xplore. Available at: https://ieeexplore.ieee.org/document/6263058 [Accessed 10 Sep. 2020].

Wachs, J. P., Kölsch, M., Stern, H. and Edan, Y. 2011. Vision-based hand-gesture applications. Communications of the ACM 54(2): 60–71.

Wachs, J. P., Stern, H. I., Edan, Y., Gillam, M., Handler, J., Feied, C. and Smith, M. 2008. A gesture-based tool for sterile browsing of radiology images. Journal of the American Medical Informatics Association 15(3): 321–323.

Whitelaw, S., Mamas, M. A., Topol, E. and Spall, H. G. C. V. 2020. Applications of digital technology in COVID-19 pandemic planning and response. The Lancet Digital Health, [online] 0(0). Available at: https://www.thelancet.com/journals/landig/article/PIIS2589-7500(20)30142-4/fulltext.

WHO. 2014. Global report on drowning preventing a leading killer. [online] Available at: https://apps.who.int/iris/bitstream/handle/10665/143893/9789241564786_eng.pdf.

Wipfli, R., Dubois-Ferrière, V., Budry, S., Hoffmeyer, P. and Lovis, C. 2016. Gesture-controlled image management for operating room: a randomized crossover study to compare interaction using gestures, mouse, and third person relaying. PLOS ONE 11(4): e0153596.

Yang, G. -Z., Nelson, B. J., Murphy, R. R., Choset, H., Christensen, H., Collins, S. H., Dario, P., Goldberg, K., Ikuta, K., Jacobstein, N., Kragic, D., Taylor, R. H. and McNutt, M. 2020. Combating COVID-19—The role of robotics in managing public health and infectious diseases. Science Robotics, [online] 5(40). Available at: https://robotics.sciencemag.org/content/5/40/eabb5589 [Accessed 25 Apr. 2020].

Yukun, Z. 2015. Unmanned aerial vehicle life buoy dropping device. [online] Available at: https://patents.google.com/patent/CN105292479A/en?oq=CN+105292479+A [Accessed 13 Sep. 2020].

3

Modelling Criminal Investigation Process, Quality and Requirements

Stig Andersen* and Jens Petter Fossdal

1. Introduction

Crime is evolving. Old crimes are now being executed in new ways with new tools, and new crimes are emerging (Farrell and Birks 2018). Our knowledge is also growing. We are constantly making discoveries that can aid in our strife towards preventing and investigating crime. But technological and societal developments are also causing challenges. The amount of data available towards a criminal investigation is increasing (Garfinkel 2010; Awadhi et al. 2015), and new methods which can furnish investigations with detailed information about the case (Smith and Mann 2015). Research in psychology has also made us aware of the risks bias can pose in human cognitive endeavours such as criminal investigations (Tversky and Kahneman 1973; Kahneman 2003; Fahsing 2016; Sunde and Dror 2019). These challenges must be consciously managed.

A fundamental part of our civilization are the human rights established in the Universal Declaration of Human Rights (United Nations General Assembly 1948) and the European Convention on Human Rights (European Court of Human Rights 2010). Essential to criminal investigation and prosecution are the 'right to a fair trial' (European Court of Human Rights 2010, art. 6) and the principle of 'No punishment without law' (European Court of Human Rights 2010, art. 7). To criminal investigation, digital and other forensic science practitioners and scientists, the right to a fair trial implies that what we as professionals base our work on, and eventually present at a trial, must be as true as we can make it. Science—and the natural sciences in particular—have been searching for universal or absolute truths for a very long time. Universal truths are hard to prove, for in their nature, they must be true always and everywhere. Still, the scientific method, described by Popper as constructing hypotheses and testing them by

Dept. of Digital Policing and Innovation, Oslo Police District, Norway.
* Corresponding author: stig.asmund.andersen@politiet.no

repeated observations (Popper 1959), has proven applicable in many fields and led to a plethora of discoveries. Criminal investigation and prosecution have an advantage over scientific research in that it does not require absolute truths. Sometimes described as 'moral certainty' (Waldman 1959, p.299), and known as Blackstone's maxim that 'it is better that ten guilty persons escape, than that one innocent suffer' (Blackstone 1799, p.358–359), the truth that we are striving for in criminal investigation is defined as truth beyond reasonable doubt. In order to reach these goals and contribute to a fair trial, each investigation needs to ensure objectives, transparency and quality in the criminal investigation process. To do that we need to identify how to describe and measure quality in a criminal investigation. And to do that we need to know and describe how such investigations are performed.

Criminal investigation is a process to discover, describe, document and explain incidents which violate criminal law (Blackstone 1799; Gudjonsson 1992; Innes 2003; Stelfox 2009; Brodeur 2010; Sennewald and Tsukayama 2015). I.e., criminal investigation—like scientific research—pursues facts through a series of targeted activities. Since the scientific method has proven to be a suitable approach to such work, criminal investigation can—as this chapter shows—be described using that tried-and-tested model as guiding template. Indeed, research conducted over the past 10–15 years in both policing and digital forensics points to the hypothetico-deductive model as the methodical standard which investigation should strive to adhere to (Fahsing 2016; Rachlew 2009; Carrier 2006). And by adopting the scientific method as the basis for a process model on investigation, we can apply the same principles of quality in criminal investigations as in scientific research; reliability and validity, to serve as measures of quality in investigations. The process model presented in this chapter aligns the investigation process with the scientific method, shows how the investigation process relates to its neighbouring processes, and delineates and details the internal sub-processes of investigation. The model shows how the hypothetico-deductive approach provides tools and methodologies for performing a reliable and valid investigation, regardless of the context in which the investigation takes place, and semi-independent of the jurisdiction governing the investigation.

2. The Criminal Case

A crime is that which violates criminal law. A criminal case is an incident, or a series of related incidents, which might violate criminal law, and all the actions, considerations and decisions made regarding this or these incidents. Criminal cases are usually processed by a law enforcement organisation, a public prosecutor and a court of law. The details of this process are dependent on the jurisdiction in which the incident takes place, but the general process is independent of legal particulars.

As shown in Figure 1, the criminal case can be divided into three phases:[1]

1. Detect and identify
2. Investigate
3. Prosecute/React

---

[1] The Business Process Modelling Notation (BPMN2.0) standard used to model the process does not specify "phase" as an entity but is used here as a synonym for the "process"-entity (Object Management Group Inc 2013).

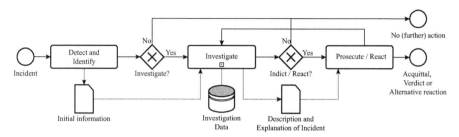

Figure 1: Criminal case process model (BPMN2.0).

For an incident to become a case it first has to be detected, identified and recognised as an incident of interest, e.g., a possible crime (phase one). This usually involves an incident being observed by, or reported to, the police or similar law enforcement organization. Based on the initial information provided and uncovered in this process, the decision on whether to initiate an investigation or not is taken. The goal of this investigation (phase two) is to gather sufficient information to describe and explain the incident. It is on the basis of this information the decision is made to either dismiss the case, if anyone can and should be indicted for the crime, or if some other reaction should be initiated. Prosecution or reaction is the third phase of the case. And though this normally involves court hearings or similar proceedings, the details of this is entirely dependent on the jurisdiction. For instance, the Norwegian criminal process includes two levels of appeal (not including revisions) (Straffeprosessloven 1981), while the Rome Statute includes only one (United Nations 1998). A criminal case is completed or solved when it is dismissed, all charges are waived or when the criminal proceedings have ended in acquittal, an enforceable verdict or a different sanction or reaction (e.g., community service or forced mental health care). Note that a situation might arise during the prosecution/reaction-phase where further investigation is required. For instance, new information may come forth or the courts might decide that an aspect of the case is insufficiently covered. When this happens, further investigative steps can be taken, effectively returning the case to the investigation phase.

Exactly at which point in time an incident becomes or is considered a crime, is also dependent on the jurisdiction and not discussed in detail here. It is sufficient to recognize that some incidents are crimes, and while these incidents are being processed by law enforcement and other parts of a justice system, they constitute a criminal case. Note also that some law enforcement organisations are also tasked with investigating incidents that are not crimes. Such cases may follow the same process, but without being subject to prosecution. Instead, they may follow different post-investigation treatment.

3. The Criminal Investigation Process

3.1 What is an Criminal Investigation?

A criminal investigation is performed to determine if a crime has occurred, and to discover, describe, and document sufficient information about the incident. As such, criminal investigation is a process of collecting, processing, interpreting and presenting information to explain the possible crime (Gudjonsson 1992; Innes 2003; Stelfox 2009; Sennewald and Tsukayama 2015). An incident is an event in time, and it can be defined and described by six basic elements or circumstances: What happened, where and when the incident took place, how the incident occurred, who was involved, and why it happened (see Figure 2). Aristotle first described these circumstances, and they figure prominently in both philosophy and rhetoric, as well as in investigation. Today they are usually referred to as "the 6Ws" or "the 5WH" of the investigation (Sloan 2010; Innes 2003; Stelfox 2009; Fahsing 2016). Only once sufficient information about these circumstances has been collected and understood can the incident can be described and explained, and the investigation completed.

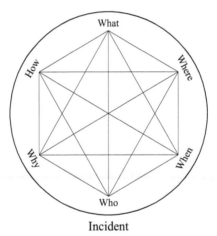

Incident

Figure 2: The six circumstances of an incident.

3.1.1 A Hypothesis-driven, Cyclic Process

In order to arrive at a reliable and valid explanation, investigators must examine all the various possible explanations of the event. These possible explanations form the different hypotheses of the incident, sometimes called lines of enquiry (Criminal Procedure and Investigations Act 1996, 1996; Innes 2003; Tong et al. 2009; Fahsing 2016). This approach resembles the scientific method and it becomes apparent that incident investigations—regardless of whether the incident is criminal or of a different nature—can be described in much the same way (Popper 1959; Platt 1964; Hilborn and Mangel 1997). Both scientific research and investigation formulate hypotheses to pose different, possible explanations for the problem at hand, both collect and process data into facts as objectively as possible to inform the different hypotheses, and both use logical inference to arrive at its conclusions. Recognizing that both endeavours are complex tasks (Glouberman and Zimmerman 2002), which require planning to be efficiently executed, investigation can be described as a four-step process similar to the scientific method:

1. Formulate possible hypotheses and identify the corresponding information needs

2. Develop a strategy and a plan to acquire the necessary information

3. Collect and process data that can respond to the information needs
4. Evaluate the hypotheses

Figure 3 shows this four-step process using Business Process Modelling Notation 2.0 (BPMN2.0) (Object Management Group Inc 2013). The process is described in further detail below but observe that the criminal investigation process—similar to the scientific process—is a cyclic process. Hypotheses are developed by formulating and updating the statement in ever-increasing detail as the amount of information increases. The strategy and plan to acquire and produce the necessary information must be adapted to the constantly changing situation and working to collect and process data involves a plethora of activities—some of which can constitute a scientific process by themselves. The cyclic loop continues until the investigation has gathered such facts as to reduce the number of probable hypotheses to one, or until it is clear that the investigation cannot be advanced any further. Note also that the complexity and amount of work required to complete each process step depends on the situation. For instance, many of the steps involved in investigations of volume crime[2] by experienced investigators at an established organisation, are probably routine. The investigators are experienced, the work is performed based on locally documented procedures, and the policies and requirements are well known and defined. Investigations of major incidents[3] on the other hand, or when an incident is investigated by someone with less experience, the circumstances are different. Nevertheless, no matter how short or long each process step takes, they are all executed. Even if the whole step occurs implicitly in the investigators mind. Studies in cognitive psychology shows that it is probably impossible for a human to perceive an incident without immediately constructing and evaluating at least one hypothesis about how it came to be based on prior experience and knowledge (Gilhooly et al. 2014).

3.1.2 Requirements and Quality

Measuring the quality of an investigation is not a simple task. The efficiency of criminal investigation as a deterrent of crime might be assessed by examining if the right cases are investigated, or if prosecution results in the expected sentences. Further, clear-up rates and studies of whether investigations are conducted according to rules and regulations—including basic human rights—can give a general measure of the quality of criminal investigation (Myhrer 2015; Brodeur 2010). However, none of these factors can indicate the quality within, and during, a specific investigation, i.e., if it will achieve its goal. For that we need to measure or assess how well the investigative process reaches its goal. In other words, we need quality factors which relate to the internals of the investigative process. In scientific research, reliability and validity are key factors when assessing the credibility and quality of a study. Reliability reflects the notion that an observation is repeatable or that an experiment can be replicated. Validation, on the other hand, is considered to be a measure of

---

[2] Volume crime is a type of crime which, 'through its sheer volume, has significant impact on the community and the ability of the local police to tackle it' (Association of Chief Police Officers 2009, p.8).

[3] A major incident is an event which requires extraordinary resources.

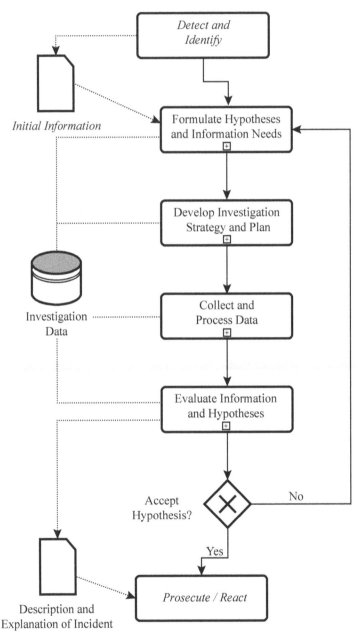

Figure 3: The crime investigation process model (BPMN2.0).

whether or not the observation or result reflects the truth. This implies that a reliable observation is stable over time, while a valid observation accurately reflects the truth.

To gain a complete understanding of the incident, the investigation needs to describe and explain all six circumstances. However, a complete explanation is sometimes not possible. Information about why, for instance, can be hard to obtain. Particularly in situations where the people involved in the incident are unable or unwilling to give information about their motivations and actions. But an absolute complete explanation may not be required for an investigation to be a success. The information must be of such quality that, when considered in its entirety, it can prove the incident beyond reasonable doubt in a criminal court (Blackstone 1859; Waldman 1959; European Court of Human Rights 2010; Bjerknes and Fahsing 2018; Innes 2003). The exact requirements for a criminal investigation to achieve this goal depends on the jurisdiction in which the case is processed,[4] the particular crimes being investigated, and on the evidence and documentation[5] provided by the investigation. The jurisdictional and legal requirements must be derived from the legal texts which form the basis for the criminal hypotheses being investigated.[6] But the requirements posed on the information can be expressed in more general terms.

The quality requirements on information can be divided into two groups with two measures each: Primary quality measures include parameters which impact directly on the resolution of the case. The two primary quality parameters are validity and reliability. Validity is a measure of to what degree the information represents a true fact. For instance, if a green car was present at the scene of the crime, validity measures if a witness or a CCTV camera actually observed and stored this fact as "green car". Reliability is a measure of to what degree the information is accurately recalled and presented. For instance, if the witness or the CCTV observed the green car but recalled or presented the fact as "red car", then the information would have low reliability. Secondary quality measures are parameters which impact on the execution of the investigation, but not on the resolution of the case. The two secondary measures are relevance and impact. Relevance is a measure of how well the data can respond to any of the information needs of the investigation (see Section 3.2.3). Impact, on the other hand, measures the force or weight of the information in relation to a hypothesis. Note that if quantified, all quality measures must be given a value between 0 (lowest score) and 1 (highest score). The quality can then be expressed as a product of all the quality measures in relation to the end result, to each hypothesis and to each information need.

As described in further detail in Section 3.1.3, information is made up of data and metadata, i.e., contextual descriptors, and a collective term encompassing evidence and evidence documentation. Information is collected and processed by investigation actions performed on or with data sources—objects, including persons—which may contain information. The relationships between the investigation actions and the various information elements (data source, data/trace, evidence and documentation) are described in Section 3.4 and shown in Figure 4. Each data source, and each investigation action affects the quality of the information. For instance, a CCTV

---

[4] Note that in some jurisdictions, a criminal investigation might also be required to collect other information related to the resolution of the case (Stelfox 2009; Riksadvokaten 1999).

[5] The terms evidence and documentation are described in Section 3.1.3.

[6] Investigations of a different nature, e.g., business internal investigations, non-criminal financial discrepancy investigations, accident and disaster investigations, derive their specific requirements from policy or other governing documents equivalent to legal texts in their respective contexts.

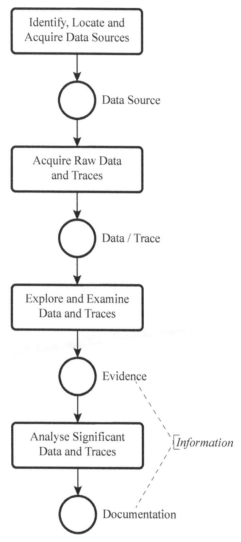

Figure 4: The relationship between the information elements and the investigation actions.

surveillance system with no microphones cannot register sound, which means that as a data source the system has no validity regarding what sounds were audible at a scene. Similarly, information collected from a witness by means of torture has no reliability because the method employed to perform the investigation action does not lead to accurate recollection and presentation of information. Further, the colour of a person's hair cannot speak to a person's intentions, thus rendering such information irrelevant to questions regarding why an incident occurred.[7]

---

[7] Assuming that hair colour was not part of the perpetrator's motivations.

3.1.3 Information—A Fundamental Problem

Investigation is 'a form of information work' involving identifying, interpreting and ordering information (Innes 2003, p.113). And though several studies conclude that most criminal cases are cleared, i.e., the perpetrator is identified and apprehended, by police patrols or based on witness statements (Innes 2003; Brodeur 2010; O'Neill 2018), the investigation is still dealing with information, even when little work is involved in obtaining or processing that information. The work which an investigation performs involves collecting and processing information in essence, information created as part of an incident is communicated—conveyed—from persons and objects to the investigation. This means that all investigations are faced with the fundamental problem of communication; reproducing as exactly as possible the information produced and transmitted by the sender (Shannon 1948). Because the collection and processing of information is perhaps the most important part of investigation, the fundamental problem of communication also becomes a fundamental problem of investigation: How to ensure that the information (re) produced by the investigation is, and is understood, as exactly as possible to the information produced by the incident?

All information carries meaning. Since the meaning can change depending on a variety of variables, information can be defined as contextualized data. Using a mathematical expression, we can say that information = data + metadata where data is understood as facts, properties or sensory output from a data source, and metadata as contextual descriptors which determine how the data is interpreted and understood. It is the meaning of the information, as it relates to the incident being investigated, that is the object of interest. And there are two parts to extracting this meaning. First, the information must be collected in such a way that the original meaning is kept intact. Second, the information must be interpreted and understood such that the original meaning is received by the investigation. This decomposition is what allows, among other things, for the method of the quality assessment described in Section 3.1.2. It is necessary to recognize, however, that the meaning carried by the information is not limited to a person's intention behind a statement. Meaning must be understood as a requirement that facts must be maintained intact in relation to their original state in case of objective facts, and to their original intention in case of subjective expressions. For instance, epithelial cells must be collected such that the DNA they might contain remains intact and free from contamination, and witnesses must be interviewed in such a way that the observations and opinions they report remain intact and free from influence.

Building on the definitions above, we can establish the following definitions:

- **Data Source:** An object, a person or a location which may contain data or traces.
- **Data:** A collection of facts sensed and stored by a data source.
- **Trace:** Material or an object which itself may, as a whole or in part, be evidence.
- **Evidence:** Data or trace with relevance to the case, i.e., which responds to a need for information or impacts a hypothesis.

- **Documentation:** A description, analysis or interpretation of evidence.
- **Information:** Evidence and documentation used to evaluate hypotheses.

Different methods must be used to collect and process data from different data sources. Data sources types are not mutually exclusive. For example, a person is both a cognitive and a physical data source. Both cognitive data, for example what the person observed, and physical traces, for example hair and fingerprints, can be collected from that source. Similarly, a mobile phone is both a physical data source and an electronic data source. See Section 3.4 for further details.

Cognitive data sources are, essentially, human minds. Currently, since mind reading technology is not available, the only recognized method for collecting cognitive data is human communication, e.g., speech, sign language, written text, etc.

Physical data sources are any and all physical objects and locations, including for example bodies, rooms/houses, audio and video recorders, photographs (the physical kind), paper documents and books, and the physical part of digital storage devices.

Electronic data sources are objects which contain electronically encoded data, i.e., data stored by a computer. This includes optical, magnetic and solid-state storage devices, wired and wireless communication.

Kuykendall (1982) describes three different types of information classified by its specificity and how it is employed in an investigation:

- **Intelligence:** General information of low specificity, e.g., a tip.
- **Lead:** Information which directs the investigation, i.e., information defining or contributing to the hypotheses or lines of enquiry of the investigation. Leads are more specific than intelligence, but less than evidence.
- **Evidence:** Information used to prove the various elements of the crime and link the perpetrator(s) to the crime.

3.2 Step One: Formulate Hypotheses and Information Needs

The first step of an investigation is to explicitly and consciously express possible and reasonable hypotheses that can explain the incident,[8] and to identify what information is missing in order to evaluate the hypotheses (see Figure 5). A hypothesis is a 'potential explanation or conclusion that is to be tested by collecting and presenting evidence', and a good hypothesis is formulated as a testable, definite statement based on observations and knowledge (Heuer and Pherson 2015, p.169). The hypotheses are essential when determining the scope of the investigation (see Section 3.3). Initially this is done based on the initial information gathered during detection of the incident. As the investigation progress, the development of hypotheses will be based on the new evidence and information uncovered through the investigation. Each hypothesis should be expressed as a complete incident, i.e., all circumstances need to be present in the articulation. At different stages of the investigation, and in particular at the beginning

---

[8] Reasonable in this instance means that the impossible, e.g., supernatural explanations like a homicidal unicorn, is excluded.

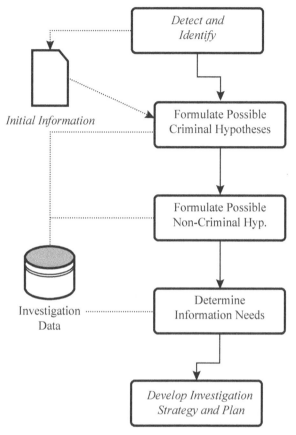

Figure 5: Formulate hypotheses and information needs (BPMN2.0).

when the only information available is that provided from the detection phase, it is likely that there will not be enough evidence and information available to construct complete incidents. When that happens, the circumstance is left blank and the missing information must be collected later.

There are several reasons for using hypotheses to guide an investigation. First of all, a precisely stated hypothesis shows us what is being investigated, i.e., what the incident might be. Second, hypotheses direct the collection of data such that all aspects are covered. From the articulation of the hypotheses it is clear what information is missing. Third, identifying several hypotheses can also reduce the risk of biases in the investigation (Fahsing 2016). And lastly, the hypotheses influence heavily both on the investigation strategy (see Section 3.3) and on the quality of the investigation (see Section 3.1.2). Hence, developing hypotheses are a vital and integral part of an investigation. Also, it is essential that the investigation goes beyond the initial information and produce hypotheses which both ignores and contradicts some of the initial information. The goal is to produce a list of hypotheses which cover all the possible explanations of the incident, thus ensuring a broad, objective and thorough investigation. This can be challenging, but brain-storming and other structured analytic techniques like Starbursting can help. Such techniques are designed to generate new ideas by focusing on quantity first under the assumption that "quantity breeds quality" (Heuer and Pherson 2015; Gilhooly et al. 2014). While they are collaborative processes consisting of explicit and transparent procedures and employed 'to increase the rigor of analysis to improve the likelihood of generating valid judgments' (Coulthart 2016, p.937), brainstorming can also be performed solo. Studies have shown that structured analysis techniques can improve the quality of intelligence analysis when employed correctly (Coulthart 2017), and similar effects can be expected when the techniques are used in comparable areas like investigation.

Initially, and early in the investigation, information about all the circumstances will probably not be available. When that is the case, the investigation should focus on what the incident was, and where and when the incident it took place. Once more information is available, further details are added to the hypotheses based on this new information, and the list of missing information is updated. Such hypothesis development can involve formulating new hypotheses, adding details about who, how or why the incident occurred to existing hypotheses, or formulating sub-hypotheses. A sub-hypothesis is a variation of a main hypothesis such that some key details are equal to all the sub-hypotheses while other details vary. Eventually, given that enough information can be collected, one hypothesis will emerge as sufficiently informed to adequately explain the incident, thus providing the means to resolve the case.

3.2.1   Identify and Develop Criminal Hypotheses

In criminal investigations, hypotheses can be divided into two, mutually exclusive, categories: Hypotheses stating that the incident was a crime (criminal hypotheses), and hypotheses stating that the incident was not a crime (non-criminal hypotheses). In a given jurisdiction, there is a finite number of possible criminal hypotheses equal to the number of crimes described by the laws of that jurisdiction. For example, if an incident is being investigated within the jurisdiction of the Rome Statue, the only possible four criminal hypotheses are genocide, crimes against humanity, war crimes and crime of aggression (United Nations 1998). In most jurisdictions the total number of possible criminal hypotheses will probably be much higher. However, different crimes can be grouped together to form categories of crime types. Violent crimes, sexual crimes and financial crimes are examples of such categories. These categories can be further divided into sub-categories.

When the criminal hypotheses are based directly on the legal text defining the criminal acts, the hypotheses define precisely what information is required to confirm each particular hypothesis. Interpreting or extracting the information requirements from the legal texts might require effort from a legal scholar versed in the particular jurisdiction. However, since these would be general information requirements relevant to each investigation where the particular crime could be posed as a hypothesis, this can be prepared beforehand. Such preparations can assist in ensuring equal treatment and considerations between investigations and reduce the amount of work necessary in each investigation.

3.2.2 Formulate and Develop Non-Criminal Hypotheses

In a purely criminal investigation, only one non-criminal hypothesis is strictly required: That the incident is not a crime. Essentially, this is the null-hypothesis. And if all the hypotheses are correctly formulated and mutually exclusive, then all the criminal hypotheses can be disproved by validating the null-hypothesis and vice versa. Criminal investigations conducted by law enforcement organisations, however, are often required to describe and explain incidents beyond determining that the incident wasn't a crime. Therefore, all possible non-criminal hypotheses should also be formulated, hence including them in the investigation. Contrary to the criminal hypotheses, no legal text contains a list of all the non-criminal incidents which might occur. Yet, it is possible to construct lists of probable or reasonable non-criminal hypotheses to be included in investigations given certain criteria. For instance, in a missing person-case, an initial list of hypotheses could include homicide, abduction, violence/injury, accident/illness, suicide, left voluntarily and not missing. It is unnecessary to spend time generating such a general list every time a person is reported missing. The general list can be used as a template, and new ones can be added depending on the situation. The particulars for each case are used to articulate the different circumstances for each hypothesis, regardless of whether the hypotheses originate from a pre-generated list or formulated uniquely.

3.2.3 Determine Information Needs

When the hypotheses have been articulated, the investigation must identify what information is required in order to evaluate the hypotheses. Information contributes to the evaluation of hypotheses first by providing candidate circumstances, e.g., by suggesting when an incident took place or who was involved, and second by supporting or discouraging a hypothesis. Early in an investigation, emphasis needs to be placed on collecting information supplying missing circumstances. Gradually, as the circumstances of the incident becomes clearer, the investigation shifts towards collecting information which supports of discourages the various hypotheses.

It can be practical to express information needs as questions. For instance, at an early stage of the investigation, relevant information needs could be 'Who were present at the scene' or 'Where did the incident take place'. Similar to lists of hypotheses, information needs like these can also be generated as templates and reused initially. However, as the investigation progress, the information needs become increasingly specific and detailed.

3.3 Step Two: Develop Investigation Strategy and Plan

Conducting an investigation requires planning. How much depends on the amount of work to be done and the available resources. Major incidents, homicide and rape, are often prioritized higher and receive more resources than volume crime cases. Also, some cases require more work than others in order to collect and process the necessary evidence and information to describe and explain the incident. The object of the second step of the investigation process is to determine the legal, administrative and practical parameters of the investigation, establish a strategy on how to proceed, and make a plan of action. These aspects will develop during the course of the investigation, and as data is collected, hypotheses are updated and events unfold, all these aspects must be reconsidered and updated accordingly. There are four parts to this step (see Figure 6):

1. Determine legal and policy requirements and priorities
2. Identify external stakeholders and requirements
3. Decide investigation orientation and profile
4. Construct/update plan of actions

The first three parts make up the investigation strategy, and guide the plan of action, which determines and describes what is to be done.

Conducting an investigation involves three types of action:

Investigation actions are performed to directly advance the investigation, i.e., hypothesis formulation and evaluation (steps 1 and 4), and data collection and processing (step 3).

Legal actions are mandated by the jurisdiction in which the investigation is performed. This includes seizing items,[9] obtaining search and arrest war-rants, and remanding an apprehended person into custody. The details of such actions vary with jurisdiction and are not discussed in further detail.

Administrative actions are performed to ensure the continued running of the investigation, including—but not limited to—strategy and planning actions (step 2). Some administrative actions are dependent on the organisation in which the investigation is conducted and are therefore not discussed further.

3.3.1 Determine Legal and Policy Requirements and Priorities

All investigations are governed by legal and organisational policies and regulations. For example, criminal investigations performed by a law enforcement organisation might have the authority to search private property when there is a reasonable suspicion towards the owner of the property. However, the same organisation might not be allowed to conduct covert telephone surveillance unless the incident being investigated is of a certain severity. Similarly, an organisation could have 50 investigators available to investigate 100 cases, i.e., 2 cases per investigator. However, policy might dictate that certain cases, e.g., homicides and rapes, have a higher priority than other cases, calling for a different distribution. Such legal and policy requirements and priorities govern how the investigation is conducted. The type of crime being investigated, and the most likely hypotheses are likely to affect these requirements and priorities.

3.3.2 Identify External Stakeholders and Requirements

All criminal cases involve people. Sometimes they also involve organisations. The situation these people and organisations are in and their status in the case (i.e., if

---

[9] Seizing an item is a legal action while locating the item and collecting and processing data from it are investigation actions.

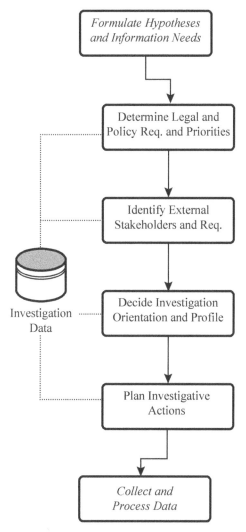

Figure 6: Develop investigation strategy and plan.

they are witnesses, victims or suspects) are likely to affect how the investigation is conducted. It can also be necessary to perform particular actions based on these issues. If, for example, the suspect speaks a different language than the investigator, it might be necessary to locate an interpreter. Such issues must be identified in order to adapt the investigation to the situation.

3.3.3 Decide Investigation Orientation and Profile

Criminal investigations can be conducted overtly or covertly. This is called the profile of the investigation. An overt investigation is one where the fact that an investigation is being conducted is known. A covert investigation is one that is conducted in secrecy. This means that a covert investigation is limited to covert investigation actions—actions conducted without the target or others knowing or noticing, while overt investigations can employ both covert and over actions. There are five aspects to consider when deciding on the investigation profile:

- Legal
- Tactical
- Technical
- Availability
- Cost

The European Convention on Human Rights require that everyone charged with a criminal offence has the right to be promptly informed of the accusation against him (European Court of Human Rights 2010, art. 6). However, this does not make covert investigations illegal *per se*, but requirements imposed by the jurisdiction must be observed. There are the legal aspects. Tactical aspects include how resources—human, financial and technical—can be disposed and how they can act and manoeuvre to achieve their goal. Technical aspects refer to what is actually possible given the available resources, e.g., if it is possible to gain entry to a place without being detected, or if the necessary technology and tools are available to eavesdrop on a wireless transmission. Availability refers simply to whether the necessary resources are free for disposition, while cost concerns how much funding can be spent.

Brodeur describes the orientation of an investigation as the direction of the investigation; if it starts from an incident and works toward identifying a perpetrator, or if it starts with a person suspected of criminal activity and works towards identifying the incident (Brodeur 2010). While this probably is be a valid description of criminal investigation from a criminology standpoint, we hold that all criminal investigations are incident oriented. While some investigations may conclude that no incident took place, and some incidents are less physical than the word first suggests, there is always an incident, or a series of incidents, at the centre of the investigation. Thus, in this context, the orientation of the investigation concerns which of the circumstances the investigation actions need to focus on. The same aspects as described above need to be considered when the orientation is selected, and the result is an important prioritizing guideline when the plan of action is constructed and updated.

3.3.4 Plan of Action

After having identified what information is needed (see Section 3.2.1), and established or updated the strategy guiding the investigation, a plan of action can be constructed and updated. Like other action plans, the investigation plan is a goal-oriented list of actions describing what is to be done, what the action is expected to achieve (i.e., why), when it is to be performed (either by a determined due date or at a fixed date and time), by whom, where, and how. Note that this does not need to be a detailed step-by-step on how to perform each action. It is a general prerequisite that the people assigned to a task is competent to perform it. Some actions require more detailed planning than others, and sometimes multiple actions can be executed together. For example, actions to search a house and apprehend the residents can be combined into an operation requiring independent planning. When constructing and updating the plan, the same aspects as described above—legal, tactical, technical, availability and cost—must be considered for each investigation action. The basis for these considerations comes from the investigation strategy, however, each action must still be independently evaluated. Each action should also be assigned a priority. The plan is updated as the investigation progress, and actions can of course be cancelled or amended as need arise.

3.4 Step Three: Collect and Process Data

Information is constructed from data and used to evaluate the hypotheses formulated in the first step of the investigation process. As described in Section 3.1.3, information is a collective term for evidence and documentation. It is the goal of the third step of this process step to collect and process data and traces from data source, identify what data and traces might be relevant (i.e., identify the evidence), and analyse that data to ensure that the evidence is correctly interpreted and understood. There are four parts to this process (see Figure 7):

1. Identify, locate and gain access to/control over sources of possibly relevant data
2. Acquire data and traces
3. Explore and examine the data/traces to identify relevant evidence
4. Analyse and document relevant evidence

Remember from Section 3.1.2 that the methods used to perform these actions have a profound impact on the quality of the investigation. This is similar to how experiments, observations and measurements are used in scientific endeavours. It is essential to ensure that the methods employed, and the sources they are employed on, can (re-)produce valid and reliable information, and that the information is relevant, i.e., responds to the information needs, and can impact the evaluation of the hypotheses. The execution of the actions, along with assessments and decisions made while performing the actions, must be documented such that they can be examined and confirmed.

3.4.1 Identify, Locate and Acquire Data Sources

The goal of this step is to identify who and where data about the incident might be located and obtain access to these data sources. In practice, this may involve finding out who might have witnessed the incident and identify their names and contact details, search for and secure physical items and traces which might be or contain data relevant to the incident, or ascertain the user account details of social media accounts belonging to individuals or organizations related to the incident.

3.4.2 Acquire Data and Traces

Acquiring data and traces involves gaining control and possession of human and digital data, for instance through communicating with a human or a digital source, and to extract and lift traces from physical objects. While data presented vocally from a

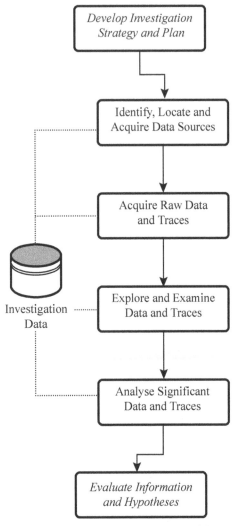

Figure 7: Data collection and processing process model (BPMN2.0).

person and stored in digital format is data, it can't be used practically by an investigator before it has been properly prepared. For example, data communicated by a witness to a police officer needs to be recorded as precisely and thoroughly as possible to maintain as much of it as possible. Current recommendations include audio and video recordings, and written transcripts or summaries. Similarly, digital data is stored on physical devices using a variety of different technologies and encodings. In order to process this data in a safe and secure manner such that the data isn't altered or lost, it needs to be copied from the original source to a different storage device.

Interviews with witnesses, suspects and victims, acquiring digitally stored data from a storage device and collecting trace material and objects are examples of data-collecting actions.

3.4.3 Explore and Examine Data and Traces

Once data has been acquired, it can be examined. The goal is to locate data which responds to the information requirements or might otherwise influence the investigation. Sometimes referred to as "reviewing" or "reading", data exploration and examination essentially means to locate significant data and traces, that is data of possible relevance. Note that to determine if a piece of data actually is relevant and why, further analysis might be required. For instance, while the content of the message "We'll get him" might appear obvious, the actual implication of the message could change dramatically when shown to have been exchanged between parents rather than between two people suspected of killing a man.

3.4.4 Analyse Data

Significant data has to be analysed to have their relevance, reliability and validity determined. Analysis of data often involves performing various scientific examinations using appropriate forensic methods to identify, classify or quantify something (Michael J. Saks and Koehler 2005; Franke and Srihari 2008; Fraser and Williams 2009), to describe and infer possible causal and historical relationships, or to assess the credibility of testimonies or statements. While several studies have found that evidence based on forensic science might not be as perfect as previously assumed (Michael J. Saks and Koehler 2005; Sunde and Dror 2019), data analysis is still an integral and necessary part of an investigation. What these studies primarily shows is that data analysis must be performed by people with the necessary competency, and that care has to be taken when evaluating the resulting information and using it as evidence.

3.5 Step Four: Evaluate Information and Hypotheses

Once information has been collected, the significance of each fact and the combined implication of all the available information must be evaluated against all the hypotheses. This is done by determining how and if each fact supports or weakens each hypothesis. To accurately perform this process, the collected information must be interpreted and understood within context and in relation to each other. Then it must be applied and assessed through logical and deliberate reasoning to each hypothesis. This mental process requires operations of what Stanovich and West, according to Kahneman (Kahneman 2003), describes as System 2 cognitive processes.

We can deduce two key requirements to performing this task:

1. Information interpretation competency
2. Information availability

The information interpretation competency requirement means that the information generated from the collected data must be considered by a person with sufficient knowledge and skill to understand what the information means. This person must also be competent to understand and assess the implications of the information when it is applied to the various hypotheses. This might sound obvious, but as Bloom's taxonomy suggests; knowledge, comprehension and application competency is required before a person is able to analyse and evaluate something (Krathwohl 2002). For instance, a timestamp collected from a message sent via an instant messaging service might have different implications when applied to two different hypotheses. The person evaluating this information in reference to the various hypotheses must be able to understand the message-data and the timestamp-data, and to assess the significance of the information in relation to the various hypotheses.

The information availability requirement means that the person performing the evaluation must be aware of and have access to all other information of relevance.[10] The implications of some information can change dramatically when considered together with other information. If the person evaluating the various information and hypotheses "can't see the whole picture", errors can easily occur. Situations where these requirements are not met result in an increased information interpretation and availability risk, i.e., the risk of erroneous evaluation of a hypothesis due to lack of information interpretation competency or missing access to relevant information. This risk is an expression of how a possible error lies with the interpretation of or access to information, rather than with the actual execution of the evaluation. The latter is a hypothesis evaluation risk, i.e., the risk of erroneous evaluation of a hypothesis due to errors in judgement. This risk stems from judgment errors when performing the hypothesis evaluation. Performing such a task involves making judgments based on available information. When performed based on impressions rather than deliberate reasoning, such mental work is subject to a number of risky heuristics like availability bias, confirmation bias, affect heuristic and tunnel vision (Kahneman 2003; Groenendaal and Helsloot 2015; Fahsing 2016). As mentioned above, studies have shown how such risks can impact criminal investigations (U.S. Department of Justice and General 2006; Kassin et al. 2013; Sunde and Dror 2019). Consequently, investigators need to apply logical and deliberate reasoning when performing this process step. Note that the risk of data error, i.e., that the data constituting the information is wrong, is not a part of this process step. Such errors are inherited from the data collection and processing steps. Hence, problems with bad data cannot be corrected during hypothesis evaluation.

3.5.1 Contextualise, Link and Assess Information

Incidents are not described and explained by separate pieces of information is solitude. All the pieces of information must be interpreted and understood in context with each other before the hypotheses can be evaluated. Presenting the information in a graph or a cross-impact matrix are two ways of contextualising and linking the information. Displaying information graphically can aid in the assessment and prepares it for the next steps of relating information to the hypotheses and subsequently assessing the hypotheses. This is also the step at which the quality of the information is assessed. This is done by considering the validity and reliability of the information chain,

---

[10] Note that this requirement goes beyond the basic requirement that the information must exist in the first place.

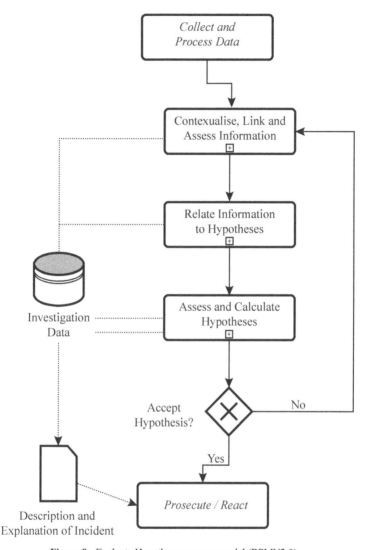

Figure 8: Evaluate Hypotheses process model (BPMN2.0).

i.e., the validity and reliability of the data source and all the methods employed to acquire and examine the data, and analyse and document the evidence.

3.5.2 Relate Information to Hypotheses

The relationship between the information (evidence and documentation) and the hypotheses is an impact assessment of the information on the hypotheses. This can be done by completing a cross-impact matrix, or by expanding an information graph. In cases with a lot of information, the result can be a large matrix, graph or list. However, performing this step explicitly and visually makes each consideration and assessment clear and available, which, in turn, enables error-detection and auditing.

3.5.3 Assess and Calculate Hypotheses

The final step before deciding whether to accept one of the hypotheses or if more information is required, is to assess the results. Based on the complete picture constructed in the previous steps, the investigation must consider how well the information describe and explains the various hypotheses. The transition from assessment to decision is not necessarily a long process, but it is important that the considerations are precise, conscious and based on a correct understanding of the information. As described above, making such assessments are cognitive processes and care must be taken to avoid bias and other risks as much as possible. They should also be documented in order to enable review at a later stage.

3.5.4 Hypothesis Accepted?

When all the hypotheses have been updated according to the collected information, a decision is made on whether or not one of the hypotheses have sufficient support (i.e., enough information) to adequately explain the incident. If one of the hypotheses does have sufficient support the case moves on. If not, the investigation process returns to step one where the hypotheses are updated, and new ones added before the process continues (see Figure 1).

4. Investigation, Forensic Science and the Digital Forensic Process

Criminal and other incident investigations can involve a variety of different forensic analyses—examinations performed to identify, classify, individualize, associate or reconstruct evidence. In the context of this book, however, it is relevant to examine how the investigation process corresponds with the digital forensics process. The digital forensics process comes in several different varieties. In a review of 21 varieties with distinct characteristics, Sachowski identified that most variants share seven common phases (Sachowski 2016):

1. Preparation
2. Identification
3. Collection
4. Preservation
5. Examination
6. Analysis
7. Presentation

The first phase in Sachowski's review finds no counterpart in the investigation process model. That is because establishing the capacity to perform investigations or to process criminal cases are considered prerequisites, and therefore outside the scope of the actual investigation process. The second of the common phases concerns the 'detection of an incident or event' (Sachowski 2016, p.19). In our process, this is the objective of the detection and identification phase, which takes place before investigation begins (see Section 2 and Figure 1). Sachowski's third, fourth, fifth and sixth phase corresponds more or less directly to the four parts in the third step of the investigation process; collect and process data (see Section 3.4, if we take into account that the two models encompass slightly different situations. As for the seventh phase, our view on presentation and reporting is that every step, part and action must be recorded. Some parts and actions involve more reporting than others, but the audit trail should be complete. Therefore, we see reporting and sharing information as an integral part of every process step and not something to be left until the end. This might appear as a disparity between the investigation process model, and the digital forensic process. However, it is not. The disparity lies with how digital forensics differs from other forensic sciences and practices.

Forensic science starts when an item is recognized as evidence and generally involve five tasks or objectives: Authentication, identification/individualization, classification, association or reconstruction (Inman and Rudin 2002). Within this definition, digital forensics can only be considered a forensic science if the electronic data source, i.e., the device, is considered the evidence. The device itself can, of course, be forensically analysed just like other physical items. However, searching for evidence—an activity shown by Sachowski's review to be included in most digital forensic processes—does not fit within Inman and Rubin's definition of forensic science. Rather, the digital forensics process combines investigation, crime scene investigation[11] and forensic analysis into one process. This has the effect of distancing the examination of digital evidence from the examination of cognitive and physical evidence, causing a disconnect between important parts of the investigation (Hansen et al. 2017). It could also have long-term effects on the digital competence of criminal investigators.

It is necessary to be aware that several studies have shown that several forensic techniques are scientifically invalid, leaving the information they provide untrustworthy. Only certain DNA testing techniques, and particular application of the information provided by such results, have shown to be consistently reliable (Michael J. Saks and Koehler 1991; National Research Council 2009; Dror and Hampikian 2011; Giannelli 2018). We must also be wary of how cognitive bias can influencing on empirical work like criminal investigation and forensic science (Tversky and Kahneman 1973; Kahneman 2012; Dror 2015; Fahsing 2016). Some have suggested that forensic practitioners should be given as little information as possible about the case to avoid biasing their judgments (Zapf and Dror 2017; Sunde and Dror 2019). While keeping information away from someone might eliminate one source of bias, it also influences greatly on those professional's possibility to apply their competence to the problem at hand. Further, it pre-supposes that the work of the forensic professional will be unscientific and that the results will be based on subjective opinions and heuristics—what Tversky and Kahneman calls system 1-type thinking—rather than the thorough, systematic, objective and empirical work—i.e., system 2-type thinking—which forensic science is intended to be. Such a situation resembles that of Kerckhoffs' Principle (Petitcolas 2011) in that the quality of the investigation rests on the forensic practitioner, rather than on the evidence and

---

[11] Crime scene investigation is the search for, collection, preservation and transportation of evidence from a crime scene to forensic examiners (National Research Council 2009).

the methods employed. The quality of the investigation should rest on the quality of the evidence in existence, and on the methods used to process and analyse that evidence. In short, if a forensic practitioner allows irrelevant information to influence the results of an analysis, then the practitioner is not practicing forensic science, and not contributing positively to the investigation quality.

As we have pointed out, it is essential to be consciously aware of the risks involved in the various investigation actions. And since humans are at the core of all these actions—including forensic analysis—extra attention should be given to the different cognitive risks, bias in particular. At the same time, we must expect that everyone involved in the investigation of crimes holds the necessary competence, executes their tasks systematically and objectively, and base their assessments and decisions on empirical data and sound logic.

5. Acknowledgements and Declarations

This chapter was made possible by financial support from the Norwegian Research Council (project 248094) and Oslo Police District.

References

Association of Chief Police Officers. 2009. Practice Advice on The Management of Priority and Volume Crime. Wyboston, UK.

Al Awadhi, I., Read. J. C., Marrington, A. and Franqueira, V. N. L. 2015. Factors influencing digital forensic investigations: Empirical evaluation of 12 years of Dubai police cases. English. *In*: Journal of Digital Forensics, Security and Law 10.4: 7–16.

Bjerknes, O. T. and Fahsing, I. 2018. Etterforskning: Prinsipper, metoder og praksis. Bergen: Fagbokforlaget. ISBN: 978-82-450-2335-0.

Blackstone, W. 1799. Commentaries on the Laws of England – Vol. IV. Second Ame. Printed at Boston by I. Thomas and E.T. Andrews.

Blackstone, W. 1859. Commentaries on the laws of England in four books. *In*: The American Law Register (1852–1891). ISSN: 15583813. DOI: 10.2307/ 3302061.

Brodeur, J. P. 2010. The Policing Web. ISBN: 9780199866083. DOI: 10.1093/ acprof:oso/9780199740598.001.0001.

Carrier, B. D. 2006. A Hypothesis-based Approach to Digital Forensic Investigations. PhD thesis. Purdue University, p. 169.

Coulthart, S. 2016. Why do analysts use structured analytic techniques? An in-depth study of an American intelligence agency. *In*: Intelligence and National Security. ISSN: 17439019. DOI: 10.1080/02684527.2016.1140327.

Coulthart, S. J. 2017. An evidence-based evaluation of 12 core structured analytic techniques. *In*: International Journal of Intelligence and Counter Intelligence 30.2: 368–391. ISSN: 15210561. DOI: 10.1080/08850607.2016.1230706.

Dror, I. E. and Hampikian, G. 2011. Subjectivity and bias in forensic DNA mixture interpretation. *In*: Science and Justice 51.4: 204–208. ISSN: 13550306. DOI: 10.1016/j.scijus.2011.08.004. URL: http://dx.doi.org/10.1016/j.scijus.2011.08.004.

Dror, I. E. 2015. Cognitive neuroscience in forensic science: Understanding and utilizing the human element. *In*: Philosophical Transactions of the Royal Society B: Biological Sciences 370.1674. ISSN: 14712970. DOI: 10.1098/rstb.2014.0255.

European Court of Human Rights. 2010. European Convention on Human Rights. English. URL: http://www.echr.coe.int/Documents/Convention_ENG. pdf.

Fahsing, Ivar 2016. The Making of an Expert Detective Thinking and Deciding in Criminal Investigations. English. PhD thesis. Gothenburg, Sweden: University of Gothenburg. ISBN: 978-91-628-9972-1.

Farrell, G. and Birks, D. 2018. Did cybercrime cause the crime drop? *In*: Crime Science 7.1. ISSN: 21937680. DOI: 10.1186/s40163-018-0082-8. URL: https://doi.org/10.1186/s40163-018-0082-8.

Franke, K. and Srihari, S. N. 2008. Computational forensics: An overview. *In*: Computational Forensics: Second International Workshop, IWCF 2008, Washington, DC, USA, August 7–8, 2008. Proceedings. Berlin, Heidelberg: Springer Berlin Heidelberg, pp. 1–10. ISBN: 978-3-540-85303-9. DOI: 10.1007/978- 3- 540- 85303- 9{_}1. URL:http://dx.doi.org/10.1007/978-3-540-85303-9_1.

Fraser, J. and Williams, R. 2009. Handbook of Forensic Science. English. New York, USA.

Garfinkel, S. L. 2010. Digital forensics research: The next 10 years. *In*: Digital Investigation 7: 64–S73. ISSN: 17422876. DOI: 10.1016/j.diin.2010.05.009. URL: http://dx.doi.org/10.1016/j.diin.2010.05.009.

Giannelli, P. C. 2018. Forensic science: Daubert's failure. *In*: Case Western Reserve Law Review 68.3: 869–941. URL: https://scholarlycommons. law.case.edu/caselrev/vol68/iss3/18/.

Gilhooly, K., Lyddy, F. and Pollick, F. 2014. Cognitive Psychology. Maidenhead: McGraw-Hill Education. ISBN: 9780077122669.

Glouberman, S. and Zimmerman B. 2002. Complicated and Complex Systems: What Would Successful Reform of Medicare Look Like? Ed. by Privy Council Office Canada. Saskatoon - Saskatchewan.

Groenendaal, J. and Helsloot, I. 2015. Tunnel vision on tunnel vision? A preliminary examination of the tension between precaution and efficacy in major criminal investigations in the Netherlands. *In*: Police Practice and Research 16.3: 224–238. ISSN: 1477271X. DOI: 10.1080/15614263.2014. 928622. URL: http://dx.doi.org/10.1080/15614263.2014.928622.

Gudjonsson, G. H. 1992. The Psychology of Interrogations, Confessions and Testimony. Chichester, UK: John Wiley & Sons Ltd. ISBN: 0-471-92663-9.

Hansen, H. A., Andersen, S., Axelsson, S. and Hopland, S. 2017. Case study: a new method for investigating crimes against children. *In*: Annual ADFSL Conference on Digital Forensics, Security and Law, p. 11. URL: http://commons.erau.edu/adfslhttp://commons.erau.edu/adfsl/2017/papers/11.

Heuer, R. J. and Pherson, R. H. 2015. Structured Analytic Techniques for Intelligence Analysis. 2nd. SAGE Publications, Inc. ISBN: 978-1-4522-4151-7.

Hilborn, R. and Mangel, M. 1997. The Ecological Detective: Confronting Models with Data. Princeton, New Jersey: Princeton University Press. ISBN: 978-0-691-03497-3. URL: http://web.b.ebscohost. com/ehost/ebookviewer/ebook/bmxlYmtfXzUyOTQ4MV9fQU41?sid=dde8b29e-375c-41fc-9bd3-e25d806bbe9a@sessionmgr104&vid=0&format=EB&rid=1.

Inman, K. and Rudin, N. 2002. The origin of evidence. *In*: Forensic Science International. ISSN: 03790738. DOI: 10.1016/S0379-0738(02)00031-2.

Innes, M. 2003. Investigating Murder: Detective Work and the Police Response to Criminal Homicide. Oxford: Oxford University Press.

Kahneman, D. 2003. A perspective on judgment and choice: mapping bounded rationality. *In*: American Psychologist 58.9: 697–720. DOI: 10.1037/0003-066X.58.9.697. URL: https://www.ncbi.nlm.nih.gov/pubmed/14584987.

Kahneman, D. 2012. Thinking, Fast and Slow. Penguin.

Kassin, S. M., Dror, I. E. and Kukucka, J. 2013. The forensic confirmation bias: Problems, perspectives, and proposed solutions. *In*: Journal of Applied Research in Memory and Cognition 2.1: 42–52. ISSN: 22113681. DOI: 10. 1016/j.jarmac.2013.01.001.

Krathwohl, D. R. 2002. A revision of bloom's taxonomy: An overview. *In*: Theory into Practice 41.4: 212–218. ISSN: 10994130. DOI: 10.1207/s15430421tip4104{_}2.

Kuykendall, J. 1982. The criminal investigative process: Toward a conceptual framework. *In*: Journal of Criminal Justice. ISSN: 00472352. DOI: 10.1016/0047-2352(82)90004-6.

Legislation.gov.uk. 2012. Criminal Procedure and Investigations Act 1996. [online] Available at: https://www.legislation.gov.uk/ukpga/1996/25 [Accessed 13 Jan. 2021].

Myhrer, T. -G. 2015. Kvalitet i etterforskningen: Særlig om påtaleansvarliges rolle og betydning [Quality in the Investigation: Particularly about the Role and Importance of Prosecutors]. Tech. rep. Oslo, Norway: Norwegian Police University College.

National Research Council. 2009. Strenghening Forensic Science in the United States: A Path Forward. Tech. rep. National Academy of Sciences, p. 352. URL: http://www.nap.edu/catalog/12589.html.

Object Management Group Inc. 2013. Business Process Model and Notation (BPMN) Version 2.0.2. Tech. rep. URL: https://www.omg.org/spec/BPMN/2.0.2/PDF.

O'Neill, M. 2018. Key challenges in criminal investigation. Bristol, UK: Policy Press. ISBN: 9781447325772. URL: https://doi.org/10.1093/police/pay040.

Petitcolas, F. A. P. 2011. Kerckhoffs' Principle. Ed. by Henk C. A. van Tilborg and Sushil Jajodia. Boston, MA. DOI: 10.1007/978-1-4419-5906-5{_}487. URL: https://doi.org/10.1007/978-1-4419-5906-5_487.

Platt, J. R. 1964. Strong Inference: Certain systematic methods of scientific thinking may produce much more rapid progress than others. Science 146(3642): 347–353.

Popper, K. R. 1959. The Logic of Scientific Discovery. ISBN: 0415278449. DOI:10.1016/S0016-0032(59)90407-7.

Rachlew, Asbjørn. 2009. Justisfeil ved politiets etterforskning. PhD thesis. Oslo. Riksadvokaten (1999). Etterforskning. Norwegian. Tech. rep. URL: http://www.riksadvokaten.no/filestore/Dokumenter/Eldre_dokumenter/Rundskriv/ Rundskrivnr3for1999-Etterforskning2.pdf.

Sachowski, J. 2016. Investigative process models. *In*: Implementing Digital Forensic Readiness, pp. 17–22. DOI: 10.1016/b978-0-12-804454-4.00002-2.

Saks, M. J. and Koehler, J. J. 1991. What DNA "Fingerprinting" can teach the law about the rest of forensic science. *In*: Cardozo Law Review 13: 361–372.

Saks, M. J. and Koehler, J. 2005. The coming paradigm shift in forensic identification science. *In*: Science 309.5736: 892–895. DOI: 10.1126/science.1111565. URL: http://www.ncbi.nlm.nih.gov/pubmed/16081727.

Sennewald, C. A. and Tsukayama, J. K. 2015. The Process of Investigation: Concepts and Strategies for Investigators in the Private Sector. 4th. Oxford, UK: Elsevier Inc. ISBN: 978-0-12-800166-0.

Shannon, C. E. 1948. A mathematical theory of communication. *In*: Bell System Technical Journal 5.3: 3. ISSN: 15591662. DOI: 10.1002/j.1538-7305.1948.tb01338.x. URL: http://portal.acm.org/citation.cfm?doid=584091.584093%5Cnhttp://ieeexplore.ieee.org/lpdocs/epic03/wrapper.htm?arnumber=6773024.

Sloan, M. C. 2010. Aristotle's Nicomachean ethics as the original locus for the septem circumstantiae. *In*: Classical Philology. ISSN: 0009-837X. DOI: 10.1086/656196.

Smith, M. and Mann, M. 2015. Recent developments in DNA evidence. *In*: Trends and Issues in Crime and Criminal Justice. ISSN: 18362206.

Stelfox, P. 2009. Criminal Investigation: An Introduction to Principles and Practice. English. First. Devon, UK: Willan Publishing, p. 248. ISBN: 978-1-84392-337-4.

Straffeprosessloven. 1981. Lov om rettergangsmåten i straffesaker [The Norwegian Criminal Procedure Act].

Sunde, N. and Dror, I. E. 2019. Cognitive and human factors in digital forensics: Problems, challenges, and the way forward. *In*: Digital Investigation. ISSN: 17422876. DOI: 10.1016/j.diin.2019.03.011.

Tong, S., Bryant, R. P. and Horcath, M. A. H. 2009. Understanding Criminal Investigation. Ed. by Wiley Series. Oxford, UK: Wiley & Sons Ltd. ISBN: 978-0-470-72726-3.

Tversky, A. and Kahneman, D. 1973. Availability: A heuristic for judging frequency and probability. *In*: Cognitive Psychology 5.2: 207–232. DOI: 10.1016/0010-0285(73)90033-9.

United Nations. 1998. Rome Statute of the International Criminal Court Rome Statute of the International Criminal Court. ISBN: 9292272276. DOI: 10.2139/ssrn.1689616.

United Nations General Assembly. 1948. Universal Declaration of Human Rights. English. URL: http://www.ohchr.org/EN/UDHR/Documents/UDHR_Translations/eng.pdf.

U.S. Department of Justice and Officer of the Inspector General. 2006. A review of the FBI's handling of the Brandon Mayfield case. *In*: Organization.

Waldman, T. 1959. Origins of the legal doctrine of reasonable doubt. *In*: Journal of the History of Ideas. ISSN: 00225037. DOI: 10.2307/2708111.

Zapf, P. A. and Dror, I. E. 2017. Understanding and mitigating bias in forensic evaluation: lessons from forensic science. *In*: International Journal of Forensic Mental Health 16.3: 227–238. ISSN: 19329903. DOI: 10.1080/14999013.2017.1317302. URL: https://doi.org/10.1080/14999013.2017.1317302.

4

Digital Investigation and the Trojan Defense, Revisited

Golden G Richard III,[1,*] *Andrew Case,*[2] *Modhuparna Manna,*[3]
Elsa A M Hahne[4] and *Aisha Ali-Gombe*[5]

1. Introduction

In recent times, digital forensics capabilities have been significantly expanded through the development of a number of new tools and techniques. Modern forensic tools can reveal data in plain sight (e.g., files containing copies of credit card statements, spreadsheets), data that was previously deleted by users (files, SMS messages, logs, etc.), illicit data (NSFW materials, sensitive documents which the user is not authorized to possess, digital contraband, etc.), evidence that systems were used to attack others (e.g., command histories), geo-location information, and more. Increasingly, digital forensics tool suites support "pushbutton forensics," which allow for a rapid recovery of digital evidence, data correlation, creation of timelines, and selective acquisition of evidence without significant effort, or in some cases, without significant expertise on the part of investigators. Making digital forensics tools easier to use and automating the tedious investigatory processes is undoubtedly useful, as it reduces investigator fatigue and case backlogs. But there is also a significant downside. As digital forensics techniques have evolved, so has the design and capabilities of modern malware. It is becoming increasingly difficult to conduct digital investigations correctly, and in the face of sophisticated malware, traditional storage forensics methods are no longer sufficient to refute the Trojan defense.

[1] Center for Computation and Technology and Division of Computer Science and Engineering, Louisiana State University.
[2] Volatility Foundation.
[3] Division of Computer Science and Engineering, Louisiana State University.
[4] Office of Research & Economic Development, Louisiana State University.
[5] Department of Computer and Information Sciences, Towson University.
Emails: andrew@dfir.org; mmanna3@lsu.edu; ehahne@lsu.edu; aaligombe@towson.edu
* Corresponding author: golden@cct.lsu.edu

Historically, malware caused disruption primarily by deleting data and limiting the performance or capabilities of computing devices (Rankin 2018). Furthermore, the incentives behind development and deployment of historical malware were often unclear. In sharp contrast, the design and development of modern malware is usually motivated by a number of distinct factors, including the potential for monetary gain or commercial advantage, revenge, the needs of nation-state actors, and more. To this end, modern malware frequently alters the state of computing devices, infiltrates and exfiltrates data, and performs unauthorized activities "on behalf of" users, such as web surfing, sending email, and downloading files. Detection of modern malware is neither straightforward nor certain, particularly if only traditional digital forensics techniques are utilized. These techniques typically examine only the contents of non-volatile storage, whereas many strains of modern malware and attack toolkits leave absolutely no traces on disk (Kaspersky Research Team 2014, 2015; Schroeder 2019; Wadner 2014). Thus, the impact modern malware can have on innocent users is enormous, as malware can perform virtually any action that a user might perform, including the download of illicit or illegal materials, such as child pornography, without being easily detected. Furthermore, while personal security products such as antivirus programs are adept at detecting historical, well-known, and established malware, detection rates for new and emergent strains remain notoriously low. Thus, "personal computer hygiene" is insufficient as a defensive measure against modern malware.

For individuals accused of wrongdoing involving digital devices, there is a very substantial burden in defending themselves when expensive technical expertise is required to recover exculpatory evidence such as proof of a malware infection. We argue that not only is a deliberate and earnest search for malware a necessary component of most digital forensics cases (where we strongly agree with (Bowles and Hernandez-Castro 2015)), but traditional forensics techniques *must* be supplemented with modern analysis techniques to "balance the scales." The most appropriate and powerful of modern techniques is memory forensics, which deeply examines the state of a system through analysis of volatile memory (RAM). By leveraging memory forensics, investigators can uncover a wealth of information that is not recorded in the file system, including signs of malware infection. Such analysis performed by experts is necessary to remove the burden of proof from suspects who have no realistic chance of discovering, analyzing, or documenting the malware capabilities themselves. This is a complicated issue, however, as substantial time and expertise is needed to properly conduct thorough memory forensics investigations across a variety of devices, operating system versions, and applications. As such, the resources and costs associated with this kind of analysis can quickly become daunting and prohibitive.

The rest of the chapter is organized as follows: Section 2 discusses the Trojan defense in more detail. Section 3 briefly surveys traditional digital forensics methodologies. Section 4 traces the evolution of modern malware and the challenges posed for digital forensics investigation, including disentangling user actions and malware effects. Section 5 outlines memory forensics capabilities and how memory forensics can be used to more accurately detect malware. Section 6 provides some concluding thoughts.

2. The Trojan Defense

Cybercrimes have escalated significantly over the past two decades (Cybercrime 2019). The entire infrastructure of computer systems and networks has changed dramatically, and crimes that once were somewhat simple to detect are now much more complicated. Law enforcement faces serious challenges, on multiple levels, in combating such crimes. While the world becomes closer and closer connected through the internet and criminals routinely access their victims' computers remotely and escape without leaving any identifiable trace, law enforcement must operate in accordance with local, state, or federal cyberlaws, which vary from one geographic area to the next (Luehr 2005). Many defendants charged with cybercrimes cite the "Trojan horse defense," stating that, without their knowledge, a malicious cybercriminal hacked into their computer to commit the crime, or planted malware responsible for said crime (Brenner et al. 2004).

Suppose someone named David is charged with possession of child pornography on his computer. If David pleads the Trojan defense, his claim is that he did not intentionally or knowingly download this content. Instead, an anonymous and unidentifiable cybercriminal or malware placed the material on his computer. Because it is often difficult or impossible for prosecutors to refute this defense, that is, proving the defendant is responsible for downloading the illegal content, many of them escape either prosecution or conviction. For example, Aaron Caffrey was charged with unauthorized computer modifications for launching a DDoS (Distributed Denial of Service) attack against a fellow chat-room user, "Bokkie." The DDoS attack passed through several servers and brought traffic at the Port of Houston to a dangerous standstill. Caffrey, however, argued that while the attack was launched from his computer, he himself did not launch it; instead, it was launched by a hacker group that had surreptitiously planted trojan malware on his computer and later wiped it away. Even though Caffrey had no evidence to substantiate his theory, he was still acquitted simply because the prosecution had no evidence to rebut it (Brenner et al. 2004).

Although the Trojan defense results in acquittals in some cases, it is not always successful. There are examples of cases where the defendant claimed the Trojan defense and still got convicted. In the Mark Rawlinson case, for instance, the defense claimed a virus was responsible for downloading the thousand pornographic photos found on his computer. The court did not accept the Trojan defense in this case, and Rawlinson was convicted (Bowles and Hernandez-Castro 2015).

There is an ongoing disagreement among academics, practitioners, and law enforcement about whether malware attacks can result in an innocent person being ultimately held responsible for crimes like possession of child pornography, tax fraud, DDoS, and other attacks. For instance, in the Miller case. When Miller was charged with possession of child pornography, he contacted the FBI agent in charge claiming a virus was responsible for the crime. Agent Kyle, the investigator in charge, refuted the Trojan defense arguments saying a virus could not do such a thing (Monterosso 2010). This might be true in some clear-cut cases, however, the modern scenario has completely changed. Nowadays, malware has become sophisticated enough to download child pornography, modify the browser information stored in the temporary cache locations, send out unwanted emails, and so on. Consider the Matthew Bandy case, where Bandy was originally charged with life imprisonment for possession of child porn until forensic investigator Tami Loehrs found more than 200 malware-infected files in his computer. After some negotiation and with the help of Loehr's findings, Bandy was finally given an 18-month probation period, during which he had to register as a sex offender (Mcelroy 2007). The Trojan defense, therefore, makes cybercrime cases highly complicated.

We emphasize that even if the defendant is finally acquitted, it does not undo much of the damage already done. Just being charged with a crime like possession of child pornography can be very costly, from both monetary and psychological points of view. The harm can include severe emotional stress, loss of reputation, employment, financial resources, and emotional support. When Michael Fiola was charged with child pornography, he lost his job with the Massachusetts Department of Industrial Accidents and was abandoned by both family and friends. Even though Fiola was ultimately acquitted, he never got his job back, and many of his relationships remain strained (PCWorld 2008).

Many authors have discussed cases where the Trojan defense played a prominent role, outlining outcomes, various legal loopholes, and how justice can somehow be guaranteed in spite of the added complications associated with this defensive strategy. One of the seminal reports in this area was drafted by Susan W. Brenner and her colleagues (Brenner et al. 2004). The report discusses the Trojan horse defense cases of Aaron Caffrey, Julian Green, Karl Schofield, and Eugene Pitts in detail, and highlights the steps the prosecution could take to verify if the defendant is guilty. This report is almost invariably cited whenever the Trojan horse defense is discussed. According to the authors, in case of a Trojan defense, there are several possible ways that the prosecution could proceed. First, the prosecution might insist that since "malware did it," the defense should produce evidence that malware is present and was installed by someone else without the defendant's knowledge. For reasons we will discuss later in the paper, our position is that while this may have been possible in the past, modern malware can be extremely difficult to detect; detection likely requires substantial technical skill and the use of forensic procedures not commonly used by law enforcement. Furthermore, transient, memory-only malware may leave no trace at all, making the production of evidence of the malware's existence virtually impossible. Another tactic that is proposed for use by the prosecution is to establish the level of computer expertise of the defendant and find out if they possessed enough technical expertise to avoid becoming a victim of malware. As we will discuss later in this chapter, the bar for self-protection is spectacularly high when sophisticated modern malware is concerned. Finally, the assertion in the Brenner paper that law enforcement can "negate the factual basis of the defense" by establishing that no malware is present must go far beyond the use of traditional forensics techniques and antivirus scans.

Though there are many theories as to how prosecutors could deal with the defendants in a Trojan defense case, things may not be so simple in practice. Each case is different, and there are no straight-forward, general recommendations on how to handle any particular case. Furthermore, forensic investigations can go terribly wrong, allowing malware to go undetected. In Julie Amero's case, she was charged with showing indecent materials to twelve-year-old kids during a class. While she was teaching, her computer started showing indecent pictures downloaded by NewDotNet spyware. Amero panicked and went to seek help while the pictures kept showing. Though the spyware was responsible for the crime, it took years for Amero to get justice. Part of the reason for her delayed justice is that the digital forensic investigation was not carried out properly. Her hard drive was imaged using the backup utility Ghost, which is not considered standard for disk imaging (Eckelberry et al. 2007). Although Ghost can be configured to perform sector-level copies of hard drives, default options must be overridden to avoid capturing only logical volume copies in at least some versions. In cases of negligence on the part of the investigator, or in the presence of highly sophisticated malware, investigations could easily fall short. Therefore, the presence of computer forensic experts as well as appropriate tools and techniques for forensic investigation of Trojan horse defense cases are extremely valuable.

Paul H. Luehr elaborates on where and how forensic investigators can find relevant evidence in cases involving digital systems. Luehr points out places such as start-up configuration files, internet browsing histories, and other places where evidence impacting a Trojan defense case might be found (Luehr 2005). Haagman and Ghavalas mention the importance of volatile and network evidence in cases of cybercrimes involving a Trojan defense (Haagman and Ghavalas 2005). The second part of the paper describes how these techniques can be used to analyze the presence of a backdoor (Ghavalas and Philips 2005).

In the past 10 years, the effectiveness of the Trojan defense has varied significantly. It has not been particularly successful in United States criminal cases, with no published acquittals in cases where it was the primary defense. On the civil side, the defense has met with more success (Steel 2014). Bowles and Hernandez-Castro have published several case studies where the defendant was able to prove that malware was present without their knowledge (Bowles and Hernandez-Castro 2015). No matter the outcome, however, thorough forensic investigations involving sophisticated tools and techniques were required.

3. Traditional Digital Forensics Investigation

Digital forensics is the branch of forensic sciences that deals with the acquisition, analysis, extraction, preservation, and presentation of digital evidence (Carrier 2003). The field is defined by sets of procedures, tools, and techniques for preserving and analyzing digital evidence recovered from a wide variety of digital devices. While the associated legal requirements governing issues such as right-to-investigate, chain of custody, qualifications for expert witnesses, and admissibility of evidence are important, we focus solely on some relevant technical issues associated with acquisition and analysis in this section.

3.1 Traditional Acquisition

In traditional digital forensics, acquisition and recovery of data specifically targets non-volatile storage, such as hard drives. The primary objective is to extract copies of storage media where the copies are as close to "bit-perfect" as possible. For fully functional media in computer systems or devices that have been powered down, bit-perfect copies can be generated fairly easily using one of a variety of methods, such as the use of open-source utilities like dd, commercial software like FTK Imager AccessData (2019a), and hardware media duplicators. The use of write-blocking hardware is generally recommended to avoid accidentally corrupting evidence sources during the acquisition phase. This type of acquisition is commonly known as "full disk forensics," wherein entire copies of hard drives are created in a digital forensics lab, or sometimes, at a crime scene. As new storage devices, such as thumb drives, external hard drives, and SD cards, have become widely used, the same approach to creating exact copies of entire storage media has prevailed using these traditional techniques. Typically, both the original media and the copies of the media to be analyzed are run through a cryptographic hashing process (traditionally, MD5 or SHA-1, but now, more likely a newer standard like SHA-256 or SHA-3) that yields an associated digital fingerprint. This fingerprint can be used to establish that the media and copies remain unaltered by subsequent investigative processes.

A standard procedure in performing acquisition of this type is the use of "dead box forensics." Upon entering a potential crime scene, all of the digital devices are powered off to prevent further changes to file systems and storage media. Depending on the type of device, either the entire device is subsequently transported to a forensics lab, or in some extenuating circumstances, just the non-volatile storage media. This "power off and then copy" approach necessarily destroys volatile evidence that is present only in RAM. The volatile evidence that is lost may include memory-resident malware, unsaved documents, and much more. It is very reasonable to expect that some of this evidence may be exculpatory. We emphasize that this volatile evidence is precisely the domain of memory forensics, which is covered in detail in Section 5.

Beyond the loss of volatile evidence, there are several technical hurdles that must be overcome during traditional acquisition. The first is how imaging of malfunctioning media might be carried out. Hard drives and other media that have been damaged due to physical abuse or normal wear and tear frequently exhibit errors during the copying process. Depending on the severity of the errors, various remedies may be required, from simply ignoring "bad" regions of the media and substituting zeros in the copy to attempts to physically repair the media, or use of sophisticated "deep" imaging provided by devices such as Deepspar's PC-3000 (DEEPSPAR Data Recovery Systems 2019), which attempt to maximize data recoverable from damaged drives by reading sectors in different orders, powering the drive up and down, and more. In many cases, these repairs are very effective; with minimal effort, storage devices can be revived. The authors have direct experience with cases in which opposing counsel in a civil case asserted that damaged media was completely unusable, but with simple replacement of electronic components, all of the stored data could be recovered. Importantly, the data on the damaged storage device had a crucial impact on the outcome of the case.

Nowadays, an even more serious hurdle commonly encountered in the acquisition phase of an investigation is related to the increasing size of modern storage media, which long ago passed a critical point. When hard drives and other storage media were significantly smaller (e.g., no larger than 10s of gigabytes), full acquisition was both feasible and relatively time efficient. With single commodity hard drives now exceeding 15TB, inexpensive network-attached storage devices allowing users to easily create drive arrays with 100s of TBs of storage, and individual drives up to 100TB on the horizon, making bit-perfect, full copies of media can be extremely time-consuming and, in many cases, infeasible. Acquisition strategies that copy only "relevant" portions of storage media in lieu of complete copies have been proposed (Grier and Richard 2015), but particular care must be taken if these selective approaches are used to generate primary copies of storage devices, or critical exculpatory evidence could easily be missed.

3.2 Traditional Analysis

Once a forensically sound copy of a storage medium has been made, forensic analysis can begin. A typical digital forensics investigation involves a number of steps, most of which are generally carried out in a commercial forensics suite, such as those offered by AccessData AccessData (2019b), Blackbag (Blackbag Technologies 2019), or OpenText Security (OpenText Security 2019), potentially supplemented with additional standalone tools to handle data such as email or databases. The investigative steps include indexing of the storage media under investigation to allow for fast keyword searches of documents and unallocated space; file carving to recover deleted files (Richard and Roussev 2005); timelining to determine when specific files were accessed or modified; scrutiny of the Windows registry (when computers running Microsoft Windows are being investigated) for evidence that external storage devices were recently used and which documents were recently accessed (Carvey 2019); investigation of web browsing history; and more. These forensics procedures are quite adept at revealing incriminating evidence (e.g., downloaded child porn or other illicit materials, web surfing activity) without necessarily establishing that a user performed these actions.

Of particular importance is the investigation of persistence mechanisms used by malware, such as modification of the Windows registry *Run* keys. Various *Run* keys specify the applications that run each time Windows is booted, for each user and for all users. Since this facility is well-known, malware that persists using this technique frequently uses an application name that closely matches commonly installed benign applications. Fortunately, scrutiny of the *Run* keys at the very least reveals applications that are deserving of further investigation. The authors have personal experience with a case in which an employee that was the victim of targeted malware was ultimately *not* terminated based solely on the discovery of the malware via its use of Windows registry *Run* keys for persistence and a subsequent complex reverse engineering effort. All of the other evidence pointed squarely at the employee accessing NSFW materials in the workplace, which was grounds for termination. Importantly, the malware sample that was discovered was *not* detected by antivirus. Screening of the sample using the Virus Total website revealed that virtually all antivirus products flagged the sample as benign, while the few that marked it as suspicious inaccurately described its behavior (e.g., as a banking trojan). Only a detailed reverse engineering effort revealed that the malware surreptitiously accessed pornographic websites "on behalf of" the innocent employee. While a full treatment of persistence mechanisms is beyond the scope of this chapter, a good treatment for Windows can be found in (Fortuna 2017).

Unfortunately, a huge number of persistence mechanisms exist. Most are neither as obvious nor as well-documented as the use of *Run* keys. Worse, modern memory-only malware may not use any persistence mechanisms at all. Our contention is that while traditional digital forensics techniques are both useful and essential, they miss a significant portion of the narrative surrounding a potential violation of law or policy involving digital devices.

4. Modern Malware and the Trojan Defense

Malware is software that performs unwanted or illicit activities on digital devices. Both the installation of malware and the actions performed by malware are generally without user consent. Over the years, malware has evolved from simple viruses designed as "pranks" to drivers for launching targeted and specialized attacks against individuals, corporations, and cyberinfrastructure. Modern malware is used on a massive scale by cybercriminals using sophisticated capabilities that can target user and corporate data, industrial control systems, equipment used for national defense, and more. These new malware attacks are explicitly designed to violate the security of a target system by breaching confidentiality, violating data and system integrity, and hiding their actions. The actions performed by modern malware include virtually anything a user might do, as well as sophisticated data infiltration and exfiltration, and attacks against other computer systems.

Broadly, malware is categorized by its mode of propagation; specifically, as viruses, worms, and trojans. We explore these briefly, although specific malware samples often exhibit behavior that spans more than one category:

- *Viruses* are malicious software that are self-propagating but not self-contained, meaning they require a host program to exist. However, they can move from one system to another by infecting programs that are subsequently copied to another machine. Viruses are the oldest form of malware that are specifically designed to inject themselves into an existing program by modifying the target binary to include the malicious code.
- *Worms* are malware that are both self-contained and self-propagating. This means that worms exist as independent pieces of code that do not require a host to exist. Usually, worms propagate to a target machine over a network.
- *Trojans* typically possess both an overt and covert functionality. Often propagated via a drive-by download or via social engineering tricks, this category of malware might be installed on user systems as legitimate applications, but unbeknownst to the user, they also have built-in malicious functionality.

Malware can also be classified by their payload or malicious behaviors. Some of these classifications include:

- *Ransomware* encrypts user files in exchange for ransom, which is typically paid using cryptocurrency.

- *Keystroke loggers* surreptitiously capture what a user types at the keyboard, including login credentials and other private data.
- *Spyware* logs and exfiltrates information about user activities, video, audio, etc.
- *Botnets* are large groups of infected machines that can be used for distributed attacks, such as mass spam campaigns and denial of service attacks.
- *Rootkits* modify the system configuration and potentially the operating system to hide its presence and ensure that attackers have continued access to a system.

According to PandaLabs, an average of 230,000 new malware samples were produced daily in 2015, and AV-TEST Institute has reported more than a 20-fold increase in registered malware from 2010 to 2019 (AV-Test 2019). The development and dissemination of malicious software has become a lucrative, international business with cybercriminals providing malware-as-a-service via the leasing of both software and hardware needed to execute a cyberattack (Laing 2018). A number of mechanisms are used to install malware on user systems, including email attachments, social engineering, drive-by downloads, vulnerable websites, and more. Modern malware is notorious for installing backdoor programs, spying on user behavior, performing ransomware attacks, mining cryptocurrency, downloading illicit materials, and more. As one example, the Emotet Trojan leverages vulnerable web services to steal financial data, inject a victim's machine with an exploit, and download additional malware to serve as spyware and/or as a backdoor (Malwarebytes Labs 2019), all without the user's knowledge. On mobile devices, malware has become a critical problem. According to the annual Internet Security Threat Report (ISTR) in 2018, the number of new mobile malware variants has increased by 54% (Symantec 2018). Android malware such as Cerberus (Doffman 2019) leverages fake websites and masquerades as a legitimate Adobe Flash Player installation. Upon installation, the malware tricks the user into granting very dangerous permissions, which then gives the attacker access to the device's screen when other legitimate apps are running. With this capability, the malware can steal user keystrokes and sensitive data, such as login credentials and contact information.

4.1 Malware Obfuscation

Anti-virus software is often used to detect malware and prevent new infections. This typically relies on signature-based detection of known malware variants. While anti-virus software is quite effective at detecting these, it frequently fails to detect new ones, particularly targeted malware and those that exhibit advanced obfuscation techniques, such as polymorphism, metamorphism, code and data encryption, kernel manipulation, and most worrisome, memory-only activity. In the case of a new malware, anti-virus software employs heuristic-based approaches to determine known malicious traits (Microsoft 2011).

Before malware samples can be analyzed, the malware must first be detected and an appropriate sample isolated for further scrutiny. This is the single most pressing issue in validating or invalidating a Trojan defense claim in a case where modern malware could be involved.

On traditional computers, advanced malware, such as kernel-level rootkits, can evade most forms of detection used in traditional malware forensics investigations. Given their power over a system, rootkits can directly choose what data is written to disk and how it is written to disk. Rootkits leverage the power to write as little of its related data to disk as possible and usually choose to encrypt or obfuscate this data. Another category of highly obfuscated malware is file-less malware. These do not create new executable files on disk, but instead embed malicious scripts inside existing files, such as shortcut files or within the registry (Armerding 2013; Majumder 2019). Detection of file-less malware requires new detection algorithms as there are no traditional executables to scan and analyze. Instead, anti-virus and other security products must implement completely new features to scan the new sources of malicious code. A recent and prominent example of a file-less malware attack was the hack on the Democratic National Convention (DNC), which leveraged a Powershell backdoor with a persistence mechanism injected into the Windows Management Instrumentation (Alperovitch 2016). For traditional computers, the most dangerous form of malware is memory-only malware, which does not persist past reboot nor write any data to non-volatile storage. Detection of such malware requires the use of memory forensics since traditional forensics techniques will completely miss all related artifacts. Duqu2 (Kaspersky Research Team 2015) is one of the most famous malware samples to employ these techniques.

On mobile platforms, other specialized programming practices such as Java reflection and the use of dynamic class loading are becoming standard techniques for mobile malware obfuscation. These techniques can help malware thwart analysis and obfuscate its payload at installation. One of the latest Android malware samples, called "Joker," was detected in September 2019 on the Google Play store after more than 400,000 downloads (O'Donnell 2019). It has both Trojan and spyware capabilities and employs dynamic class loading to install an extra component with more enhanced features capable of subscribing to premium SMS, information stealing, etc.

Given these advanced obfuscation and hiding mechanisms, it is apparent that traditional on-disk malware forensics is under threat as the primary technique for postmortem investigations of cybercrime, especially when stealthy malicious software is involved. We briefly discuss malware analysis in the next section. Evaluating a Trojan defense claim requires *accurately* determining what actions the malware can perform. Without better detection strategies, incorrect decisions regarding Trojan defense claims may be inevitable.

4.2 Malware Analysis

As malware becomes more sophisticated, there is an increasing need to understand not only the malware's actions at the time of execution, but its provenance, persistence, dynamic injection methods, and both internal and external remote communications. Thus, to understand the causality as well as the functionality of a cyberattack in its entirety, especially those involving malware, the security community has adopted a postmortem investigative process called *malware forensics*. This technique involves examining malware code and its effects to identify how an attack happened, what data and resources were compromised, and what actions were executed (Malin et al. 2008). When malware is identified in a case, it is imperative to understand precisely what actions can be attributed to the malware vs. a human user.

Once a malware sample is available, there are two primary approaches: static analysis and dynamic analysis, although these are frequently used together for additional insight. With static analysis, a malware sample's code is examined for any malicious functionality, often using predetermined signatures, patterns, code sequences, semantics, and strings. Static analysis can often be a fast and efficient technique, particularly to understand variants of known malware. Unfortunately, deep static analysis often requires specialized reverse engineering skills and extensive experience, which are in short supply.

Dynamic analysis on the other hand, involves executing a sample in a contained environment and then monitoring its behavior at runtime. With this technique, unwanted or illicit behavior can often be detected and understood much more quickly than via an in-depth static analysis effort. Expert knowledge is typically required in building the execution and analysis environment, although some systems like Cuckoo (Cuckoo Foundation 2019) ease this burden. While dynamic analysis methodologies such as taint analysis (Schwartz et al. 2010) perform an excellent job in program tracing, drawbacks include significant resource overhead, contamination of the analysis environment with analyst code, and limited path exploration. Specifically, dynamic analysis may not reveal "hidden" malware behaviors, which are triggered only by certain user actions or the passage of time. In this regard, static analysis is superior.

While online services that evaluate malware samples by running antivirus products against them and reporting the results are useful in judging the accuracy of antivirus products, this practice does not constitute "malware analysis" and should not be used for evaluating a Trojan defense claim. In our direct, personal experience, antivirus software is frequently woefully inaccurate in either detecting or categorizing new malware samples. Sometimes antivirus simply fails to detect malware at all, and sometimes the malware is identified as a variant of existing malware with which it actually has no relationship at all.

Of course, analysis procedures to get to the bottom of whatever actions a malware sample might perform are useless if the malware isn't detected in the first place. Memory forensics offers both better detection and understanding of sophisticated malware.

5. Memory Forensics vs The Trojan Horse Defense

Memory forensics encompasses the set of techniques to first acquire and then analyze a sample, or snapshot, of physical memory at a particular moment in time. The dawn of memory forensics began when malware authors realized that through anti-forensics techniques they were able to bypass many or all of the traditional forensics analysis procedures. For example, security researchers documented that, contrary to popular belief, an application does not ever have to be written to disk to be executed. Publicly available research papers document memory-only execution of applications and libraries as far back as 2004 (Skape and Turkulainen 2004;

grugq 2004). These techniques are now commonplace and implemented in popular open-source offensive security projects, such as Meterpreter (Wadner 2014) and PowerShell Empire (Schroeder 2019), as well as a wide variety of malware used during real attack campaigns.

Besides hiding executables in memory, malware can also be programmed to hide the rest of its presence on the live system. This can be accomplished via a technique known as API hooking, which allows malware to filter the types of information viewed and accessible by end users of the system, as well as other software running on the system. Common hiding techniques on Windows systems include hiding the malware's processes from Task Manager, files from Explorer, and network connections from *netstat*. Other tools to investigate system resources will similarly be affected by the hooking, and the malware will be hidden from them also. We note that the ability to run executables that reside only in memory and to hook APIs is widely abused on all major platforms, including Linux and Mac, and not just on Windows.

Beyond malware, other types of applications have similarly worked to avoid traditional digital forensics. The most prominent examples are applications that implement a "private" usage model, such as private browsing modes that do not log browsing history or cookies to disk, and chat applications that use end-to-end encryption on the network and do not keep local records of chat history. These efforts to specifically circumvent traditional forensics analysis have contributed to an increased awareness of the rising need for memory forensics and demands for ongoing advances in this field.

5.1 Techniques for Acquiring Memory

There are two categories of techniques for acquiring memory: software-based acquisition and hardware-based acquisition. Hardware-based acquisition was initially popular due to the fact that widely-accessible protocols, such as Firewire and PCMCIA, allowed direct access to physical memory by attaching hardware devices and using DMA. Specialized hardware devices take advantage of these protocols to acquire memory from systems after being attached. Hardware-based acquisition bypasses the need to log into systems, which requires valid credentials, or to load custom software. While initially popular, hardware-based acquisition is now less commonly used due to the inability of pervasive technologies such as USB devices to access all of physical memory, as well as operating system protections against DMA-based attacks. For example, Mac OS X systems prevent attached devices from performing DMA operations while the system is locked. Only after valid credentials are entered do the devices gain access. The requirement of valid credentials substantially reduces the power and scope of hardware-based mechanisms. Now, the use of software-based mechanisms is much more common.

Software-based acquisition utilizes kernel-level code to access all of physical memory. The memory contents are typically written to the file system of an external storage device or delivered securely over a network connection to a remote machine. Software-based acquisition has an advantage over hardware-based solutions in that it can successfully acquire memory from a variety of operating systems and hardware configurations, as it does not rely on specific hardware protocols being present or active. While widely supported, software-based acquisition does have two main drawbacks. First, to load a kernel driver, valid administrator credentials are required. This is generally not an issue in enterprise networks where the IT team manages user accounts but is a major stumbling point in law enforcement operations when the suspect may not be legally required to reveal their credentials, or the operation is supposed to be covert and the suspect not alerted. Second, malware running on the system at the time of acquisition has the potential to interfere with the acquisition process. This capability has been demonstrated in many research projects and several malware samples found in the wild have implemented interference techniques. Fortunately, most attempts to interfere with the acquisition process are rather obvious, such as completely blocking acquisition when it would otherwise work or tampering with in-memory data in a way that produces easy-to-detect discrepancies during analysis.

5.2 Analyzing Memory Samples

After a valid memory capture is made, the sample is then analyzed in a forensic lab using appropriate software. Relative to the Trojan horse defense, analysis of a memory sample provides numerous benefits, including the ability to detect stealthy malware, uncover precise user actions not accessible by traditional analysis techniques, and help prove intent, or lack thereof, on the part of the person under investigation.

5.2.1 Memory Forensics and Modern Malware

The true power of memory forensics is illuminated when applied to the investigation of modern malware. Since memory forensics provides the ability to examine the entirety of the state of a system, there is little room for malware to hide or act in a covert manner. This presents a significant advantage to the investigator as they can operate with increased confidence that any malware that is present will be found. In the case of memory-only malware, which is essentially invisible to traditional forensics techniques, memory forensics can provide three distinct benefits. First, it can detect that something is "off," based on the fact that active code and data structures in memory are not associated with a file on disk. This is not a situation that occurs using legitimate application development practices. Second, besides simply detecting that something malicious in on the system, tools can pinpoint precisely where the malicious code is active in memory and then automatically extract it for further scrutiny. This allows retrieval of code and data that was never actually written to the file system of the machine under investigation. Third, data that malware hides from live and traditional forensics methods, such as running processes and open network connections, are fully visible to memory forensics tools. Leveraging these benefits, memory forensics provides not only the ability to detect malware, but also mechanisms for deep understanding of malware behavior.

Volatility (Volatility Foundation 2017) is the most widely used and powerful framework for memory forensics, containing an entire suite of analysis plugins dedicated to the GUI subsystem of Windows (Ligh 2012a,b). This subsystem powers all interactions the end user has with the keyboard, mouse, monitor, and other devices.

For malware to fake user keystrokes, such as typing in the URL of an illegal website, this subsystem must be used. To detect such behavior, Volatility has several analysis plugins that specifically look for code performing such actions. In situations where these plugins report active code, that code must then be investigated to determine its precise actions and reasons for controlling hardware devices. In some cases, actions such as the implementation of hot keys or custom mouse controls turn out to be legitimate, but in other cases, this analysis ends up pointing directly to the malware responsible for framing an innocent party.

Another type of analysis concerns malware programmed to contact a list of illegal websites from a victim's computer. When assessing whether the websites were accessed intentionally by the user or programmatically by malware, the list of accessed URLs can often be extracted from the acquired sample. This can potentially reveal many details to the investigator, including which applications were referencing the URLs; which files, if any, contained the URLs; and the context of the URL within applications, such as them appearing inside an advertisement shown in a browser, or in the copy/paste buffer on the user's system. By analyzing the full context of illegally accessed material, the investigator can build a strong and defensible case about the guilt or innocence of the person under investigation.

5.2.2 Anti-Forensics Applications

Investigating computer systems where anti-forensics techniques are in place can be extremely difficult. The purpose of anti-forensics tools is to either erase or scramble the digital artifacts investigators rely on to perform their work. In cases where the Trojan defense is employed, the use of anti-forensics can and does remove the exact artifacts relied upon during traditional analysis to tie activity back to either the end user or malware. Fortunately, memory forensics is not as easily affected by anti-forensics techniques. Even artifacts that have been mangled on disk can still be recoverable in memory. A common example of this is when a user securely deletes a file from disk using a third-party wiping utility. For the subset of utilities that implements secure deletion properly, the file is truly gone and unrecoverable from non-volatile storage after the wiping operation completes. Using memory forensics techniques can circumvent such deletion, however, as remnants, or even a complete copy, of the file may remain in memory.

5.2.3 "Private" Applications

As mentioned previously, web browsers, chat programs, and other common applications routinely implement private usage modes. The purpose of these operational modes is to ensure that passive monitoring of an application's network traffic, as well as traditional forensic investigation of the system's hard drive, reveals little to no detail of the activity that occurred. This is problematic for all sides in a legal investigation. The lack of on-disk browser history can make it difficult for the investigator to tie visiting specific websites to the user, and inversely, difficult for the user to show that they did not visit those websites.

As with malware and anti-forensics applications, memory forensics can still recover most or all of the activity that occurred in these private usage modes. This is possible because all of the activity that happens in the applications—typing text, viewing pictures, sending and receiving chat messages, browsing web pages, choosing file names, and more—all leave traces in memory. In the case of end-to-end encrypted chats, which are only visible to the actual participants in the chat, entire plaintext copies of conversations will be left in memory. This occurs because memory buffers that are created after decryption to display the plaintext data in the chat window remain in memory.

Browsers suffer a similar fate under the scrutiny of memory forensics techniques, even for data that was sent and received using HTTPS. Again, for the browser to display a page's content in a readable form, the decrypted network traffic must be stored in memory. Similarly, before an encrypted request is made by the browser, the plaintext data must first be stored in memory for encryption. The data generated by applications, such as browsers and chat programs, often stays in memory long after the application is closed.

Many forensic tools exploit the gap between what traditional forensic analysis can uncover versus what memory forensics can uncover. Bulk Extractor (Garfinkel 2013) is one of the most widely used, analyzing every byte of a memory capture to look for data, including URLs, emails, DNS lookups, social media usage, web searches, and other artifacts. By simply running Bulk Extractor against a memory sample, investigators can uncover a wealth of forensic data that may be inaccessible to traditional digital forensics.

5.2.4 Encrypted Stores

The use of encryption is now widespread, even for novice users. Mainstream operating systems provide full disk or partition encryption by default and this is now the expectation when configuring a new computer. Windows, Linux, and Mac all also natively support creation of encrypted containers. These containers are stored as a single file on disk, but then internally have an encrypted file system. The use of containers is very attractive as they can easily be moved to different devices using email, removable storage devices, or cloud storage. They are also useful in that a user's sensitive files can be enveloped by an extra layer of protection beyond full disk encryption. Of course, criminals are well aware of these encrypted containers and use them to store information they would prefer law enforcement and digital investigators not to find.

When a system is examined, investigators will often use forensic software that is designed to find encrypted containers. Finding the containers is only the first step, however; the credentials to unlock them must be obtained. In countries where users do not have to divulge their credentials to law enforcement, this can immediately derail an investigation. Fortunately, memory forensics can be used to gain access to encrypted containers in cases where the credentials are unknown. By focusing on keystrokes, such as the user typing in their password(s), as well as the contents of open files, including text files of passwords or a password manager's database, tools can still access protected information in memory. This might allow an investigator to build a password-cracking dictionary that is closely tailored to the user under investigation. In many cases where encrypted containers are present, the use of a memory sample to crack the container is the difference between a guilty person going to jail or walking free.

6. Conclusion

This chapter has considered the Trojan horse defense and whether traditional forensics techniques are sufficient to definitively detect cutting-edge malware and disentangle the actions of legitimate users from those covertly executed by malware. In general, the answer is no. Modern malware is often weaponized, extremely stealthy, and in many documented cases, leaves no trace on non-volatile storage. Furthermore, modern malware can secretly perform virtually any action a user might perform on a computer system, including actions that place human users in serious legal jeopardy, such as launching attacks against other systems or downloading illicit materials. Traditional approaches to detecting malware that might impact a legal case include executing antivirus software and using "pull the plug" forensic techniques that target only non-volatile storage devices. Unfortunately, in many cases when investigators restrict themselves to these techniques, they will be completely unable to detect malware, much less establish whether malware played a substantial role. When malware is in fact responsible for illegal actions, this choice of tools tips the scales heavily against innocent parties.

Memory forensics is already widely adopted in digital forensic and incident response teams in both the private and the public sphere, as it often provides the sole viable solution for detecting and understanding modern malware, especially strains that are memory-only or file-less. Organizations have rushed to train their investigative teams in how to use memory forensics and put processes in place to increase the likelihood of success in real investigations. While the use of memory forensics tools currently require substantial expertise, improving their reliability and usability is an area of active research. Unfortunately, the use of memory forensics is not particularly widespread in the law enforcement community, especially in smaller, local organizations and departments. Given the power of memory forensics to provide investigators with viable tools for properly detecting and analyzing modern malware, memory forensics simply must become part of the modern digital forensics toolkit used by law enforcement.

7. Acknowledgments

The authors would like to thank LSU Law Professor Ken Levy for helpful comments on early versions of this chapter.

References

AccessData. 2019a. AccessData FTK Imager. https://marketing.accessdata.com/ftkimager4.2.0.
AccessData. 2019b. Forensic Toolkit (FTK). https://accessdata.com/products-services/forensic-toolkit-ftk.
Alperovitch, D. 2016. Bears in the Midst: Intrusion into the Democratic National Committee. https://www.crowdstrike.com/blog/bears-midst-intrusion-democratic-national-committee/.

Armerding, T. 2013. Advanced Volatile Threat: New Name for Old Malware Technique. http://www.csoonline.com/article/2132995/malware-cybercrime/advanced-volatile-threat--new-name-for-old-malware-technique-.html.

AV-Test. 2019. Malware. https://www.av-test.org/en/statistics/malware/.

Blackbag Technologies. 2019. Blacklight. https://www.blackbagtech.com/blacklight.html.

Bowles, S. and Hernandez-Castro, J. 2015. The first 10 years of the Trojan Horse Defence. Computer Fraud & Security, vol. 2015.

Brenner, S. W., Carrier, B. and Henninger, J. 2004. The Trojan Horse Defense in cybercrime cases. Santa Clara High Technology Law Journal, vol. 21.

Carrier, B. 2003. Defining digital forensic examination and analysis tools using abstraction layers. International Journal of Digital Evidence, vol. 1.

Carvey, H. 2019. RegRipper. https://github.com/keydet89/RegRipper2.8.

Cuckoo Foundation. 2019. Cuckoo Sandbox Automated Malware Analysis. https://cuckoosandbox.org.

Cybercrime. 2019. Bureau of Justice Statistics. https://www.bjs.gov/index.cfm?ty=tp&tid=41.

DEEPSPAR Data Recovery Systems. 2019. PC-3000 Data Extractor. http://www.deepspar.com/products-pc-3000-data.html.

Doffman, Z. 2019. Warning as Devious New Android Malware Hides In Fake Adobe Flash Player Installations (Updated). https://www.forbes.com/sites/zakdoffman/2019/08/16/dangerous-new-android-trojan-hides-from-malware-researchers-and-taunts-them-on-twitter/#70c2245c6d9c.

Eckelberry, A., Dardick, G., Folkerts, J. A., Shipp, A., Sites, E., Stewart, J. and Stuart, R. 2007. Technical Review of the Trial Testimony State of Connecticut vs. Julie Amero. https://web.archive.org/web/20090124121203/http://www.sunbelt-software.com/ihs/alex/julieamerosummary.pdf.

Fortuna, A. 2017. Malware Persistence Techniques. https://www.andreafortuna.org/2017/07/06/malware-persistence-techniques/.

Garfinkel, S. L. 2013. Digital media triage with bulk data analysis and bulk extractor. Computers & Security 32: 56–72.

Ghavalas, B. and Philips, A. 2005. Trojan Defence: A forensic view Part II. Digital Investigation, vol. 2.

Grier, J. and Richard, G. G. III. 2015. Rapid forensic imaging of large disks with sifting collectors. Digital Investigation, vol. 14S.

grugq. 2004. FIST! FIST! FIST! It's All in the Wrist: Remote Exec. http://phrack.org/issues/62/8.html#article.

Haagman, D. and Ghavalas, B. 2005. Trojan Defence: A forensic view. Digital Investigation, vol. 2.

Kaspersky Research Team. 2014. Kaspersky Lab Uncovers "The Mask": One of the Most Advanced Global Cyber-espionage Operations to Date Due to the Complexity of the Toolset Used by the Attackers. https://usa.kaspersky.com/about/press-releases/2014.

Kaspersky Research Team. 2015. The Mystery of Duqu 2.0: A Sophisticated Cyberespionage Actor Returns. https://securelist.com/the-mystery-of-duqu-2-0-a-sophisticated-cyberespionage-actor-returns/70504/.

Laing, B. 2018. Malware-as-a-Service: The 9-to-5 of Organized Cybercrime. https://www.lastline.com/blog/malware-as-a-service-the-9-to-5-of-organized-cybercrime/.

Ligh, M. H. 2012a. MoVP 3.1 Detecting Malware Hooks in the Windows GUI Subsystem. https://volatility-labs.blogspot.com/2012/09/movp-31-detecting-malware-hooks-in.html.

Ligh, M. H. 2012b. OMFW 2012: Malware in the Windows GUI Subsystem. https://volatility-labs.blogspot.com/2012/10/omfw-2012-malware-in-windows-gui.html.

Luehr, P. H. 2005. Real evidence, virtual crimes. Criminal Justice, vol. 14.

Majumder, B. G. 2019. New Malware Infects Thousands of PCs, Confirms Microsoft and Cisco Talos. https://www.ibtimes.sg/new-malware-infects-thousands-pcs-confirms-microsoft-cisco-talos-32615.

Malin, C. H., Casey, E. and Aquilina, J. M. 2008. Malware Forensics: Investigating and Analyzing Malicious Code. Syngress.

Malwarebytes Labs. 2019. 2019 State of Malware. https://resources.malwarebytes.com/resource/2019-state-malware-malwarebytes-labs-report/?utm_source=blog&utm_medium=post&utm_campaign=0119_ws_stateofmalwarereportq119_mb.

Mcelroy, W. 2007. In Child Porn Case, Technology Entraps the Innocent. http://www.independent.org/news/article.asp?id=1894.

Microsoft. 2011. What is Antivirus Software? http://web.archive.org/ web/20110411203211/http://www. microsoft.com/security/resources/antivirus-whatis.aspx.

Monterosso, F. S. 2010. Protecting the Children: Challenges that Result in, and Consequences Resulting From, Inconsistent Prosecution of Child Pornography Cases in a Technical World. XVI Rich. J.L. & Tech., vol. 11.

O'Donnell, L. 2019. Joker Spyware Found in 24 Google Play Apps. https://threatpost.com/joker-spyware-google-play-apps/148053/.

OpenText Security. 2019. Encase Forensic. https://www.guidancesoftware.com/encase-forensic.

PCWorld. 2008. A Misconfigured Laptop, A Wrecked Life. https://abcnews.go.com/Technology/PCWorld/story?id=5188541.

Rankin, B. 2018. A Brief History of Malware Its Evolution and Impact. https://www.lastline.com/blog/history-of-malware-its-evolution-and-impact/.

Richard, G. G. III and Roussev, V. 2005. Scalpel: A frugal, high performance file carver. Digital Forensics Research Conference (DFRWS), pp. 71–77.

Schroeder, W. 2019. PowerShell Empire. https://www.powershellempire.com/.

Schwartz, E. J., Avgerinos, T. and Brumley, D. 2010. All you ever wanted to know about dynamic taint analysis and forward symbolic execution (But might have been afraid to ask). In 2010 IEEE Symposium on Security and Privacy, pp. 317–331.

Skape and Turkulainen, J. 2004. Remote Library Injection. http://www.hick.org/code/skape/papers/remote-library-injection.pdf.

Steel, C. 2014. Technical Soddi Defenses: The Trojan Horse Defense revisited. Journal of Digital Forensics, Security and Law, vol. 9.

Symantec. 2018. Internet Security Threat Report, vol. 23. https://www.symantec.com/content/dam/symantec/docs/reports/istr-23-2018-en.pdf.

Volatility Foundation. 2017. The Volatility Framework: Volatile Memory Artifact Extraction Utility Framework. https://github.com/volatilityfoundation/volatility.

Wadner, K. 2014. An Analysis of Meterpreter during Post-Exploitation. https://www.sans.org/readingroom/whitepapers/forensics/paper/35537.

Part 2
Digital Forensics

5

Law Enforcement Agencies in Europe and the Use of Hacking Tools During Investigations

Some Legal Informatics, Civil Rights and Data Protection Issues

Giovanni Ziccardi

1. Introduction

The future of digital forensics in Europe is, in our opinion, conditioned by several factors that are not always well balanced between them. The first factor is the need for a common strategy and shared tools: today, crime crosses borders (Picotti 2004), especially in the era of cloud and big data, and it is unthinkable to manage complex (and very fast) criminal phenomena using investigative strategies designed for the analogical era (Lupária 2009). However, there is not always a technical, legislative and investigative uniformity between the various European Countries (Lupária and Ziccardi 2007).

Secondly, there is a need to use the best technological tools, often the same ones used by criminals, in order to counter their actions (Ziccardi 2013). However, these are very invasive instruments that can endanger the protection of citizens' fundamental rights (Perri 2007b). We will see, for example, how there is an interesting debate going on in Europe about the use of hacking tools by law enforcement (Ziccardi 2018).

Finally, in Europe, in recent years, the GDPR has come into force: a rule which, albeit with exceptions and while allowing law enforcement a certain freedom in

Professor of Legal Informatics, Jean Monnet Chair of 'European Union Data Governance, Cybersecurity and Digital Fundamental Rights', Director of the Information Society Law Centre (Department of Legal Sciences 'Cesare Beccaria') of the University of Milan, Italy.

processing data for investigation purposes, protects the citizen with reference to his personal data and, also, to his judicial data (Sartor and Monducci 2004).

The core issue is that data are, today, at the centre of the information society, and this is well known. That is the reason why data protection, over the last twenty years, has become a central topic of political, technological, social and legal analysis (Schneier, 2008 and 2012). In recent years, the national and international legislators have pointed out that, on the one hand, a strong automation process has caused the loss of control over the circulation of data and, on the other hand, it is necessary to raise the level of protection in order to guarantee the rights of the individual in the technological society. In the age of algorithms, artificial intelligence and big data, the individual is protected through the protection of his data, also in the States where the individual lives (Rodotà 2014).

This picture of great diffusion of data has also involved the world of investigations: today each individual generates millions of data that can be interesting from an investigative point of view (e-mail, WhatsApp messages, data on the cloud) but which become extremely difficult to manage in a "manual" way and must necessarily be collected, analysed and selected with automated tools during the investigation (Solove 2008).

In 2016, the GDPR significantly renewed the traditional protection tools, trying to adapt the data protection rules to the diffusion of social network platforms and to the practice of commercial and behavioral profiling (seen as a new frontier for online marketing).

Let's clarify, right from the start, that the GDPR is not a normative provision expressly dedicated to digital investigations, but it is still, for us, an interesting source both from the point of view of the level of data protection that is established in Europe and from that of security measures (Schneier 2013) and possible data breaches (which, obviously, also concern data collected for investigative purposes).

A year later, in 2017, the LIBE Committee of the European Parliament addressed, in a very complex and innovative study, the issue of data protection and information systems during the investigations concerning the digital data of individuals (with particular regard to the suspects).

The study was commissioned by the European Parliament's Policy Department for Citizens' Rights and Constitutional Affairs at the request of the LIBE Committee. It is very interesting because it presents concrete policy proposals on the use of hacking techniques by law enforcement and, most of all, these proposals are driven by a comparative examination of the legal frameworks for hacking by law enforcement across six EU Member States and three non-EU Countries, in combination with analyses of the international and EU-level debates on the topic and the EU legal basis for intervention in the field (Ziccardi 2018).

The two documents, although related to norms and areas only partially overlapping, are linked by a common thread: the idea that data, in today's society, must be considered as a fundamental good, linked to the rights of the individual (Perri 2007a).

The protection of data becomes, in fact, the instrument to guarantee the protection of rights as well.

This means that the scholar, today, who wants to analyse how the "digital investigations of the future" will appear, will always have to take all these elements into great consideration.

The subject of investigations, for the individual legal systems of the various European Countries, it's not new.

There are already decisions, by the Courts, that have tried to outline the limits of using similar strategies and investigative actions both in relation to the investigative system in general and with reference to the tools used, especially if these tools are particularly invasive.

In some Countries, attempts have been made to identify the types of crimes for which such use of instruments is permitted, for example mafia crimes, corruption, or computer crimes. There were, then, specific draft laws to try to regulate the technical aspect of the management of these instruments, in order to be able to control every single operation.

In this chapter we will first analyse the notion of data protection, and the rights of the person, in the GDPR. A special mention will be made to the topic of security measures (Mele 2018a) and data breach management which are two elements that can be easily connected to the topic of digital investigations. Then, we will dedicate attention to the LIBE commission document, more specific with regard to the new technological tools of investigation and the limits in the use of particularly invasive strategies towards the rights of freedom of the individual. Finally, we will try to draw from the two documents some predictions on the policy of investigations of the future.

2. Common Digital Forensics Activities and the GDPR

A new element, which has been added in recent years in Europe to the already complex framework of investigations, is the advent of the GDPR, the European data protection regulation which, while providing for various exceptions to the world of data processing carried out by law enforcement agencies, has made the topic of data protection, and the rights of people with information and big data, a topical issue.

The recent GDPR clearly lays down additional obligations on private companies and public authorities that process personal data, through a new and proactive approach.

Many of these rules directly concern companies and individuals who manage data used for digital investigations. In many European Countries, in fact, it is common practice for Courts and Prosecutors to delegate to the outside most of the technological and IT activities, including the collection of evidence.

The purpose of the GDPR, in fact, is to protect personal data in the information society, and is permanently applicable in all EU Countries as of 25 May 2018.

It is a new, important Regulation that has impacts on daily work activities and introduces, in case of violations, a penalty system that aims to protect individual's rights and data. GDPR penalties consist of fines, possible claim for damages, and criminal penalties (if introduced by national legislations).

Fines are imposed by a Data Protection Supervisor, following investigations or claims; this Authority can, in minor cases, enact warnings, formal notices, process inhibitions or monetary fines, and it is always possible to appeal to the Court against the Data Protection Supervisor's decisions (Ziccardi 2018).

On 18 July 2018, the Italian Data Protection Supervisory Authority explicitly reported to the Italian Parliament the data protection problems related to digital investigative activities after the implementation of the GDPR.

Several events, also described by the Italian media, demonstrated in fact, in Italy, the risks likely to derive from the recourse, for investigative purposes, by private companies, to certain software whose peculiar characteristics would deserve, in the Authority opinion, a specific discipline.

The Report refers, in particular, to computer programs connected to apps, not directly inoculated, therefore, only in the suspect's device, but placed on platforms (such as 'Google Play Store') accessible to all. Where made available on the market, even if only by mistake in the absence of the necessary filters to limit the acquisition by third parties—as would appear to have been the case in Italian events—these spy apps would risk becoming dangerous surveillance tools (Lyon 2002).

According to the Italian Data Protection Authority, the use of IT collectors for judicial purposes is undoubtedly useful in light of the evolution of available technologies. It allows, in fact, to disregard the physical installation of the collection devices to carry out interception of communications and conversations between present, directly inoculating the spy software in the host device.

However, the innovative features typical of these software—and more generally, the telematic intercepting activity on smartphone-type mobile terminals or similar IT devices—are such as to determine a substantial, very significant change in the effects and potential of a medium of proof research, such as the interceptive one, designed and regulated with reference to other realities.

Some intruding agents would, in fact, not only be able to 'concentrate', in a single act, a plurality of investigative tools (searches of the contents of the personal computer, stalking activities with the satellite system, wiretapping of any kind, acquisition of records) but also, in some cases, to eliminate the traces of the operations carried out, sometimes even altering the acquired data.

The guarantees established by the Italian criminal code, to protect the suspect (from the actual confirmation of the judge on the acts performed by the investigators and on the respect of the conditions established by the law for each act, to the adversarial test) would thus be strongly weakened by the appeal, not adequately circumscribed, to these methods of investigation, due to the peculiar characteristics that make them difficult to classify in the traditional legal-procedural categories.

The Italian Authority recalls that this difficulty in dogmatic qualification is, moreover, at the base of the interpretative contrast composed, in April 2016, by the United Sections of the Court of Cassation, which specified the conditions of use of computerized sensors to carry out interceptions of conversations and communications between present individuals, also in the home environment.

The particular characteristics of these methods make, in fact, the 'itinerant' environmental interception as it is arranged on a mobile device and, for this reason alone, ontologically incompatible with the indication of the place and the particular protections accorded to the confidentiality of the conversations carried out in the home environment.

Seizing many of the indications of the United Sections, the Italian legislator has recently regulated the use of computerized data collectors, admitting it in particular for interceptions only between those present and delegating to a subsequent ministerial decree the definition of the technical requirements of the computer programs functional to the execution of such operations investigation.

During an opinion both on the draft legislative decree reforming the regulation of wiretapping, and on the draft ministerial decree implementing it, the Italian Authority has provided the Government with some proposals for integrating the text, useful for surrounding the use of IT scanners with greater guarantees for investigative purposes.

In the opinion on the draft legislative decree, in particular, the Government was invited to evaluate the opportunity to include in the authorization decree—also for crimes within the competence of the District Attorneys—the indication of the places and time of collection in order to strengthen, also in this area, the guarantees connected to a more incisive control by the judge on the investigative activity. Moreover, it was represented how this modification would have contributed to develop the criterion of the separation of the phase of insertion of the sensor from that of actual activation of the microphone, in order to limit as far as possible the invasiveness of this means of searching for evidence and to guarantee the due correspondence of the intercepting operations to the object of the authorization decree.

Furthermore, the Authority invited the Government to specify some parts of the legislative decree that could legitimize, by way of interpretation, the acquisition (albeit without possibility of use in court) of personal data even outside the time and space limits established by the magistrate authorization decree.

Finally, it was stated that the opportunity to introduce an express prohibition (with the relative sanction in the event of non-compliance) of the knowability, disclosure and diffusion of interceptions carried out by sensors, concerning subjects extraneous to the facts for which it is proceeded, was also in accordance with the criteria of delegation.

Therefore, according to the Data Protection Authority interpretation, it seems appropriate to reflect on the limits of use of these software for intercepting purposes, also evaluating the possibility of a prohibition or, subordinately, the adoption of further, specific precautions.

In the opinion on the draft ministerial decree, on the other hand, the Authority had underlined the need to specify in greater detail the software modules that can be used, among those that commonly make up an interception system using an IT sensor (for example the software that, installed on the target devices, the information acquisition operates, the inoculation system, the management system, etc.).

Furthermore, it was noted, in this 'letter to the Government', that it was necessary to indicate in a precise manner the technical measures to be adopted in order to guarantee the confidentiality of the data on the systems functional to the execution of the interceptions by means of the computer, specifying for example the methods of access to the systems by the operators authorized, the functionalities of recording of the operations carried out there, the modalities of transmission of the acquired data through sensor.

Finally, it was suggested to exclude recourse to sensors whose operation lowered the security level of the guest device to prevent third parties from compromising it, with possible negative repercussions on the protection of personal data contained therein, as well as on the confidentiality of the activity itself.

Most of these indications have not been incorporated in the definitively approved texts. They lack, above all, the provision of adequate guarantees to prevent, due to their extraordinary intrusive potential, these investigative tools, from precious auxiliaries of the investigating bodies, degenerate instead into massive surveillance means (Campbell 2003) or, conversely, into multiplication factors exponential vulnerability of the evidentiary compendium, making it extremely permeable if allocated in unsafe servers or, worse, delocalized even outside national borders.

Some judicial investigations, which the press reported, have in fact demonstrated the risks associated with the use of IT collectors in the absence of the necessary guarantees and, above all, with the use, by the companies in charge, of particular, worthy techniques of further precautions, due to their particular characteristics and specific potential.

The Authority refers, in particular, to the use, for wiretapping purposes, of software connected to apps, which therefore are not directly inoculated in the suspect's device only, but placed on platforms (such as Google Play Store) accessible to all. Where made available on the market, even if only by mistake in the absence of the necessary filters to limit its acquisition by third parties—as would appear to have been the case in the known cases—these spy apps would, in fact, risk turning into dangerous mass surveillance tools.

Furthermore, it is extremely dangerous, in the Authority's opinion, to use cloud systems for archiving, even in non-European Countries, the data captured, even if it appears to have been done in cases investigated by investigators. The de-localization of servers in areas not subject to national jurisdiction is, in fact, an obvious defect not only for the protection of the rights of the parties concerned, but also for the same effectiveness and secrecy of the investigative action.

The use of these two types of systems (apps or in any case software that are not directly inoculated on the guest device but downloaded from platforms freely accessible to all and, on the other hand, archiving through cloud systems in servers located outside the national territory) should, therefore, be the subject of a specific prohibition.

Alternatively, if it were not deemed to sanction an express prohibition of recourse to these techniques, it could be envisaged—also in this case, preferably with a primary rule—that the actual installation in the portable electronic device and the consequent acquisition capabilities of the computer can completely be realized only after having verified the univocal association between the device affected by the software and the one considered in the judicial authorization provision.

In any case, also because of the rapid evolution of the features and functionalities of the software available for wiretapping purposes, it would be advisable to introduce—in the legislative or even just revealing the aforementioned ministerial decree—an express prohibition of recourse to suitable sensors to delete the tracks of the operations performed on the host device.

In fact, for the purposes of correct probative reconstruction and the completeness and truthfulness of the investigative material collected, it is essential to have suitable software to reconstruct in detail every activity carried out on the host system and on the data therein present, without altering its content.

In this sense, the requirement of the 'integrity, security and authenticity of the captured data' could be explicitly stated, that the software used must ensure, in accordance with article 4, paragraph 1 of the Italian ministerial decree, thus effectively guaranteeing the completeness of the 'Chain of custody of the computer test'.

More generally, at the application level, if not through a specific integration of the ministerial decree itself, it could also be envisaged to adopt a single data transmission and management protocol destined to flow onto the servers installed in the interception rooms of the Public Prosecutor's Offices for their conservation, avoiding possible unevenness in the levels of security.

It could also be considered, according to the Authority, the opportunity to make available management software suitable to allow the analysis of data concerning the features of access to the servers used for the intercepting activity by private suppliers, for the realization of maintenance activities. In this way, it would be possible to make the storage systems of the access logs to the instrumentation through which the captive activity is carried out accessible to the companies themselves, strengthening the guarantees of the secrecy of the investigative documentation.

Moreover, it would be appropriate to define the management criteria, by each Public Prosecutor, of interceptions carried out by other judicial offices and relating to proceedings, the documents of which have subsequently been transmitted for competence or otherwise acquired for use in different proceedings.

Particularly important for the purposes of this chapter is, on the other side, the fact that the GDPR has considerably strengthened monetary fines, bringing them up to twenty million euros or up to four per cent of the company global turnover of the previous year (Ziccardi 2018). The amount of the fine depends on the nature and severity of the data breach, length of behaviour, negligent or intentional nature of the conduct (for example knowingly ignoring a non-compliant situation), recidivism, and the presence of aggravating or mitigating factors.

Anyone who has suffered damage can claim compensation, both from the interested party (the Data Controller) and from third parties (for example, from companies that used the data); compensation can be claimed for asset damage (for example financial loss) and non-asset damage (for example loss of reputation).

The request shall be lodged with the judicial authorities against the Data Controller or Data Processor responsible for the violation, and the Data Controller (or Data Processor) is exempted from damages only proving that the harmful event is not imputable to it.

The GDPR does not directly provide for criminal penalties, but provides for the possibility of EU Countries to issue laws with criminal penalties for data processing breaches (Ziccardi 2018).

Concerning the individual protection, the GDPR is applicable to data relating to natural persons (in the EU, regardless of nationality and residence), including data under the control of the Controller or Processor established in the EU, data that is being processed in the EU and data processed in a public cloud (because the geographic location of the data cannot be determined). It is not applicable to data relating to legal persons or to data processed for personal (or household) use; some exceptions apply, also, in the interest of the freedom of expression and freedom of the press.

In the text of the GDPR it is possible to intend 'data protection' in many ways (Ziccardi 2018).

The first interpretation describes data protection as the person's sovereignty over their own personal data. The person ('data subject') must be always 'informed' (with an 'Information Statement') about the processing of the data, and has the possibility to take decisions (for example: the exercise of some rights) on the basis of this information. The statement will explain who is processing the owner's data, how data will be processed, what data is being processed, where data will be processed (geographically or in the cloud), the purpose of the processing activity and the rights that the person can exercise.

'Personal data' means any information relating to an identified or identifiable natural person, such as, for example, name/first name, surname/last name, place and date of birth, location data (home, personal or work address), identification codes (credit card, bank account), online ID (identification codes, IP address) and sensitive personal data (health status, habits, chronic diseases, hereditary diseases, diets), daily activities, membership in trade unions or political parties, sexual life and orientation and racial or ethnic origin.

The processing of personal data is forbidden unless specifically agreed by the data subject, except under special circumstances, such as the need to exercise a right related to work and social security, when life protection is threatened or for reasons of public interest.

Special categories of personal data (sensitive data) concern political opinions, religious or philosophical beliefs, trade union membership, health, sexual orientation, racial or ethnic origin, genetic data or biometric data. At the same level of importance are data relating to criminal matters, such as criminal convictions, offenses committed, security measures related to criminal convictions (for example probation, restraining order).

A very interesting category of data are 'risky data', which imply high risks for the dignity and freedom of the person, and are subject to specific measures based on the 'impact assessment' (prior checking). Such data include profiling, mass data processing, video surveillance, geolocation, data that makes identity theft easier (for example IP addresses, identification codes, bank account, credit card information, etc.).

The processing is any operation, or set of operations, which is performed on personal data, whether or not by automated means, from collection to destruction or erasure, including consultation.

Each person shall have the right not to be subject to a decision based only on automated processing, including profiling, which produces legal effects for him or similar effects. In particular, 'profiling' in the GDPR means any form of automated processing of personal data consisting of the use of personal data to evaluate certain personal aspects relating to a natural person.

The Data Protection Supervisor is an independent authority, acting in full autonomy, with a mandate that has a variable duration depending on each country.

The Data Protection Supervisor is responsible to supervise and ensure the application of the rules in the country, promote awareness and foster understanding of the EU Regulation, examine claims from interested parties, investigate the application of the rules, impose administrative penalties, monitor technological developments that can affect people's privacy (Faulkner 2003) and collaborate with the supervisory authorities of the other EU Countries.

A new professional role, the Data Protection Officer (DPO), is placed at the heart of the data protection framework: the DPO supervises data protection within the company, and should not have conflicting interests with other functions that he may be required to perform. The DPO provides advice to the Data Processor and Data Controller, supervises compliance with the regulations and company provisions regarding data processing, supervises the proper staff training and information regarding data processing obligations and cooperates with the Data Protection Supervisor. The DPO must be promptly and adequately involved in data protection issues, must be supported with necessary resources, must be independent and not receive instructions, and must report directly to top management. Moreover, he can be contacted directly by any party, can perform other tasks (if not in conflict of interest), and cannot be removed from the fulfilment of its tasks. Contact details of the DPO are communicated to the Data Protection Supervisor and reported on all Privacy Statements.

The Officer is appointed by a Data Processor or by a Data Controller and shall be a person who meets requirements of professionalism (legal, IT and other skills and expertise), experience in the field of privacy and the ability to perform the assigned tasks. Such an appointment is mandatory for public entities, while for private companies is mandatory only in specific cases (e.g., for companies dealing with big data such as private hospitals or insurance companies that can handle large amounts of sensitive personal data).

One of the central issues of the GDPR is the security of data processing (Schneier 2004). The security system must adequately protect personal data at each stage of processing, and must protect the security of company assets that are used for processing. The aim is to prevent the risk of damage to data subjects.

The Data Controller and Data Processor must identify and adopt security measures, must provide the staff involved in processing operations with instructions and training on the topic, must check the effectiveness of the system and monitor the security system constantly and keep it updated. Staff involved in processing operations must treat the data according to the instructions received, be aware of the risks and act accordingly.

Last but not least, general protection and safety of data is linked to the concept of 'accountability': it is compulsory to provide documentation and proof of the correct processing of personal data in accordance with the provisions of the GDPR, the availability, integrity and confidentiality of data, the resilience of systems and services, the use of pseudonyms or data encryption systems, the capacity to restore the system in the event of an accident and to perform efficacy tests.

The aspects of the GDPR summarized above place data protection at the center of the new legal framework. In particular, one should note the reference to 'sensitive' data, for example information that in today's society have become particularly serious and able to harm the rights of the individual, the new approach to the idea of security and accountability, and the new role of the Data Protection Officer who acts as a guardian to ensure a higher level of protection of the individual and respect for the law during data processing activities.

The purpose of the GDPR is to raise the level of information protection in a highly automated context, managed in many cases by algorithms and artificial intelligence and capable of profiling citizens with great precision.

3. The LIBE Commission Study of 2017

In March 2017, the European Parliament (Directorate-General for Internal Policies, Policy Department, Citizens' Rights and Constitutional Affairs) published a study of over one hundred forty pages entitled 'Legal Frameworks for Hacking by Law Enforcement: Identification, Evaluation and Comparison of Practices'.

It is a very complex study, urged by members of the LIBE Commission, which aims to draw several concrete legislative proposals that are appropriately preceded by a schematic (but accurate) review of the regulatory framework of six European Union States, and of three non-European states. In addition, it presents a comprehensive analysis of the ongoing political debate on the subject, and calls for a solid (and common) legal basis to regulate the phenomenon in a way that is respectful of the fundamental rights of citizens (Ziccardi 2018).

The underlying premise of the whole study is that the so-called 'hacking by law enforcement' (that is, the use of hacking techniques in investigative activities) is presented as a relatively new phenomenon (at least in its 'official' and 'visible' form) within the older (and traditional) political problem of finding a constant balance between security requirements and protection of data and privacy in the information society (Ziccardi 2018).

On the one hand, law enforcement agencies and law enforcement practitioners justify the use of such strategies (and actions) on the basis of the assertion that the use of hacking techniques has now become indispensible to bring more security, representing the only solution to the challenge that encryption has placed in the search for the elements of a crime. In fact, this challenge could not be overcome by trying to systematically weaken encryption (for example, by introducing backdoors, a process that would be very complex not only from a technical point of view, but also from a 'political' one), but only by 'anticipating' the issue and penetrating directly into the information system. In simpler terms: if encryption exists, and it has been applied to data, the only two ways to overcome it are either attacking and weakening it, or by inoculating into the system a trojan that acquires data in the 'plain' and 'clear' communications environment, just before someone activates the encryption system to 'close' the information (Ziccardi 2018).

On the other hand, civil society actors and the scholars who are more concerned with the respect for privacy and the rights of the individual, have argued that hacking is an extremely invasive investigative tool, able to significantly impinge on fundamental rights and on the privacy of individuals. But not only that: the use of tools that should 'crack' and make systems insecure could also have a direct impact on the security of the Internet itself, and on the technology infrastructure in general. Using techniques, viruses and exploits to 'poison' the common information systems would result in a widespread insecurity and vulnerability. Very recent is the case of viruses, worms and ransomware circulating worldwide, infecting critical systems in over a hundred States, which were originally developed by enforcement or intelligence agencies: 'technological weapons' produced by States that, suddenly, began to circulate and attack the entire civil infrastructure.

The study, and this is certainly a very good point, has a highly interdisciplinary approach: firstly, it analyzes the debate at the international level and then proceeds, from a procedural standpoint, to propose possible 'legal foundations'. Finally, with a more practical approach, the relevant regulatory framework is analyzed in six European Countries (France, Germany, Italy, the Netherlands, Poland and the United Kingdom) and three non-European countries (Australia, Israel and the United States of America).

The conclusions, which we will comment on in the second half of this short contribution, takes the form of an interesting piece of legislative policy proposals (with accompanying recommendations). 2016 has been repeatedly indicated, among the lines of the study, as a crucial year for the subject of computer State-trojans and hacking tools: all States have shown a regulatory interest (including, ad hoc reforms) or have started drafting a legislative strategy for the foreseeable future (Ziccardi 2018).

The study wants to be probably an 'answer' to such a sudden 'change of course', and wants to raise the level of attention in all the operators, investigators, politicians, magistrates, lawyers and scholars dealing with human rights.

The debate from which the study originated has developed, over the last few years, moving from a clear awareness of the legal challenges posed by encryption (in general), to the modern possibilities of investigation (in particular).

This awareness has given rise to a period characterized by what the study defines as the 'going dark' phenomenon: a framework in which there has been a growing lack of power in accessing data 'legally' during investigation and in effectively acquiring and examining sources that are today 'resident' on the most commonly used electronic devices, or 'constantly moving' through communication networks. Such 'darkening' of the digital sources would cause blocking of investigations, and encryption techniques are seen as one of the strongest barriers to this access.

At the same time, however, a political (and commercial) analysis reveals that it is still clear that the intention to support strong encryption around the world, especially in products and services sold by 'big players' of the Internet, and that the ideas of 'institutional backdoors' appear unattainable.

This has led, in practice, to the use of hacking techniques during investigations to bypass encryption, by borrowing and refining the operating modes used by hackers.

At the same time, however, the study highlights clear risks for the fundamental rights to the protection of privacy and freedom of expression of thought and information: hacking techniques are, in fact, extremely invasive, especially if compared to the more traditional 'intrusive' techniques (such as interceptions, inspections, searches and seizures). Through hacking, Law Enforcement Agencies can access all data in a device or in a system. This means the management of a very large amount of data: a recent investigative activity carried out by the Dutch authority, mentioned in the study, led to the collection of seven Terabytes of data, more or less eighty-six million pages of this Journal. At the same time, the data being processed are not only significant, but are also particularly sensitive: the geographic location, movements in everyday life, communications that the subject spreads and receives, all the data stored relating to his/her life, including the most intimate ones and possibly not of interest in that specific investigation (Ziccardi 2018).

All these worrying aspects have not, however, prevented the political world from perceiving these tools as necessary. There was, in particular, no great public debate about the opportunity (or not) to admit similar proofs in front of a Court. They have entered slowly, in investigative everyday life, and have been used for years in many States. The discussion on the eligibility of hacking tools has never come to a real political confrontation, and has never directly involved citizens (except, perhaps, in Germany and in the United States of America, where some issues related to the matters at hand have been recalled also in the mainstream media).

A second risk is purely technological, and would ask a re-examination of the security of the Internet itself and its infrastructure: the hacking activities of Law Enforcement agencies may go beyond the targeted system, and cause damage to other unrelated systems. All in conjunction with possible ethical problems (the obligation, or not, for the Law Enforcement Agencies to report the discovery of digital weapons that they would rather prefer to reuse for investigative purposes).

There would then be a risk that involves the broader idea of territorial sovereignty: the device hacking activity could be located in another state or even 'in transit'. The same tools used to do hacking (such as a 'Remote Administration Tool') could be sold to governments or agencies with little regard for human rights, and could be used for illicit purposes (to investigate journalists, dissidents or political opponents).

In conclusion, hacking practices by Law Enforcement Agencies are seen as necessary (and admitted) in all six Countries analyzed by the Authors of the report. Four States (France, Germany, Poland and the United Kingdom) have already adopted specific rules; Italy and the Netherlands are experiencing a phase of legislative development, which, according to the study, generated a sort of 'gray zone' (hacking techniques are used by Law Enforcement Agencies, but without an express legislative framework that allows it).

The study mentions France, a State that has reported a major reform in 2011 of the Code of Criminal Procedure that has significantly increased the interception powers, reformed by Law 3 June 2016 no 731, which allowed remote access to computers and other devices. In Germany, the issue arose following a well-known decision (BvR 370/07) by the Constitutional Court which established a new fundamental right to the confidentiality and integrity of computer systems (Bundesverfassungsgericht 2008). Strictly speaking, German law allows the use of hacking tools both in the Criminal Procedure Code and in the Federal Crime Police Act. In Italy, use has been made, over the years, of these instruments, although not expressly governed by law. There is, however, a specific bill on the subject (with a very technical approach) and case law. In the summer of 2017, a broad reform of the whole Criminal Procedural Code included the generic possibility to use hacking tools. In Poland, regulatory reform took place in 2016 with the reform of the Police Act and the explicit provision for the possibility of hacking systems. Also the United Kingdom, since November 2016, has established a solid regulatory basis for similar practices in the Investigatory Power Act.

Such a complex legal and technological framework must inevitably provide several guarantees: the report deals with 'ex ante' guarantees and 'ex post' guarantees that in some States have already been implemented.

'Ex ante' guarantees are, in fact, the conditions under which, when and how (with what formalities) such tools can be used. In this case, particular attention is pad to the fact that the use must be proportionate and necessary, that there must be a Court decision as a legal basis (the report usually defines it as a 'judicial authorization'), and that there must be guarantees of duration, purpose and the limitation of such investigative techniques to a certain type of crime.

'Ex post' guarantees are related to the presence of a supervisor, the ability to view log files and remedies to be put in place in case of incorrect use of such tools (resulting in compensation for damages or compulsory mitigation of harmful effects).

Concerning the limitation on the use of such tools based on the crime or the maximum duration of the prison term for specific offenses, all six States restrict the use of hacking tools on the basis of the severity of the crime. In some States, legislation provides for a specific list of crimes where hacking is permitted. In other States, however, the possibility of the use of such tools is provided only for those crimes that are punished with a high maximum of prison's years (in this case, the study records significant differences between the various States). Some States, moreover, limit the timeframe in which hacking activities can be carried out: from one month (France and the Netherlands) to six months (UK), although time extensions are allowed.

Such 'ex ante' guarantees, coupled with additional, specific 'ex-post' guarantees (such as target notification of illegal hacking practices, log file keeping of all activities, and activation of audit and control systems) should ensure a balanced and as fair as possible picture of everyone's rights.

4. Conclusions

There are some aspects that link the two documents that we have described above, and which allow us to draw some interesting considerations on the treatment and protection of data in today's society.

First of all, the idea behind the GDPR is to address matters regarding personal data in a 'more modern' way which is more closely linked to the era of smartphones, fitness bracelets, social networks, profiling algorithms, data mining activities and automated decisions. Secondly, in addition to the more traditional concept of personal data, which remains, the focus is on data that are connected to the electronic life of the individuals and their identity on social networks and that deserve, today, the same level of protection.

At the same time, the LIBE document highlights the level of dissemination that data have achieved in our society—data that are controlling the citizens, that crosses the boundaries and that requires, in its treatment, a necessary cooperation between public and private, especially in case of computer crimes or big data breaches and security flaws.

The conclusions of the LIBE report are very interesting and useful to analyse not only the present, but also the future of digital investigations.

First of all, the Report makes clear that the use of hacking techniques by law enforcement agencies evolved organically to solve the challenge of 'Going Dark' (a term used by law enforcement agencies to describe their decreasing ability to lawfully access and examine evidence at rest on devices and evidence in motion across communications networks). A significant barrier to this access is encryption. Thus, the argument follows that lack of access to such evidence places public safety at risk and will, to a certain extent, result in impunity. Overcoming this barrier resulted in law enforcement use of hacking techniques to bypass encryption technologies.

Despite the investigative benefits of increased data access, law enforcement hacking also presents several significant risks. Primarily, police hacking risks significantly impacting the fundamental right to privacy. Furthermore, it may have potential implications for the security of the internet and, to a lesser extent, territorial sovereignty.

In the Report, risks to fundamental rights are enucleated as follows:

Risk to the fundamental right to privacy: hacking techniques are extremely invasive, particularly when compared with traditionally invasive investigative tools (for example: wiretapping). Thus, their use is inherently in opposition to international, EU and national-level legislation protecting the fundamental right to privacy.

Risk to the security of the Internet: hacking techniques, by their very nature, use vulnerabilities to gain access to an IT system. As such, the discovery and exploitation of such vulnerabilities presents risks to the security and functioning of the hacked system and the wider internet.

A specific example, and the primary focus of debates on the topic, is the discovery and exploitation of zero-day vulnerabilities by law enforcement agencies. Civil society actors argue that, if discovered, governments should immediately report zero-day vulnerabilities at risk of undermining the security of the internet, given the potential damage that can be done if such a vulnerability is discovered by a malicious actor.

Risk to territorial sovereignty: given the nature of the internet, the expansion of cloud computing services and the fact that these services and channels are owned and controlled by private international companies, many services are provided across borders. Therefore, the target data of a law enforcement hack may be located anywhere in the world. This 'loss of knowledge of location' means that, when conducting investigations using hacking techniques, law enforcement agencies risk extraterritorial hacking and breaching the international legal principle of sovereignty.

The idea is that the use of hacking techniques and the implementation of specific legislation at the national level should be subject to EU and international fundamental rights principles (Franklin 2013). As such, prior to the use and legislation of such techniques, an informed decision should be taken on the necessity of law enforcement hacking capabilities on the basis of national context, the particular challenges facing national police forces and the abovementioned risks. It is thus concluded that the right for law enforcement agencies to use hacking techniques should not be assumed but must be deemed necessary within the specific context of a Member State (Mele 2018b).

References

Bundesverfassungsgericht, 1 S. 2008. Bundesverfassungsgericht-Decisions-Provisions in the North-Rhine Westphalia Constitution Protection Act on online searches and on the surveillance of the Internet null and void. [online] www.bundesverfassungsgericht.de. Available at: https://www.bundesverfassungsgericht.de/SharedDocs/Entscheidungen/EN/2008/02/rs20080227_1bvr037007en.html [Accessed 7 Jan. 2021].

Campbell, D. 2003. Il mondo sotto sorveglianza. Echelon e lo spionaggio elettronico globale. Eléuthera, Milan. Italy.

Faulkner, W. 2003. Privacy. Il sogno americano: che cosa ne è stato. Adelphi, Milan. Italy.

Franklin, M. I. 2013. Digital Dilemmas. Power, Resistance and the Internet. Oxford University Press, Oxford. UK.

Lupária, L. and Ziccardi, G. 2007. Investigazione penale e tecnologia informatica. L'accertamento del reato tra progresso scientifico e garanzie fondamentali. Giuffrè. Milan. Italy.

Lupária, L. 2009. Sistema penale e criminalità informatica. Giuffrè, Milan. Italy.

Lyon, D. 2002. La società sorvegliata. Tecnologie di controllo della vita quotidiana. Feltrinelli, Milan. Italy.

Mele, S. 2018a. I principi strategici delle politiche di cybersecurity, https://tinyurl.com/yd9j4k2w.

Mele, S. 2018b. Cyber-Weapons: Legal and Strategic Aspects. https://tinyurl.com/yakopzdl.

Perri, P. 2007a. Protezione dei dati e nuove tecnologie. Aspetti nazionali, europei e statunitensi. Giuffrè, Milan. Italy.

Perri, P. 2007b. Privacy, diritto e sicurezza informatica. Giuffrè, Milan. Italy.

Picotti. L. (ed.). 2004. Il diritto penale dell'informatica nell'epoca di internet. CEDAM, Padova. Italy.

Rodotà, S. 2014. Il mondo nella rete. Quali i diritti, quali i vincoli. Laterza, Roma-Bari. Italy.

Sartor, G. and Monducci, J. (eds.). 2004. Il codice in materia di protezione dei dati personali. Commentario al D.Lgs. 30 giugno 2003, n. 196. CEDAM, Padua. Italy.

Schneier, B. 2004. Secret and Lies: Digital Security in a Networked World. Wiley, Indianapolis. USA.

Schneier, B. 2008. Schneier on Security. Wiley, Indianapolis. USA.

Schneier, B. 2012. Liars and Outliers: Enabling the Trust that Society Needs to Thrive. Wiley, Indianapolis. USA.

Schneier, B. 2013. Carry on: Sound Advice from Schneier on Security. Wiley, Indianapolis. USA.

Solove, D. J. 2008. Data mining and the security-liberty debate. The University of Chicago Law Review 75: 343–362.

Ziccardi, G. 2013. Resistance, Liberation Technology and Human Rights. Springer, Berlin. Germany.

Ziccardi, G. 2018. The GDPR and the LIBE Study on the Use of Hacking Tools by Law Enforcement Agencies. The Italian Law Journal 1. https://www.theitalianlawjournal.it/ziccardi/.

6

Mobile Forensics
Tools, Techniques and Approach

Manish Kumar

1. Introduction

Digital forensics is a branch of forensic science focusing on the scientific approach for the extraction and analysis of digital evidence. With the exponential growth in digital devices, computers, laptops and mobile phones, demand for digital forensics has also grown-up. The objective of the digital forensic process is to extract the evidence from the digital gadgets and devices without any alteration. The entire process should maintain the integrity of the evidence. Digital forensics is very mature field and has multiple specialized branches such as Computer Forensics, Network Forensics and Mobile Forensics, etc.

Mobile forensics is a branch of digital forensics which deals with the techniques to extract and analyze the digital evidence from mobile phones in forensically sound manner. It's important to understand that any evidence is admissible in court of law only if the integrity of the evidence is maintained during the entire process of investigation. Maintaining the integrity of evidence is most challenging. Forensics tools and software need to interface with mobile phones to extract evidence, which may alter the data.

In some situations, the investigator may encounter a mobile phone which may be partially damaged or may not be in working condition. In such circumstances, more advanced methods are required, which may involve removing a chip and installing a boot loader on the mobile phone. Whatever the approach adopted for the extraction of evidence, it should make sure that the evidence is not tampered with in any way else it will not be admissible in the court.

Assistant Professor, Department of Master of Computer Applications, M S Ramaiah Institute of Technology, Bangalore – 54, India.
Email: manishkumarjsr@yahoo.com

Forensics investigation follow a standard search and seizure procedure. It's an initial step taken by any forensics examiner. The investigating officer faces many challenges while seizing the mobile devices. The officer may find a device in an ON or OFF state. If the device is in the OFF state, there are easy steps for the officer and he just needs to seize the device safely. He can keep the device in a faraday bag to prevent it from any accidental damage. However, if the device is found in the ON state, it increases the task for examiner.

From a forensics point of view, a mobile phone in the switched on state contains much vital information, which are then important as evidence. If the phone is in the switched on state, it is possible that the offender can remotely erase the data. Hence the device should be first disconnected from all the active network connections (Wi-Fi, GPS, Bluetooth, Hotspot, etc.). However, most of the time mobile phones are locked using PIN, Password or Biometric authentication which makes it difficult for the officer to access the device and disable the network connections. Hence the device must be put in faraday bag to protect the device from any remote connectivity and protect from any accidental damage of data. Once the device is seized safely it can be transported to a forensics lab, where the examiner can extract the evidence from the device using specialized forensic acquisition tools. Forensic examiners should also take care about the battery backup left out in the device while seizing it. Battery may exhaust if the evidence extraction process delayed. Evidence from the mobile which is seized in the ON state, should be extracted in the ON state. The examiner will lose vital evidence, once it is switched OFF.

Mobile phones present many other challenges to the forensic examiner. Rapid changes in mobile phone technology and operating systems, makes data acquisition a tough job. A single tools and technology do not support different makes and models for mobile forensics. Hence sound knowledge and expert skills are required for the forensics examiner for data acquisition and analysis. Makes of the mobile phone means the manufacturer or brand of the mobile phone and models refers to the specific model of mobile phones (Chernyshev et al. 2017).

2. Challenges in Mobile Forensics

Mobile forensics is different from computer forensics and presents unique challenges to forensic examiners. There are many challenges in mobile forensics. Mobile devices can store and access data across multiple devices. As the mobile data is volatile, it can be quickly deleted. It can also be accessed remotely and hence extreme precaution is required for the preservation of data (Zareen and Baig 2010).

Law enforcement agencies and forensic examiners face many critical issues to obtain digital evidence from mobile devices. Some of the major challenges are as follows:-

- **Hardware differences:** The market is flooded with various models of mobile phones and new models emerge very frequently. These phones have different specifications running on different types of customized operating systems. Forensic examiners come across different handsets. It's important for the examiner to have the knowledge about updated models and the information about tools, which can support the new models for forensic examination.

- **Mobile operating systems:** There are various mobile OS available in market among which only a few OS are popular and used in most of the mobile devices. Among all the mobile OS, the Android operating system is leader in mobile OS market share. It's an open source mobile OS from Google which is based on Linux kernel. Android OS possess many challenges for forensics analysis as it has number of variants. Though there are only a few OS which have a large market share, this does not ease the task. Forensic tools and examiners should be capable to examine all types of mobile OS and devices, which also increase the challenges. Though the forensics tools and software support well known mobile OS and handset, sometime it may not support customized OS and new handset with modified hardware and firmware.

- **Mobile platform security features:** Most of the modern mobile phones have an in-built advanced security features to protect the user data and privacy. There are various layers of security features implemented with advanced hardware and software techniques. Though these features are advantageous for the end user, it creates hurdles for data acquisition and analysis.

- **Preventing data modification:** One of the fundamental rules of forensics is to make sure that evidence in the device should not be modified by any means during the investigation and analysis process. In other word, any attempt to extract data from the device should not alter the data present on that device. It's one of the most challenging issues as many times device need to be switched on or switch off. A sudden transition from one state to another may result in the loss or modification of data.

- **Anti-forensic techniques:** Anti-forensic techniques like advanced encryption, data hiding, data obfuscation, secure wiping, make investigations difficult and complex.

- **Factory reset:** All most all the mobile phone provide the option for factory reset. Mobile phones provide features to reset everything. Resetting the device accidentally while examining may result in loss of data.

- **Passcode recovery:** Mobile device protection with passcode or biometric is very common. If the device is protected with a biometric or passcode, the forensic examiner needs to gain access to the device without damaging the data on the device. Though there are plenty of tools available to bypass the passcode, it may not work all the time on all the models.

- **Communication shielding:** Mobile devices communicate over cellular networks, Wi-Fi networks, Bluetooth, and Infrared. As it is always possible to access the device remotely and alter the data, it is important to shield the device immediately after seizing.

- **Lack of resources and tools:** There are various mobile sets available in the market of different makes and models. Frequently new mobile set models emerge in market. However, there is no single software which can support all the models and it's really a challenging issue to keep the tools updated to support the investigation for all the latest mobile phones.

• **Legal issues:** Sometime the cybercrime case and mobile phone investigation are multijurisdictional issue and involve cross geographical boundaries. In order to tackle these multijurisdictional issues, the forensic examiner should be aware of the nature of the crime and the regional laws.

3. Classification of Mobile Phones

We generally classify mobile phones in two categories, i.e., feature phone and smartphone. Features phones normally have the basic features of calling, SMS and camera for still and video captures of low to medium quality. Smartphones adds-on many features with high quality camera and Global Positioning Systems (GPS) that equally substitute the features of laptop and desktops.

With the advancement in technologies, mobile phones are becoming more compact with more and more features. The architecture of mobile phone is similar to computer architecture but it's not same as the objective of mobile device is totally different. It has a Processor, Memory Storage, Radio Module, Signal Processor unit, Microphone, Speaker, Compact Screen, Keyboard or touch screen interface. Typically, the mobile device OS is stored in NAND or NOR memory while application is executed through RAM.

Mobile phones available in market available with a varying storage capacity up to 128 GB of internal memory. Most of the mobile device support extended memory supporting up to the capacity of 2 TB of Storage capacity. Smartphone support for many other communication features like Infrared, Bluetooth, Near Field Communication, Wi-Fi, etc. (Ayers et al. 2014; Jansen et al. 2007). Comparative analysis of feature phones and smartphones is shown in Table 1.

Table 1: Feature phone vs. smartphone features.

	Feature phone	**Smartphone**
Processor	Limited speed (~ 52 Mhz)	Superior Speed (2.9 Ghz)
Memory	Limited Capacity (~ 5 MB)	Superior Capacity (~ 128 GB)
Display	Small size color, 4k–260k (12-bit to 18-bit)	Large size colour, 16.7 million (~ 24-bit)
Memory Slots	None, MicroSD	MicroSDXC
Camera	Still, Video	Still, Panoramic, and Video (HD, 4K)
Keypad	Numeric Keypad, QWERTY-style keyboard	Touch Screen, Handwriting Recognition, QWERTY-style keyboard
Network	Voice and Limited Data	Voice and High Speed Data
Positioning	None, GPS receiver	GPS receiver
Communication	Bluetooth	Bluetooth, Infrared, WiFi, and NFC
Battery	Fixed/Removable, Rechargeable Li-Ion Polymer	Fixed/Removable, Rechargeable Li-Ion Polymer

4. Mobile Device Memory and Storage

Mobile device have two types of memory, i.e., volatile and non-volatile memory. RAM is a volatile memory that is used for storing dynamic contents. It requires continuous power supply to maintain the state of data. Once the power is drained it will lose all the data. Non-volatile memory is persistent as its contents are not affected by loss of power. RAM which is used in mobile devices are technically called as DRAM, where D stands for dynamic. The structure of DRAM is array of capacitor where each capacitor can store a bit. The capacitors leak charge and thus require constant "refreshing" to maintain the state (Ayers et al. 2014; Jansen et al. 2007). Memory configuration of mobile phones are shown in Figure 1.

The mobile phone has internal storage which is used for storing the operating system for the mobile phones. These are non-volatile flash memory. Typically, two different types of non-volatile memory are used. These are NAND and NOR.

NAND flash memories are available in much higher density compared to NOR flash typically comes in capacities of 1 Gb to 16 Gb. NAND flash has much smaller cell size with higher speed of write and erase compared to NOR flash. The disadvantage is the read speed is slower and does not allow random access. The code execution form NAND is achieved by shadowing the contents of NAND to a RAM. One of the major disadvantage of NAND flash is the presence of bad blocks. NAND flash memory is generally used for application data storage.

Compare to NAND flash, the NOR flash memory provides enough address lines to map the entire memory range. This is advantageous for random access and makes it easy for code execution. The disadvantage of NOR flash is that it has a larger cell size and which cost more for per bit storage. It also has slower write and erase speeds. NOR flash memories range in density from 64 Mb to 2 Gb.

Smartphone contain NAND and RAM memory which support for higher transaction speed, greater storage density and lower cost.

Most of the smartphones today come with eMMC (Embedded Multi Media Card). The eMMC architecture integrate the flash memory and flash memory controller on the same silicon die. It simplifies the interface design and frees the host processor from low-level flash memory management to facilitate the lack of space

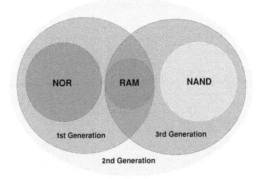

Figure 1: Mobile phones memory configuration.

on mobile device mainboards and the demand for higher density storage space (i.e., 2 GB–128 GB). The new Embedded Multi Media Cards (eMMC) style chips are present in many of today's smartphones.

Apart from Internal and External memory storage, mobile phones also have a SIM (Subscriber Identity Module) card which has limited memory storage capabilities but important for forensics analysis. SIM card is in fact a Universal Integrated Circuit Card which help the mobile phones to connect it to its nearest cellular network for communications. SIM card contains an embedded EEPROM memory chip. It's similar to the memory chip used in pen drives and SSDs. Generally, the SIM card has the capacity to hold data from 16 to 64 KB but recent trends in the market shows SIM cards with storage capacity from 512 MB to 1 GB.

5. Mobile Phones Artifacts Extraction

Data acquisition from a mobile phone basically depends on make, model and OS. There are several frameworks and methodologies developed by many professionals and researchers to streamline the process of mobile forensic. However, the ground reality is, there is no single framework and methodology which will suit for all types of cases.

For complete analysis of mobile evidence, we need logical and physical extraction of the device. Logical extraction is quick, easy and reliable. It can extract data such as contact, call details, SMS, Chat text, Images, etc. but not all the data. Logical extraction may also change the data in the device while accessing the evidence. For example, an unread SMS status may change to read. Logical extraction also cannot help extract deleted data, log files and many other artifacts which may be important for investigation.

Mobile acquisition techniques are broadly classified in five-different levels as shown in Table 2. All the data acquisition tools used for forensics purpose can be categorized in five levels based on their capabilities of data extraction. The different level of extraction required based on the complexity of the case. Each level of extractions has its own advantages and disadvantages. A comparative analysis of different levels of extraction methods are shown in Table 2.

Level 1 is the simplest and less time consuming process. As we move from Level 1 to Level 5, data acquisition become more complex, time consuming and expensive as shown in Figure 2.

The level wise approach is further classified in destructive, semi-destructive and non-destructive method based on the physical characteristics of the method.

5.1 Non-Destructive Methods

Non-Destructive or Non-invasive method is the process of extracting and analyzing the evidence without destroying the device or system. Generally non-destructive methods are used when the seized device is in working condition. It can also be used on the device with minor damages provided the device is responding to the forensic software, tools and forensic workstations.

Table 2: Comparative analysis of different level of extraction method.

Level	Method	Advantages	Disadvantages
LEVEL 1	Manual Extraction	• Easy Process. • Do not require much expertise. • Tools are easily available. • Complexity is less. • Cost and Effort required is less. • Will work for all make and models of mobile phones. • No specific cables are required.	• Time-consuming. • Risk of data modification. • Deleted data and Metadata cannot be recovered. • Not feasible with damaged devices.
LEVEL 2	Logical Extraction	• Fast • Technical complexity is less. • Tools are easily available. • Cost and Effort required is less. • Support for foreign language and different time zone is available. • Software generate the report in standard report format.	• Risk of data modification. • Limited access to data. • Access to Log Files are limited. • Specific compatible cables are required.
LEVEL 3	Hex dumping/ Joint Test Action Group (JTAG)	• Device with minor damage can be analyzed. • Allow access to deleted data, metadata and log files.	• Semi-Destructive method. • Data parsing and decoding is difficult. • Do not guarantee access to all memory section. • More expertise is required.
LEVEL 4	Chip-off	• Provides a complete binary image.	• Destructive method. • Expensive. • More expertise is required. • No Standard Report Format.
LEVEL 5	Micro read	• Viable last-resort option. • Able to extract and verify all data from device memory. • Most authentic and reliable information.	• Most time consuming. • Destructive method. • Very Expensive. • Technically challenging. • Hard to interpret/convert. • No Standard Report Format.

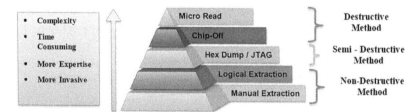

Figure 2: Different level of mobile data extraction.

5.1.1 Level 1 (Manual Extraction)

In manual extraction techniques the forensic examiner manually browses the data of mobile devices and searches for the important evidence. The examiner also photographs and video records the visible data on the mobile screen as a

Figure 3: Manual extraction of mobile phone evidence.

Table 3: Manual extraction (Level 1).

Evidence Types and Format	Evidence collected through manual extraction is photographically documented.
Pros	• Extraction is simple • Works on almost all type of mobile phones
Cons	Will not get all types of data like • Metadata • Log files and • Deleted files
Skill Set	Basic skill set and knowledge to explore the files and content of mobile phone is sufficient.
Time and Effort	Time required to complete the documentation process depends on the volume of data stored in the device. Comparatively time and effort required for manual extraction is less than the other extraction methods.
Tools	• Ramsey's STE3000FAV • Eclipse 3 • ZRT • Project-A-Phone, etc.
Cost of Tools	$200 to $2800 Approx.

documentation process (Figure 3). The manual process of extraction is simple and can work on all the devices. However, it has many limitations. Browsing through the file is only possible when examiner has the access on the mobile phone. If the devices are locked by password or PIN, manual extraction will not be so easy. Manual extraction will also not help to explore many artifacts, metadata and log files. Most of the time examiner would be interested in deleted files. Manual extraction may not help in restoring the deleted files. Manual extraction may also change the state of the device, e.g., unread Email, SMS files may change to the read state which is not advisable as a standard process of forensic examination. Table 3 represents various facts about manual extraction process.

5.1.2 Level 2 (Logical Extraction)

Logical extraction can be done by connecting the device with forensic workstation using USB cable, Bluetooth or Infrared. Much proprietary software is available for logical extraction which supports different types of make, model and OS. Logical

Table 4: Logical extraction (Level 2).

Evidence Types and Format	Memory image in software specific proprietary format.
Pros	• Extraction is simple. • Many tools and software are available. • Standard Report Format.
Cons	• Limited access to data. • Access to Log Files are limited.
Skill Set	Examiner should have knowledge of Forensic tools and software.
Time and Effort	Time and effort required to complete the analysis process depends on the size of storage in device and the performance of forensics acquisition workstation.
Tools	• Paraben's Mobile Forensics • Susteen's Mobile Forensics • Radio Tactics Aceso (RTA) • Oxygen Forensic Suite • AccessData Forensic Toolkit (FTK) • Universal Forensic Extraction Device (UFED) • XRY Logical • EnCase Mobile Investigator, etc.
Cost of Tools	$3000 to $15000 (Cost varies based on the package and software suite used for investigation. Cost of software depends on brand and features).

extraction requires little bit of experience for handling the extraction. However, in rare case this technique may inject some piece of code and data in mobile device to facilitate the extraction which alter the integrity of the evidence. Table 4 represent advantages, disadvantages and cost factors for Logical Extraction.

5.2 Semi-Destructive Methods

Generally Semi-Destructive methods are not discussed in mobile forensics literature. When Non-destructive methods do not give fruitful results, we need to do some manual or physical alteration in device to get closer access to the memory. With the advancement in technology the minor alteration for the forensic purpose do not completely destroy the device and it can be restored in useful condition. Hence the process is called as semi-destructive process.

5.2.1 Level 3 (Hex Dump/JTAG)

JTAG: It's a semi-destructive method. JTAG Forensics is the process that uses Test Access Ports (TAPs) on a PCB. In several occasions the investigating officer gets a damaged mobile phones. Generally, such a device does not sync with the forensic workstation through normal mode of communication channel and forensic software. In such a scenario data is accessed by connecting to the Test Access Ports (TAPs) of a device which instructs the processor to transfer raw data from memory chips. In this process generally a JTAG Box (Riff, Z3X, ATF, etc.) are used which can be connected to TAPs on a PCB by solder, molex or jig as shown in Figure 4. It's a low

Figure 4: JTAG for mobile phone evidence extraction.

level interface normally used by the device manufacturer for testing the devices. It's a direct access to memory without any interference from mobile OS.

eMMC and eMCP memory are the standard in today's smartphones, and the ISP practice enables examiners to directly recover a complete data dump without removing the chip or destroying the device. Identifying the taps that connect to the memory chip using a multimeter is required in ISP technique. Thus, for each evidence phone, a second identical phone that can be destroyed will be needed.

Hex Dump: Hex dump is another popular method used for physical extraction of device memory. There are specialist tools that are designed for repairing and servicing of the mobile devices. Forensics examiners make use of these tools, which allow the examiner to dump the device's memory. Figure 5 shows the screenshot of software used for a memory dump. An image copy of the device memory in binary format can be retrieved using hex dump. The hex dump image copies of the device contain abundant amount of data consisting of deleted data. Though the tools are available to make the entire process easy, the examiner should have good technical skill to carry out the work smoothly. One has to be cognizant of the fact that hardware and tools used for hex dump are not officially provided by the manufacturers. Table 5 shows the advantages, disadvantages, tools and cost details for JTAG and Hex Dump.

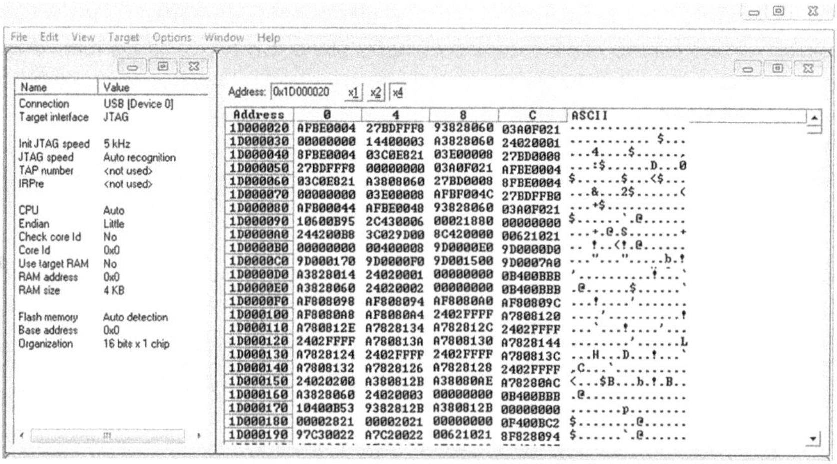

Figure 5: Screenshot of hash dump.

Table 5: JTAG and hex dump (Level 3).

Evidence Types and Format	Memory image of device in raw format.
Pros	• Device with minor damage can be analyzed. • Allow access to deleted data, metadata and log files.
Cons	• Semi-Destructive method. • Data parsing and decoding is difficult. • Do not guarantee access to all memory section. • More expertise is required.
Skill Set	Examiner should have good understanding of Mobile Phone circuit board and TAPs.
Time and Effort	Time required to complete the evidence analysis depends on the storage size of target device, tools and techniques used for evidence extraction and analysis.
Tools	• RIFF Box • AccessData Forensic Toolkit (FTK) • Universal Forensic Extraction Device (UFED) • XRY Physical, etc.
Cost of Tools	$3000 to $15000

5.3 Destructive Methods

Destructive methods are where device is physically broken and cannot be restored back to the normal working condition. Destructive or invasive methods are used when device is non-functioning because of severe physical damage. Typically, destructive methods are time consuming and complex. In some circumstances, it may be possible that the device is in good working condition but forensic examiner may require the chip for data acquisition.

5.3.1 Level 4 (Chip-Off)

As the term 'Chip-off' is self-explanatory, is the process where the memory chip is removed from the device and a reader is used to acquire the raw data from chip. The major difference between chip-off and JTAG is that chip-off method is more destructive compare to JTAG. Since the Chip is physically removed from the device so the device cannot be returned to normal operation and cannot be examined further by any other forensics tools and software.

According to the preparations pertinent to this level, the chip is detached from the device and a chip reader or a second phone is used to extract data stored on the device under investigation. Figure 6 shows the chip-off process and Adapter for Data Recovery. It should be noted that this method is technically challenging because of the wide variety of chip types existing in the mobile market. Also, the chip-off process is very expensive. Expert training for the examiner is required, and the examiner should procure specific hardware to conduct de-soldering and heating of the memory chip. Bits and bytes of raw information that is retrieved from the memory are yet to be parsed, decoded, and interpreted. Even the smallest mistake

Figure 6: Mobile phone chip-off process and Adapter for Data Recovery.

may lead to damages to the memory chip, which, in effect, would render the data irrevocably lost. Chip-off method should be used only when all the other methods of extraction is used but complete evidence could not be extracted.

The whole process consists of five stages:

1. Detect the memory chip typology of the device.
2. The memory chip is physically removed. This is accomplished using appropriate heat (de-soldering) and chemicals (adhesive removal).
3. The chip is cleaned and repaired (or re-balled) as necessary.
4. The raw data is acquired or "imaged" from the chip using specialized chip programmers and adapters.
5. The raw forensic image is then analysed using industry standard forensic tools and custom utilities.

The last two phases coincide with those of the non-invasive methods. However, the phases of physical extraction and interfacing are critical to the outcome of the invasive analysis. Table 6 represent various facts about chip-off method.

Table 6: Chip-off (Level 4).

Evidence Types and Format	Memory image in software specific proprietary format.
Pros	• Provides a complete binary image.
Cons	• Destructive method. • Expensive. • No Standard Report Format.
Skill Set	Examiner should have sound knowledge of chip unsoldering, extraction and reading data from it.
Time and Effort	The overall process is slightly complex and required expert man power. Since the entire process is not completely automize and human intervention is require, the time and effort is significantly high.
Tools	• Xeltek • H-11 Chip-Off Tool Kit • Gillware Chip-Off, etc.
Cost of Tools	$1000 to $5000 (Cost of tools used in Chip-Off is comparatively less. However, the expert man power will be significantly high, which will increase the overall cost of evidence extraction and analysis).

5.3.2 Level 5 (Micro Read)

It's a manual process involves recording the physical observation of the memory chip with the help of electron microscope. Figure 7 shows Scanning Electron Microscope (SEM) used for Micro Read and Figure 8 shows SEM Image of Micro Read. Its manually taking an all-around view through the lenses of an electron microscope and analyzing the NADN or NOR gates on the memory chip. No doubt, it's very time consuming and a costly effort.

In a nutshell, micro read is a method that demands utmost level of expertise, it is costly and time-consuming, and is reserved for serious national security crises. Data acquisition at this level requires a team of experts. Micro read is last resort for data acquisition and normally used for high profile cases related to national security. Table 7 represent advantages, disadvantages and cost factors for Micro Read process (Courbon et al. 2017).

Figure 7: Scanning electron microscope (SEM) used for micro read.

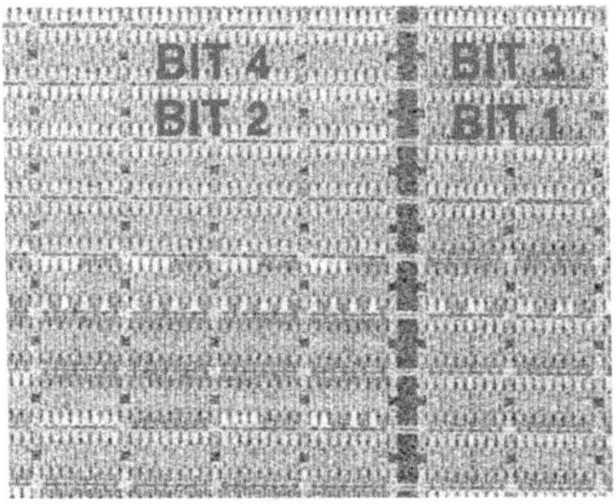

Figure 8: SEM image of micro read.

6. Conclusion

Whatever the techniques and methodology used for investigation, maintaining the integrity of mobile device evidence is a major concern. Strong security features in the latest mobile phone makes it hard for accessibility and data acquisition. Its common that accused person from whom the device has been seized, may not cooperate with

Table 7: Micro read (Level 5).

Evidence Types and Format	Sting of 0's and 1's.
Pros	• Viable last-resort option. • Able to extract and verify all data from device memory.
Cons	• Most time consuming. • Destructive method. • Very Expensive. • Technically challenging. • Hard to interpret/convert. • No report format.
Skill Set	Examiner should have sound knowledge of • Circuit depackaging. • Layer by layer deprocessing. • SEM acquisitions for each layer. • Cross-layer alignment. • Individual element annotation. • Netlist reconstruction and analysis.
Time and Effort	Its very time consuming process. The examiner uses an electron microscope and analyzes the physical gates on the chip and then translates the gate status to 0's and 1's to determine the resulting ASCII characters.
Tools	Hitachi - Scanning Electron Microscope (SEM).
Cost of Tools	Exact Estimation of cost is difficult. Various brands of Scanning Electron Microscope (SEM) are available in market between the costs of $50000 to $1 Million. The overall cost of evidence extraction and analysis depends on the Expert Man Power and Time required for data extraction and analysis.

investigator and does not provide the PIN and Passcode. In such circumstances data acquisition process is very challenging. Though the tools are available for Brute-Force and to bypass the authentication, but it's always a risk for evidence integrity. Another issue related with the mobile device is volatility of its data. Mobile apps do not only store the data in local device but also store significant data on cloud storage. Many such apps require a separate authentication apart from device authentication. In many cases data from individual apps are crucial for investigation but unfortunately the complete evidence cannot be extracted from device and need to be extracted from cloud storage. Mobile malware is another growing concern which may put evidence integrity at risk, if not taken care properly.

There are a variety of tools available in the market by different vendors for a similar kind of forensic analysis. However, the reports generated by different tools for the same device and evidence analysis may not be same. Forensic tools are software developed by experts and it's possible that two different software might have been developed using different algorithm and approach. Hence there is always possibilities of differences in result. In such a scenario, it's a challenging task for the examiner to select the admissible evidence.

As there is continuous development in forensic techniques, anti-forensic techniques are also getting an edge. Anti-forensic techniques used for data hiding, artifacts wiping and trail obfuscation purposefully used to divert the digital investigation. Its uses all the tools and techniques to make the artifact undetectable and evade the investigation.

In many cases the forensics examiner needs support from the Handset manufacturer and OS vendor. In general vendors are very reluctant to support, using their customers/user privacy as a concern. Though the vendors support can improve the forensics evidence extraction and analysis but user's obligation and privacy issues are taken more seriously than individual case. It is also important to understand that device and OS vendors may be from different country and hence international level cooperation and legal support is required.

References

Ayers, R., Brothers, S. and Jansen, W. 2014. Guidelines on Mobile Device Forensics. https://doi. org/10.6028/nist.sp.800-101r1.

Chernyshev, M., Zeadally, S., Baig, Z. and Woodward, A. 2017. Mobile forensics: advances, challenges, and research opportunities. IEEE Security & Privacy 15(6): 42–51. https://doi.org/10.1109/ msp.2017.4251107.

Courbon, F., Skorobogatov, S. and Woods, C. 2017. Reverse engineering Flash EEPROM memories using scanning electron microscopy. Smart Card Research and Advanced Applications Lecture Notes in Computer Science 2017: 57–72. https://doi.org/10.1007/978-3-319-54669-8_4.

Jansen, W. and Ayers, R. P. 2007. Guidelines on Cell Phone Forensics. https://doi.org/10.6028/nist.sp.800-101.

Zareen, A. and Baig, S. 2010. Notice of violation of IEEE publication principles – mobile phone forensics: challenges, analysis and tools classification. 2010 Fifth IEEE International Workshop on Systematic Approaches to Digital Forensic Engineering. https://doi.org/10.1109/sadfe.2010.24.

7

Digital Forensics of Cyber Physical Systems and the Internet of Things

Sandhya Armoogum,[1,*] *Patricia Khonje*[1] and *Xiaoming Li*[2]

1. Introduction

According to the National Institute of Standards and Technology (NIST 2017), Cyber Physical Systems (CPS) consists of interacting networks of physical and computational components, and thereby allow the physical world to connect to the digital world by means of sensors and actuators, which can sense and act in the physical world. In a recent publication by Greer et al. (2019), the lack of consistent distinguishing metrics between CPS and the Internet of Things (IoT), and the convergence of definitions of CPS and IoT as well as the underlying technology used by both, there is consensus around the equivalence of CPS and IoT concepts. Thus the term CPS and IoT can be adopted interchangeably. Traditionally, CPS was not connected to the Internet, but merely standalone systems whereas nowadays with the advent of communication technology, they have the capability of being connected to the Internet. Today, CPS is closely associated to the fourth industrial revolution also known as Industry 4.0, Industrial Internet or the Industrial Internet of Things (IIoT), whereby manufacturing plants are embracing technology for advanced automation, enhanced local and remote monitoring and communication between components, as well as self-diagnosis and analysis of data at different levels to significantly improve productivity.

CPS/IoT systems are characterised as having limited computing and storage capability, but they often generate massive amount of data (even big data), which require large storage and high processing power to do any computation on the data. The cloud, on the other hand, has the characteristic of being capable of providing

[1] School of Innovative Technologies and Engineering, University of Technology Mauritius.
[2] School of Computer Science and Technology, Tianjin University, Tianjin, China.
* Corresponding author: sandhya.armoogum@umail.utm.ac.mu

high storage and computing power. Thus, it is logical that CPS/IoT systems are being integrated to the cloud whereby the terminology "Cloud of Things (CoT)" is often used (Atlam et al. 2017). As such, CoT represents the next generation embedded intelligent systems that are interconnected, autonomous, and collaborative. Such systems enable more efficient monitoring and control.

The key technological trends underlying CPS and IoT systems include large scale machine-to-machine (M2M) communication between smart objects, Big Data technologies, and Cloud computing amongst others. CPSs are predicted to transform critical infrastructure services to improve quality of life in general. Typical application domains for CPS/IoT include intelligent transportation systems, water purification and distribution systems, smart energy grid, smart homes, smart healthcare system, smart vehicles, etc. CPS areas of application are constantly developing at a rapid pace. For example, many CPS are also integrating human participation instead of just devices interaction, i.e., crowdsensing applications where humans use their smart phones as a sensor to capture and send data (Jian et al. 2015; Merlino et al. 2016); and the use of social relationships or other relating parameters to help disseminate a message in a realistic network communication, for instance in the case of a natural disaster in a region (Yaakobi and Goldenberg 2014). Figure 1 illustrates a simple CPS/IoT architecture.

CPS/IoT systems have several major benefits. Haque et al. (2014) identified the following advantages of CPS/IoT: (1) network integration of sensors, actuators, multiple computational platforms and storage networks; (2) support human interaction allowing to capture human perception for decision making; (3) greater adaptability to the environment as CPS/IoT can evolve and operate with changing environment

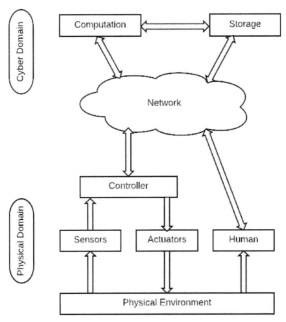

Figure 1: Basic CPS/IoT architecture.

parameters; (4) better performance as CPS/IoT uses real-time data from sensors and high computational resources; (5) scalability; (6) autonomy as in CPS components interacts to assess the physical environment and take decisions; (7) faster response time due to the enhanced processing capability of computing resources (i.e., on cloud) and faster communication capability of CPS/IoT components and network; (8) flexibility; and (9) optimization capability of CPS.

The number of IoT devices to be connected to the Internet will only increase with time. Gartner predicts 20 billion internet-connected things by 2020 (Hung 2017). Though many of the IoT devices are consumer devices such as smart vehicles, smart TVs, fridge and digital set-top boxes, the Industrial Internet of Things will also contribute to the rising number of connected devices. The IoT market is expected to grow from \$472B in 2014 to \$890B in 2020 for industrial manufacturing; and from \$520B in 2014 to \$1.335T in 2020 in the area of healthcare life sciences (Statista). According to GrowthEnabler (2017), the global IoT market share will constitute mainly of the three sub-sectors: Smart Cities (26%), Industrial IoT (24%) and Connected Health (20%); followed by Smart Homes (14%), Connected Cars (7%), Smart Utilities (4%) and Smart Wearables (3%).

In the Section 2, the security of CPS/IoT environments as well as security incidents are described. Section 3 presents the traditional computer forensics process and its challenges. In Section 4, the challenges faced during a forensic investigation in IoT systems are discussed. The IoT forensics process is presented in Section 5. The challenges related to Cloud forensics and the different cloud forensic framework is discussed in Section 6. Finally, Section 7 concludes this chapter.

2. Security Attacks on CPS/IoT

Today critical infrastructure such as smart grids, water purification and distribution systems, chemical plants, oil refinery and transportation systems are being modernized and transformed into CPS for improved efficiency. However, this may render critical infrastructure CPS more susceptible to cyber-attacks due to the increased attack surfaces in CPS. Such attacks can have disastrous impacts on the physical world and on human lives. According to the Industrial Control Systems Cyber Emergency Response Team (ICS-CERT) Annual Assessment Report (2016a), the largest number of incidents was reported in the following sectors in descending order: Critical Manufacturing, Communication, Energy, Water and Waste water management systems, Government facilities, and Transportation Systems.

Attacks on industrial control system (ICS) infrastructure date back to June 2010, where the first cyber-weapon called the Stuxnet worm emerged. Stuxnet infected 14 industrial sites in Iran, including the Natanz nuclear facility (Kushner 2013). The Stuxnet worm re-programmed the programmable logic controller (PLC) to take command of the centrifuges of the nuclear plant. In March 2013, a malware named "DarkSeoul" paralyzed three major South Korean banks, thus preventing South Koreans to access ATM's and two of the largest news broadcasters (Sang-Hun 2013).

Another example of CPS is Smart grids. The ICT infrastructure as well as the different smart grid components that are used to operate, control, and monitor Smart Grids are vulnerable to a multitude of attacks. Attacks on Smart Grids may cause inconvenience and even loss of human lives, i.e., power disruptions during the coldest winter months can cause death. On the 23rd of December 2015, 230 000 people in Ukraine were deprived of electricity for six hours after hackers compromised several power distribution centres. The "BlackEnergy" malware was used to remotely control the computer networks of the electricity company so as to make the distribution system components go offline, resulting in a blackout (ICS-CERT 2016b). In 2016, a similar energy outage was observed, where one substation (Pivnichna) was affected resulting in loss of about one-fifth of Kiev's power consumption at night (BBC News 2017). This attack was more elaborate and complex and it is suspected that the "Industroyer" malware was used (Osborne 2018). Such attacks could take place on the smart grid in any other country.

Likewise, in October 2016, a Distributed Denial of Service (DDoS) attack launched against the control systems, which regulated the heating of two apartment buildings in eastern Finland, resulted in the residents being left in the cold (with temperatures well below freezing) for about a week (Kumar 2016). Such electricity disruptions due to cyber-attacks have also been reported in Israel in January 2016 (Times of Israel 2016) and in Turkey in December 2016 (Ankara and Kocaeli 2016). In 2013, cyber-attacks were attempted on the small Bowman Dam north of New York City. A successful cyber-attack on a major dam like the Hoover Dam in the US could be devastating to tens of millions of people (Charette 2018). Such attacks can be considered as cybercrime and even cyber-warfare. Al-Mhiqani et al. (2018) examined 18 security incidents related to CPS and categorized the 18 incidents as follows: 8 cases of Cyber-warfare (highest category), 5 Cybercrime incidents, 4 Hacktivism incidents, and 1 case of cyber-espionage.

According to Kaspersky Lab experts (2016), around 13,000 ICS, connected to the internet, were remotely accessible and a staggering 90% of these ICS hosts were observed to have known vulnerabilities. Similarly, Positive Technologies (2016) reported that 743 vulnerabilities in components from approximately 500 ICS vendors were identified. Large number of vulnerabilities was also discovered in SCADA components, PLCs, industrial network devices, software, human–machine interfaces (HMIs), and in remote access and management terminals. The most vulnerability was of either high or medium risk (47% high, 47% medium). It was also reported that there were vulnerabilities in the embedded firmware running on CPS/IoT devices, which eventually results in a vast number of critical systems and data at risk. Security is fundamental for CPS as with the increasing dependency on ICT systems, IoT devices have to be properly secured to decrease the risk of disruptive and detrimental incidents against CPS. The unprecedented Mirai botnet DDoS attack, which harnessed 360000 vulnerable IoT devices to launch the attack on Dyn DNS Service provider in October 2016, is a clear example of the impact of unsecured IoT (Dignan 2016). In January 2017, it was reported that implantable cardiac devices (St. Jude Medical) had vulnerabilities that could make them remote accessible to an attacker who could drain the battery of the device or command the device to administer incorrect pacing or shocks (Larson 2017).

Smart homes are becoming more popular. Smart homes consist of a range of sensors (e.g., temperature, motion, light, baby monitors, etc.), systems (e.g., heating, lightning, security, etc.), and devices (e.g., smart home appliances such as smart meters, smart lights, smart thermostat, washing machine, refrigerator, microwave, etc.), which can be monitored, controlled and automated through a smart phone or computer, locally or remotely, via the Internet. Such digital devices can communicate and regulate themselves based on the sensed physical state of the home. Atlam et al. (2017) identified the different attacks possible in an IoT based Smart Home such as physical intrusion leading to burglary or physical ransom, death (i.e., block signal to sound alarm in case of fire), leak of behavioural patterns, leak of private data as IoT devices may be collecting and processing private information, extortion and direct financial loss. In October 2017, Checkpoint security researchers discovered "HomeHack" in LG SmartThinQ smart home devices which could allow hackers to gain unauthorised remote access and control to the millions of SmartThinQ home appliances such as robot vacuum cleaner, refrigerators, ovens, dishwashers, washing machines/dryers, and air conditioners. The hacker could exploit the integral video camera of the Hom-Bot vacuum cleaner to spy on users. By July 2016, more than 400000 Hom-Bot robotic vacuum cleaner were sold. There was an increase of 64% sales of smart home devices in 2016 and some 80 million smart home devices were delivered around the world (San Carlos 2017). There is the potential for cybercriminals to exploit software flaws, cause disruption in users' homes and access their sensitive data. Fortunately, LG addressed the security vulnerability to prevent exploitation based on the identified vulnerability.

This growing likelihood of ever-escalating cyber-attacks in CPS/IoT makes it necessary to urgently address security issues in such systems. Moreover, there is also growing importance to conduct digital forensic investigations in such heterogeneous networked CPS/IoT environments as cybercrimes and cyberattacks escalate in CPS/IoT systems. In civil and criminal investigations, data from consumer wearable devices in cases of personal injury and murder is already accepted and used (Hauser 2017).

3. Traditional Computer Forensics

Digital forensics is about conducting a precise investigation in the aftermath of a cyber-incident to investigate what has led to the incident, to retrieve lost data and to gather evidence to be used against the person or entity which caused the incident. Digital forensics includes the forensics of all digital technologies and mainly focuses on reactive measures. The electronic data uncovered and interpreted in digital forensics is to be preserved in its original form as evidence. Traditional digital evidence includes data from computers/servers, printers, scanners as well as mobile devices such as tablets, smart phones due to their increased daily usage. With the growing digital dependence, digital evidence is finding its way into the world's courts and the area of digital forensics is quite new but growing. Not all investigations are the same and this can be a challenge when coming up with standard procedures for forensic analysis. In 2012, the ISO/IEC published the "Guidelines for identification, collection, acquisition and preservation of digital evidence (ISO/IEC 27037)" and the ISO/IEC 27043 "Incident investigation principles and processes" in 2015 as well as a few other related standards in the next years (ISO/IEC 27037:2012). As in any forensics fields, preserving the integrity of evidence is fundamental. Given that software applications and tools used in digital forensics investigations must be reliable and repeatable, the NIST is working on the Computer Forensics Tool Testing (CFTT) project to establish a methodology for testing computer forensic software tools by development of general tool specifications, test procedures, test criteria, test sets, and test hardware (NIST). However, given that there are fast paced changes in the area of digital technology, it is quite challenging without rigorous and extensive frameworks, and standards to keep up in the area of digital forensics.

According to Kumari and Mohapatra (2016), digital forensics can be traditionally split into five branches: (1) Computer forensics; (2) Network forensics; (3) Mobile forensics; (4) Memory forensics; and (5) E-mail forensics. Because it encompasses different disciplines like law, ethics, criminology, information and communication technology, computer science, computer engineering and forensic science, digital forensics is multidisciplinary and interdisciplinary (Losavio et al. 2016). The aforementioned disciplines are shown in Figure 2 below.

Ken Zatyko (2007) defined an eight-step digital forensics scientific process, which is illustrated in Figure 3.

The digital forensics methodology mainly consists of three stages namely: (1) Acquisition; (2) Authentication; and (3) Analysis. This is in line with the European Union funded project 'Cyber Tools Online Search for Evidence (CTOSE)', which propose a systematic methodology for identifying, preserving, analyzing and presenting digital evidence as described in (Sansurooah 2016; Sriram 2013). During the acquisition stage data from the live system and/or from storage system such as hard drives are captured. If the suspect computer is OFF, the hard drive is removed from the computer and connected to the forensic analyst's workstation via a write blocker. The write blocker ensures that no changes occur in the original drive during the acquisition of the drive. At least two bit-stream copies or image of the data are made. A bit stream copy unlike a typical backup copy, which only copies active files, is a sector-by-sector/bit-by-bit copy of a hard drive such that it exactly replicates

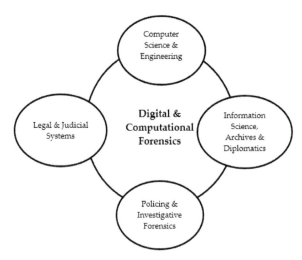

Figure 2: Multiple domains of digital forensics (Losavio et al. 2016).

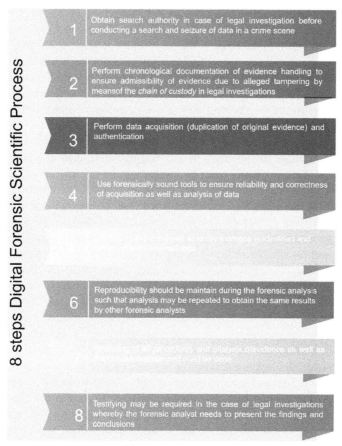

Figure 3: Eight steps digital forensics process.

all files and ambient data. Either a bit stream copy of the original drive is done on sanitised external media storage or a bit stream image copy is done.

If the computer is ON, it is useful to also capture data from the volatile memory as such data would be lost once the computer is powered down. Memory forensics allows to capture a snapshot of the system when it is running. Using a tool such as Access Data's FTK Imager, Belkasoft RAM Capture, or Rekall Forensics a snapshot of memory, called a memory dump, can be captured. The memory dump can later be examined, for example by using the Volatility Framework, to analyse and interpret the data from the memory dump. Such data can provide information about processes running, open files, executables files running on the system, clipboard contents, logged users, browsing history, chat messages, passwords, open sockets and ports, IP addresses as well as other networking information amongst other, which may otherwise not be available if only analysing the hard drive contents. Memory forensics is particularly crucial in such cases where the whole hard drive is encrypted. Password or encryption keys are cached in memory and may be retrieved from the memory dump to decrypt the data in the hard drive. It is also possible for the computer to be running a live OS such as Ubuntu Live, or Knoppix whereby the OS is not installed on the hard drive, but only run on memory from a USB stick. In such a case, all data is in the RAM while the memory acquisition is being done on the suspect machine. Nowadays, some malware and rootkits, known as fileless malware and memory rootkits respectively, run from memory and leave no trace of its activity on the system's hard drive. Without memory forensics, it would be impossible to identify such malware and their activity. A few examples of fileless malware include Powerliks, Angler, Meterpreter and PHOSPHY.

For post-mortem forensics involving acquisition of the hard drive, to prove that the copies made are identical to the original drive data, the copies must be authenticated. This is usually done by computing the cryptographic hash value of the original drive and comparing with the hash value of the copies made. If the hash values are the same, then it is unequivocal that the copies made are exactly the same as the original drive data. The forensic tools used to make the acquisition also support features that allows the authentication to be performed as well as generating reports to confirm authentication. It is important to use tools which are forensically sound. Popular forensic suite includes Guidance Encase and FTK. Popular tools for extraction of data from mobile phones include Oxygen Forensic Suite, Cellebrite UFED Physical Analyzer, and MSAB XRY (Seung JeiYang et al. 2015).

Analysis is done on the acquired data rather than the original drive to maintain integrity of the original drive. During the analysis process, evidence is extracted, analysed and findings are documented. Logical and/or physical extraction of evidence is often performed. Logical extraction is easiest to perform as it involves relying on the file system to find and retrieve evidence. Such evidence includes active user and system files, and deleted files. Information such as file properties can be viewed. Physical extraction is more difficult, takes longer and requires a good knowledge of the system being investigated. Here extraction of data is done at the physical level, i.e., the binary data stored in the sectors. For example, the partition table of the computer can be examined to identify the different partitions on the computer. To analyze the data extracted related to the case, several different analysis approaches can be adopted namely timeframe analysis, data-hiding analysis, application and file analysis, and ownership and possession analysis. Time frame analysis allows understanding when a computer is used or what events occurred before or after a given event. During data-hiding analysis, the forensic analyst has to discover and retrieve any data that may be hidden by the suspect. Various data hiding techniques can be used by suspects to hide information on the computer such as the use of steganography techniques, hidden partitions, hiding data in alternate data streams in NTFS, etc.

Some of the challenges when performing a digital forensic investigation include the overabundance of digital information, the fleeting nature of evidence, the multidisciplinary nature of forensic investigations requiring knowledge in different domains, and the ability of a suspect to hide data using various tools and techniques (Vincze 2016). Digital evidence is also fragile by nature and can be very easily altered, erased, or subjected to claims of tampering if it is not handled properly. The existing standards related to forensic investigations are not yet extensive and they do not cover certain aspects of the process such as generating digital forensic reports

(Nickson 2019). Finally, suspects may use anti-forensics techniques which make it difficult to find and extract evidence. Typical anti-forensic techniques include the secure deletion of data, use of steganography and encryption, use of a TOR browser, and manipulation of file properties and header. Nickson and Venter (2015) present a taxonomy of challenges for digital forensics where they classify the challenges in the following four categories: (1) Technical Challenges; (2) Legal Systems and/or Law Enforcement Challenges; (3) Personnel-related Challenges; and (4) Operational Challenges.

4. Challenges of IoT Forensics

CPS/IoT systems have proliferated into all areas and they play an important role in society. Such systems can be hijacked and compromised by attackers, which could have dangerous consequences as discussed in Section 2. The CPS/IoT system is also more complex, involving a large number of heterogeneous devices, various communication protocols, and different data formats which give rise to new security challenges while traditional security problems become more severe. Given that IoT devices are usually small devices with limited hardware resources, they are streamlined for providing the required functionality and not to be inherently secure. Thus, they can be easily targeted for cybercrimes as it may not be possible to install security measures such as anti-virus software for instance on such devices. There is an ever growing need for the development of forensically sound methodologies and procedures to acquire and examine digital evidences found in these CPS/IoT systems.

Digital forensic investigators need to be able to detect perpetrators' breach and actions in CPS/IoT systems to be able to uncover evidence so as to identify the culprits. The traces of evidence found in such systems, which autonomously or in response to some human action or some event generate data, have a high likelihood of being scrutinised in the course of forensic investigations with the increased adoption of such systems in our society. Kebande et al. (2017) describes the Smart Refrigerator Crime Propagation (SRCP) model which is used to explore how vulnerabilities of IoT home appliances can be exploited to gain control and perpetrate different kinds of attacks or cybercrime. Investigators need to be able to identify the location of devices and extract data from different smart objects which can be useful for investigating any type of offense including cyber attacks and physical assaults.

Despite the fact that smart objects constitute an invaluable source of evidence from real world CPS/IoT applications in investigations, there are some major challenges faced by forensic examiners. Watson and Dehghantanha (2016) emphasize on the importance of research and development in the area of IoT forensics to address serious issues such as a lack of tools, methodologies and standards such that forensics is at pace with the emerging technologies.

4.1 Large Number and Variety of IoT Devices

One of the main challenges of IoT forensics is the wide variety of devices from which evidence may be collected as compared to traditional forensics where data is mainly acquired for analysis from computers/servers/laptop, and more recently from mobile phones. In CPS/IoT systems, data with evidentiary value may be found on a vast variety of devices such as wearable devices like smart watches or fitness trackers, medical devices, drones, connected appliances, home appliances, home automation devices, 3D printers, RFID devices, IP cameras, glasses, smart vehicles, and sensor networks. Identifying the devices which are involved in the incident at the crime scene, as well as where the data came from, or the data attributes that are stored, is not obvious. Could the smart coffee maker or baby monitor be involved in the crime being investigated? The IoT device being too small, disconnected, switched OFF or distributed geographically may not be easily identified. Moreover, forensic investigations requires shutting the IoT/CPS system down. However, this may not be a viable option in critical CPS such as water treatment system, power grid, transport control systems, manufacturing plants and healthcare systems.

Oriwoh et al. (2013) introduces the Next Best Thing (NBT) model, whereby evidence from devices at hand is examined, as it might not be possible to obtain evidence from all devices in a forensic investigation. Harbawi and Varol (2017) suggest that location of evidence can be facilitated using the Last-on-Scene (LoS) algorithm whereby the last node in the communication chain is investigated first and progressively within the current zone and other zones. The digital process to include LoS algorithm is depicted in Figure 4.

Data on such devices may be stored on onboard storage and/or may simply be transmitted to a server on the Internet or the Cloud. Subsequently, it is difficult to use a single tool or a standard approach to identify and extract data from a given IoT device due to the different proprietary hardware and software, operating systems, and file systems that could be present on the device. Typically these devices consist of a microcontroller; memory (RAM), flash memory, I/O peripherals and networking capabilities (e.g., Bluetooth, WIFI, GSM). Data stored on firmware usually consists of a bootloader (e.g., U-Boot), the operating system (OS) kernel and file system (e.g., SquashFS, JFFS2, UbiFS) and different binaries and scripts which constitute the device's functionality.

On low end devices such as a remote control, the firmware could consist of a single binary handling all functionality of device. The firmware OS is either an embedded OS or an IoT OS. An embedded OS is designed for a dedicated purpose and to run on resource constrained devices. Typical examples of embedded OS include embedded Linux, Windows CE and Google Brillo. The IoT OS is an embedded OS but designed to enable data transfer over the internet for connectivity. Some popular IoT OS includes Ubuntu Core, Contiki, RIOT OS, TinyOS, Windows 10 IoT, Amazon FreeRTOS and WindRiver VxWorks. Many devices also use Android OS.

Data onboard may not be easily accessible in some cases. If the device can be connected to a computer, then the internal storage can be forensically imaged in any chosen format using traditional forensic imaging utilities such as FTK, and X-ways forensics. The data acquired can be analyzed using traditional forensic tools.

Alternatively, if data cannot be connected to a computer, data from firmware can be extracted by using JTAG. Most firmware supports debugging functions through interfaces such as UART, JTAG or SPI. Joint Test Action Group (JTAG)

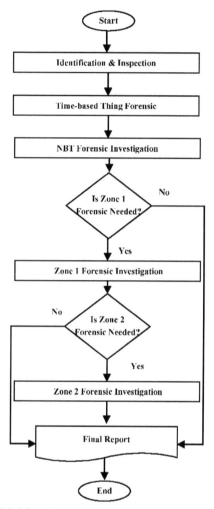

Figure 4: Digital forensic procedure's flowchart (Harbawi and Varol 2017).

is standardized as the IEEE 1149.1 Standard Test Access Port and Boundary-Scan Architecture. It specifies the use of a dedicated debug port—Standard Test Access Ports (TAPs)—implementing a serial communications interface to directly interact with the firmware. Most embedded devices support JTAG when they have enough pins. Instructions can be sent to the processor to transfer raw data stored on the memory chip on the device by connecting to the TAPs of the device. The data is transferred in a raw format which could be parsed into usable formats. Examples of JTAG/Chip-off tools include easy JTAG Plus and RIFF boxes. However, if the proper instructions/signals are not sent, there is the risk of causing modification or damage to the device circuitry. JTAG is often used to extract data from phones and other devices that cannot be acquired by other means (Seung JeiYang et al. 2015).

Data can also be extracted from firmware by UART. The Universal Asynchronous Receiver Transmitter (UART) is simply a serial port. Most IoT firmware have enabled UART for debugging but it is possible to get full root access and to extract data from the device via the UART interface. According to Vasile et al. (2019), UART is currently the most common and exploitable debugging interface found in IoT devices. 45% of the examined IoT devices were found to be vulnerable to firmware extraction via UART.

IoT devices, being quite small, energy efficient storage is required for storing the firmware on such devices. Serial flash is often used for storing the firmware in IoT devices, given that it has a small form factor, needs few wire connections on the board and it uses low power flash memory. The Serial Peripheral Interface (SPI) is an industry standard protocol for providing access to the data on the serial flash. By connecting to the serial flash chip pins and using a tool such as Attify Badge or Bus Pirate, it is possible to capture a data dump of the flash memory.

Embedded MultiMediaCard (*eMMC*)—NAND flash memory—are also commonly used in IoT devices due to their low cost, speed, multitude of storage sizes, smaller footprint, lower power usage, and integrated controller. Etemadieh et al. (2017) describes how to identify the correct eMMC pinout, and how to connect pins of eMMC to an appropriate SD card adapter to easily access the content of the flash storage.

Choosing the approach to extract data from an IoT device is not as simple as extracting data from a hard drive and must be done on a case to case basis. Forensic investigators with more experience in working with such devices may be needed. Boztas et al. (2015) describe the digital forensics procedure for extracting potential artifacts such as network information, app activity, web browsing history, and media files from a smart TV, namely a Samsung smart TV. Davies et al. (2015) present PlayStation 4's potential information sources as well as a method for acquiring information from the PlayStation 4. Similarly, Clark et al. (2017) describes the forensic analysis of the DJI Phantom III drone. Horsman (2016) describes the acquisition of a test Parrot Bebop unmanned aerial vehicles internal storage to extract the on-board flight data, captured media as well as operating system files. The paper also includes discussion of forensic analysis of the controller device. The investigation of radio equipment is described by Kouwen et al. (2018). Smart vehicles store a wealth of digital information such as GPS coordinates of recent destinations, favourite routes, call logs, and phone contacts. Nhien-Anle-Khac et al. (2018) discusses the challenges relating to the forensics extraction and analysis of data from smart vehicles. Shin et al. (2017) describes how to collect data from (1) Amazon Echo, (2) Home Area Network consisting of a central controller, sensors, and Z-wave devices like Thermostat, Smart Lockers (touchscreen or lever lockers), Wireless Water Valve, etc., and (3) home routers. Li et al. (2019) also describes the acquisition and analysis of data from Alexa (Amazon Echo). Servida and Casey (2019) present smart home evidence extraction from iSmartAlarm, Cube One, Netgear Arlo Base Station, Wink hub as well as the corresponding applications from the smart phone. Forensics extraction of data from Almond+ smart home system is presented (Awasthi et al. 2018).

4.2 Data Formats and Communication Protocols

Data acquired from some IoT devices may also not be readable and be more challenging to analyze. Reverse engineering of application binaries running on the IoT device may be required to understand the functionality of the device as well as where it is saving and/or sending data. Moreover, data extracted may be encrypted or in a non-standard data format which severely limits the ability to produce human-readable evidence from IoT devices. For example, the DJI Phantom III drones store data in its nonvolatile internal storage in proprietary DAT files which are encrypted and encoded (Clark et al. 2017). Ariffin et al. (2013) describe the challenge of recovery of proprietary-formatted video files with their time stamps from digital video recorders in video surveillance and closed-circuit television (CCTV) systems. Similarly, IoT systems may be using different communication protocols (IPv6, 6LoWPAN, ZigBee, Bluetooth Low Energy (BLE), Z-Wave, Near Field Communication (NFC)), and physical interfaces, which makes the process of extraction and analysis of evidence complex. IoT sensors and actuators, being low-power chips typically use customised energy-efficient routing and application layer protocols such as the Routing Protocol for Low-Power and Lossy Networks (RPL) and the Constrained Application Protocol (CoAP) for connectivity and data transfers.

4.3 Data Location and Jurisdiction

Given that IoT devices have limited storage capacity, very little data is stored onboard; data captured or generated is often simply transmitted to another device such as a server, a mobile phone, and/or a cloud infrastructure via a network connection. In systems where data is stored locally in the IoT device, the duration of evidence survival poses a challenge as data can be easily overwritten over a short period of time due to the limited storage capacity of the device. Moreover, the cumulative dataset may exist in multiple locations, which may be unknown to the user. Information about the destination of data being transferred from IoT devices can be obtained by analyzing the network traffic from the IoT device.

The storage of data in multiple locations, which may have multiple jurisdictions whereby different laws and regulations apply, is an important issue when conducting forensic investigations. Different data protection laws may apply to data depending on the country where it is located. If the investigator is from one jurisdiction, and the data resides in another jurisdiction, then the different laws have to be considered before accessing the data. An example of legal ramifications is the case of the US government appeal to get Microsoft to hand over emails held on its servers in Dublin, which were relevant in a drugs case. The case had been dragging on for four years due to the major implications it entails for the cloud provider and privacy of the cloud customers (Edward 2017).

Similarly, if IoT data is being stored on the Cloud, physical access to the Cloud for collection of evidence may be challenging for the forensic investigator. In traditional forensics procedures it is assumed that the investigator has physical access to the device such as computer/server, router or mobile device. However, in cloud it might be difficult for the investigator to identify where the data is stored on the cloud. Conducting forensic investigations on data stored on the cloud is further discussed in Section 6.

4.4 Large Amount of Data

IoT systems are capable of generating enormous amount of data. In some cases the data is stored in silos, while in more complex IoT ecosystems, IoT data from multiple systems, and organisations provide rich data sets for analysis. Capturing and analysing such huge volume of data in the case of a forensics investigation is not trivial. Making a bit-stream copy of a 500 GB hard drive takes around 24 hours. Data reduction techniques can be applied to reduce the volume of data during the acquisition and/or analysis stage. Data reduction involves excluding the extraction of standard operating systems or applications files as they have no evidentiary value. Large scale cryptographic hash databases for known files can be used to discard these known files. The National Software Reference Library (NSRL) is a NIST project which is designed to collect software from various sources and incorporate file profiles computed from this software into a Reference Data Set (RDS) of information. By using the RDS, forensic investigators can match files with file profiles in the RDS for data reduction. Thus, only a selection of key files and data are extracted for analysis. Such files of interest include registry, user documents, email, browser history and temp files, logs, images, videos, etc. Quick and Choo (2016) show that when data reduction is applied to real world cases, there is tremendous reduction in the volume of data whilst retaining key evidentiary data. This data reduction allows forensic analysis of data to be done in a timely manner and is very useful in cases such as kidnapping, and terrorism. Quick and Choo (2018) also present a process of bulk digital forensic data analysis including disparate device data by using data reduction techniques.

IoT forensics also involves capturing large volume of network traffic for analysis. Chhabra et al. (2018) propose using the Wireshark's DumpCap utility for capturing continuous IoT traffic, and MapReduce and Apache Mahout (machine learning) running on a Hadoop cluster to translate traffic, extract, and analyze the dynamic traffic features for identifying network malware. By using a cluster to analyze data instead of one computer, analysis can be done faster. Unfortunately, most of the current forensic tools are not designed to run on a cluster. Given the difficulty in analyzing IoT traffic, Koroniotis et al. (2019) have created a BoT-IoT dataset which provides a baseline for allowing botnet identification across IoT-specific networks.

4.5 Preserving Integrity of Evidence

Chain of custody allows to prove the reliability of evidence. It gives assurance about the integrity of evidence in a court of law by documenting how the evidence was seized and handled in a forensically sound manner. However, in the context of IoT, evidence is dynamic and volatile as it may not stay on one node for a long time due to the resource limitations. Data could be quickly overwritten by more recent data or transferred from one device to another, for example in ad-hoc wireless sensor networks; until it reaches an edge node from where the data may be transferred to cloud storage. Such data often undergo aggregation along different points during the transfer. Proving the integrity of such dynamic data is problematic.

Data in transit could also be of a sensitive nature and pose privacy risks. It is not easy to identify devices which hold private data or to present data collected from an IoT environment to a jury. To maintain the privacy and integrity of IoT data and evidence, in their FAIoT model, Zawoad and Hasan (2015) introduce the "Secure Evidence Preservation Module" and the "Secure Provenance Module". The Secure Evidence Preservation Module consists of an evidence repository which preserves and stores evidence from IoT devices securely while ensuring that the IoT data from different owners are segregated to maintain privacy. Moreover, only the forensic investigators have access to the data in the repository. The "Secure Provenance Module" maintains the chain of custody of the evidence by preserving the access history of the evidence. Nieto et al. (2017) propose a Privacy-aware IoT-Forensic Model (PRoFIT) which takes privacy into consideration and incorporate privacy in the requirements of ISO/IEC 29100:2011 throughout the investigation life cycle. It highlights the importance of collaboratively gathering data from surrounding devices based on the cooperation of individuals. The methodology was applied on the case of a possible social malware in a public space such as a coffee shop.

5. IoT Forensics

IoT forensics is where evidence from IoT infrastructures is used for the establishment of a crime or attack. Similar to computer forensics, in IoT forensics the IoT device can play one of the following three roles: (1) IoT device is a target of crime; (2) IoT device is a tool used to commit crime; and (3) IoT device is a witness of a crime whereby it has captured evidence related to the crime, e.g., Amazon Echo recordings used as evidence during a murder case. Figure 5 depicts an IoT Forensic Model proposed in (Li et al. 2019a).

Moreover, IoT forensics follows the main process of traditional forensics such as identification and extraction of evidence, analysis and documentation of evidence found. Preservation of evidence as well as maintaining the chain of custody to provide assurance of integrity of the evidence applies. The difference lies in the evidence sources as in IoT forensics evidence sources include computers/servers on the Internet or the Cloud, mobile devices such as smartphones as well as smart vehicles, sensors, home appliances, medical appliances, medical implants, tag readers, etc.

Zawoad and Hasan (2015) proposed a Forensics-aware IoT (FAIoT) model for supporting reliable forensics investigations in the IoT environment which is depicted in Figure 6. The FAIoT model identifies IoT forensics as a combination of three digital forensics schemes (three zones), namely device level forensics, network forensics, and cloud forensics. Device level forensics involves the identification of IoT devices and the collection of data from such devices. Network forensics is the capture and analysis of network traffic or network logs from the IoT network to find evidence. Typically, the IoT network could consist of a Personal Area Network (PAN), Local Area Network (LAN) and Wide Area Network (WAN). Given that the IoT devices have constrained processing power as well as limited storage, data from IoT devices are usually processed in the cloud. Thus Cloud forensics is an intrinsic

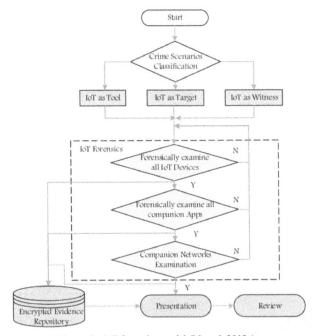

Figure 5: IoT forensics model (Li et al. 2019a).

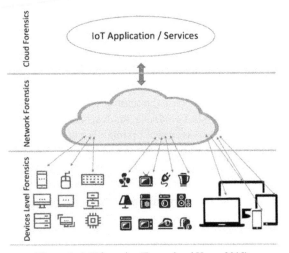

Figure 6: IoT forensics (Zawoad and Hasan 2015).

part of IoT forensics. Khan et al. (2016) presents and discusses the different cloud network forensic approaches.

Perumal et al. (2015) proposed a more comprehensive IoT Based digital Forensic Model which details the start of an investigation till the evidence is archived as shown in Figure 7.

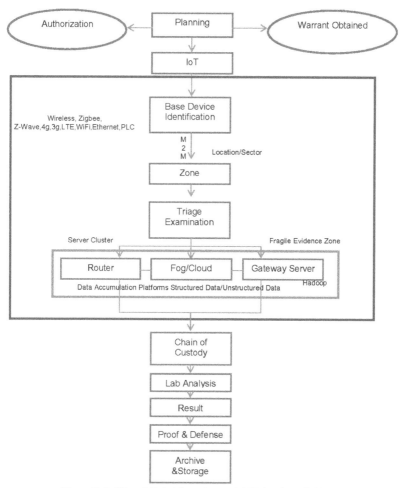

Figure 7: IoT based digital forensics model (Kebande et al. 2017).

Kebande and Ray (2016) agree with Watson and Dehghantanha (2016) that the field of digital forensics has to develop further to include IoT infrastructures. They proposed the generic Digital Forensic Investigation Framework for IoT (DFIF-IoT), which is compliant with the ISO/IEC 27043:2015 for incident investigation principles and process, to support investigation of IoT systems. The proposed framework, if incorporated in future digital forensic tools, would facilitate effective forensics for IoT systems as it is comprehensive enough to cover all the aspects of a digital forensics investigation. The DFIF-IoT is a combination of four distinct modules which include: the Proactive process, the IoT forensics, and the Reactive process as shown in Figure 8.

The Proactive process focuses on the digital forensic readiness for the IoT environment; it involves planning and preparation guidelines about potential IoT incidents that can occur in the IoT system and consists of the following tasks: IoT incident scenario definition (identifying potential IoT incident), IoT evidence source

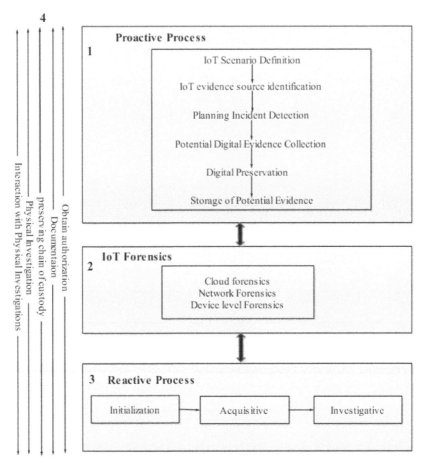

Figure 8: Digital forensic investigation framework for IoT (DFIF-IoT) (Kebande and Ray 2016).

identification, planning incident detection (how to detect incidents and respond to such incidents), potential digital evidence collection, digital preservation, and storage of potential evidence. The IoT forensics module focuses on the extraction of evidence from the IoT infrastructure and aligns with Zawoad and Hasan (2015) and finally the Reactive process focuses on the actual methodology once the incident/crime has been reported. It follows the traditional approach and consists of the following three stages: Initialization (incident detection, first response, planning and preparing for an investigation); Acquisitive (acquiring potential evidence from IoT environments); and investigative (analysis, interpretation and reporting of evidence). The fourth module, namely the Concurrent processes, defines concepts that enable effective investigation and includes such tasks as obtaining a legal mandate to start an investigation, documentation of a crime scene, maintaining the chain of custody, and the documenting processes carried out as part of the physical investigation.

Kebande et al. (2018) further extends the framework and proposes the Integrated Digital Forensic Investigation Framework (IDFIF-IoT) for an IoT ecosystem consisting of complex relationships between the different interconnected smart objects that makes them intelligent, programmable, and highly interactive among themselves as well as with humans. A high level view of the IDFIF-IoT is depicted in Figure 9 and a detailed view of the IDFIF-IoT is shown in Figure 10.

Servida and Casey (2019) present a methodology consisting of the following six steps, which can be adopted by a forensic investigator to study a new device, and discover which artifacts are available on the device, where and how to collect them: (1) preliminary analysis (survey of existing research on device), (2) testbed setup

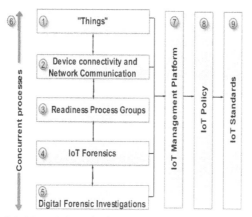

Figure 9: Integrated digital forensic investigation framework (IDFIF-IoT) (Kebande et al. 2018).

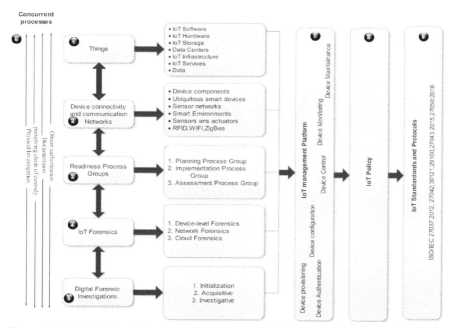

Figure 10: Detailed view of the integrated digital forensic investigation framework (IDFIF-IoT) (Kebande et al. 2018).

(to study the IoT device in a controlled environment), (3) network analysis (to study the communication aspect of device), (4) smartphone application analysis (study of the application code to connect/control IoT device), (5) vulnerability analysis (to identify how device could be exploited for attack as well as for accessing device), and (6) physical analysis (to acquire data from the storage of the device directly). Such an approach can, in due course, allow the development of new tools or extend existing tools to automate the process for any new devices.

Hossain et al. (2017) presents a Trust-IoV, a Trustworthy Forensic Investigation Framework for the Internet of Vehicles (IoV). Similarly, Goudbeek et al. (2018) have proposed a forensic framework for Smart Home environment which consists of the seven phases as depicted by Figure 11.

Rahman et al. (2016) argue that a more proactive approach to Cyber Physical Cloud Systems (CPCS) forensics is needed. It is proposed that CPCS be *designed* for forensic readiness whereby they can collect and preserve forensic data continuously prior to a security incident. Data collected would reduce the complexity and time required in the forensic investigation. This forensic readiness in CPCS can be achieved when forensic requirements are integrated during the CPCS design and implementation phases, i.e., forensic by design. Figure 12 illustrates the conceptual

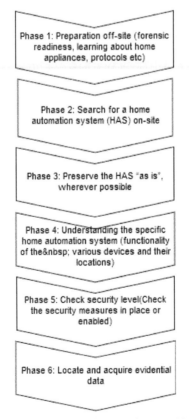

Figure 11: Forensic framework for smart home environment (Goudbeek et al. 2018).

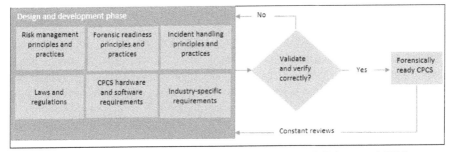

Figure 12: Conceptual forensic-by-design framework for a CPCS (Rahman et al. 2016).

forensic-by-design framework which includes six factors to facilitate forensic investigations. The six factors consist of risk management principles and practices, forensic readiness principles and practices, incident handling principles and practices, laws and regulations, CPCS hardware and software requirements, and industry-specific requirements.

Similarly, Al-Masri et al. (2018) proposes a fog-based IoT forensic framework (FoBI) that uses fog computing to proactively collect and preserve evidence. Such data captured can help detect and protect the IoT/CPS against cyber-attacks and facilitate digital investigations. IoT systems often use fog computing—computing and storage resources on the edge of network in proximity to IoT devices—for several functions such as data filtering and aggregation. Such data that transits through the fog computing towards the cloud could constitute of important digital evidence (e.g., a fog node could store the last known location of an IoT device) as well as data that could help diagnose the health status of the IoT devices. The FoBI framework is depicted in Figure 13 and it consists of six modules (device monitoring manager,

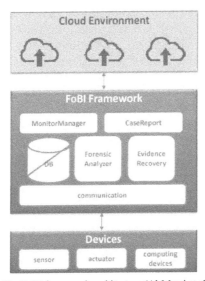

Figure 13: FoBI framework architecture (Al-Masri et al. 2018).

forensic analyzer, evidence recovery, case reporting, communication and storage) which run on a fog gateway or node.

Probe-IoT (another proactive forensic solution) is a blockchain based forensic investigation framework for IoT (Hossain et al. 2018) whereby IoT entities (CSP, users, and IoT device hub) implements a distributed ledger which stores transactions (blocks in the Blockchain) of interactions that take place among the various entities. The blockchain in Probe-IoT records a chronological history of interactions in the IoT system in a secured, confidential, non-deniable, highly available and tamperproof manner. The public ledger can be probed to acquire evidence in case of a cyber-attack and/or cyber-crime and from any entity accessible to the forensic investigator. The inherent authenticity and integrity of the records in the blockchain, ensures that evidence from the ledger is trustworthy. Similarly, Brotsis et al. (2019) proposes the use of a permissioned blockchain for evidence collection, preservation and investigation for IoT environments in the smart home domain. Several features of the smart home gateway provide information about the state and behavior of IoT devices along with metadata which can be correlated to identify attacks as well as investigate cyber-attacks. Likewise, Li et al. (2019b) proposes an IoT forensic chain (IoTFC) blockchain based solution for recording details of evidence, preserving digital evidence, and analysis of evidence in IoT and social system environments which involves evidence in different jurisdictional countries.

6. Cloud Forensic

Given the limited storage and processing capacity of IoT devices, IoT devices typically transfers data on an IoT Cloud, which provides large scale storage, on-demand accessibility, scalability and high processing capability. Some popular examples of IoT Cloud solutions include Thingworx 8 IoT Platform, Microsoft Azure IoT Suite, Google Cloud's IoT Platform, IBM Watson IoT Platform, AWS IoT Platform, Cisco IoT Cloud Connect, Salesforce IoT Cloud, Kaa IoT Platform, Oracle IoT Platform, and Thingspeak IoT Platform.

Such IoT cloud solutions allow the cloud customer to collect data on separate channels and store sensor data to the cloud, remotely monitor smart objects, analyse and visualise data from an app on the Smart Phone. Data captured from IoT is often stored in raw or processed form in the Cloud. The Google IoT platform provides structured but schema-less databases, such as Cloud Datastore and Firebase Realtime Database for IoT data storage. Most of the IoT cloud platforms also support high speed messaging to send real time notifications to the user devices. Authentication and secure communication can also be established between the IoT devices and the Cloud. IoT data processing and analytics is often done on the cloud itself.

Typically, there are four basic cloud deployment models namely public cloud, private cloud, hybrid cloud, and community cloud. Cloud service providers (CSP) such as Amazon, Google, Microsoft, Oracle, have massive infrastructure in their data centres and they offer cloud to the general public. In public clouds, the resources of the data centres are shared among numerous customers from different companies. Private cloud is a cloud infrastructure solely operated for a single organisation, while community cloud is cloud infrastructure shared by several organisations in a community that share the same concerns and policies. A typical example of a community cloud is a university cloud for several universities. Hybrid clouds are composed of two or more cloud deployment models (often private and public) that remain unique entities but are bound together by standardized or proprietary technology that enables data and application sharing. The cloud also supports three service delivery models: Infrastructure as a service (IaaS), Platform as a service (PaaS), and Software as a service (SaaS).

Another characteristic of cloud environment is the use of virtualisation whereby virtual machines run on the physical server infrastructure of the cloud. An IoT cloud customer could have several virtual machines (VM) deployed and running to capture and analyse IoT data in real-time. With virtualisation, several customers' VMs run on the same physical server and share the resources of the server. In this, multi-tenant environment, it is difficult to know where a customer's machine is running and who are the neighbours of the customer on that physical server without support from the cloud service provider (CSP). Moreover, the VM and/or data in the cloud do not stay in the same location, i.e., VM can be migrated from one physical server to another physical server to perform load balancing on the cloud.

6.1 Challenges of Cloud Forensic

As stated in (Zawoad and Hasan 2015), IoT forensics involves the three stages of Device Forensics, Network Forensics and Cloud Forensics. In the cloud environment, there are virtual machines and containerized apps running on physical servers. Traditional forensics and even IoT device forensics involve identifying which devices hold evidence and extracting evidence from the device, which assumes that the investigator gets physical access to the devices. However, such assumptions, i.e., physical access to evidence, may not be valid in the Cloud, especially in Public clouds. The physical servers may be located in a data centre in a different continent. There is the legal aspect whereby the data to be examined is under a different jurisdiction and legal authorisation may have to be sought before access to the data is allowed. The international co-operation policy of different countries may vary whereby access to data may be denied. Moreover, given the multi-tenant environment of the cloud, it is would be a violation of privacy of other customer sharing the same physical server in the cloud, if the physical server hard disk is to be acquired. Additionally, given that the location of VM and/or data is not known and that location is dynamic, it may be difficult to request a warrant as a warrant must specify a location. Moreover, the data stored on the cloud may be typically encrypted for protection, e.g., Google Cloud Platform encrypts customer data stored at rest by default. Virtualisation also results in dynamic use of physical storage, i.e., deleted files are quickly overwritten by another user's data or VM making it difficult to recover previous data on the disk. Identifying and analysing evidence may also pose a problem as data could be spread out across several applications and servers in the cloud (Taylor et al. 2011).

Evidence in the context of cloud forensics includes files, network and process logs. CSP often provide no tools or support for accessing low level logs and usually encourage customers to implement application level logs in their applications running on cloud. Major CSPs allow customers to view log accesses to stored objects and logging of activity. Amazon offers AWS CloudTrail that enables customers to log, continuously monitor and retain account activity related to actions across the customer's AWS infrastructure. CloudTrail provides event history of the AWS account activity, including actions taken through the AWS Management Console, AWS SDKs, command line tools, and other AWS services (Amazon). Similarly, the Google's Stackdriver management tool supports Cloud Audit Logs which maintains three audit logs for each Google Cloud Platform project, folder, and organization: Admin Activity, Data Access, and System Event (Google). Azure Active Directory (Azure AD) tracks user activity and sign-in metrics and creates audit log reports. By using such services, the forensic investigator could collect data from the cloud related to a particular user's activity. However, examining logs from clouds can be quite tedious given that the logs can be in different formats. Marty (2011) proposed some guidelines to handle such logs.

The VM basically consists of a number of files. In the case of VMware (the leader in vitualisation), the main files which constitutes a VM are the configuration file (.vmx) which is a plain-text file that stores the settings of VM; a VM log file (vmware.log); BIOS file (.nvram); the disk descriptor file (.vmdk) which is a text file containing descriptive data about the virtual hard disk; the disk data file (..flat. vmdk) where the actual content of the disk is stored; a suspended state file (.vmss) which stores the state of a suspended VM; and snapshot files (.vmsn, .vmsd, ..delta. vmdk), which preserve the state as well as data when a snapshot of the VM is taken. The actual virtual disk (...flat.vmdk) is usually stored in a VMFS datastore on a same physical server or on a different server in the cluster. If the VM files are available, a VM instance could be run and evidence extracted. For the VM files to be trustworthy, it should be authenticated, i.e., hash of VM files on cloud compared with hash of VM files made available to the investigator. However, there is no support for authentication of VM image. Moreover, in the case of VMs that have been terminated, CSPs often do not keep the files associated with such VMs and thus evidence related to such VMs are not available from the Cloud. Capturing network traffic to and from the cloud could however allow to get some evidence regarding ongoing attacks or other security incident.

Forensic investigators often rely on the CSP to supply forensic data. To ensure admissibility of such evidence, the CSP must preserve evidence and prove its authenticity; otherwise the trustworthiness of such evidence would be questionable. For instance, if the cloud employee who is assigned to collect data colludes with the suspected cloud user, then the employee may provide incomplete data or tampered data to the investigator.

Finally, there is the issue of the storage of data. The cloud offers large and elastic storage capacity to its customers. For forensic investigators to collect and examine such large amount of data may pose to be problematic. Only data relevant to the case should be extracted and analysed (triaging of evidence). Finally, identifying the actual suspect in the cloud may not be easy as compared to traditional forensics where the device is seized from the suspect's home or workplace, and can be easily tied to the suspect. In public clouds, which offer limited free services such as the free Dropbox account, the account is created only after weak verification based on

Table 1: Challenges to digital forensics in cloud environments (Grispos et al. 2012).

Phase	Action	Challenges
Identification	Identifying an illicit event	Lack of frameworks
Preservation	Software tools	Lack of specialist tools
	Sufficient storage capacity	Distributed, virtualized and volatile storage; use of cloud services to store evidence
	Chain of custody	Cross-jurisdictional standards, procedures; proprietary technology
	Media imaging	Imaging all physical media in a cloud is impractical; partial imaging may face legal challenges
	Time synchronization	Evidence from multiple time zones
	Legal authority	Data stored in multiple jurisdictions; limited access to physical media
	Approved methods, software and hardware	Lack of evaluation, certification generally, but particularly in cloud context
	Live vs. Dead acquisitions	Acquisition of physical media from providers is cumbersome, onerous and time consuming data is inherently volatile
	Data integrity	Lack of write-blocking or enforced persistence mechanisms for cloud services and data
Examination	Software tools	Lack of tested and certified tools
	Recovery of deleted data	Privacy regulations and mechanisms implemented by providers
	Traceability and event reconstruction	Events may occur on many different platforms
Presentation	Documentation of evidence	Integration of multiple evidence sources in record
	Testimony	Complexity of explaining cloud technology to jury

a working email address and requires no credit card number of the user or any other credentials of the user. Table 1 presents the challenges as identified in (Grispos et al. 2012).

6.2 Cloud Forensic Frameworks

The support of the CSP is fundamental for digital forensics in the Cloud for collecting logs and data from the cloud. A subpoena or warrant is often required to get access to such information and there needs to be a mechanism to verify integrity and trustworthiness of such logs and data provided by the CSP. Simou et al. (2018) proposes a conceptual model for designing cloud forensic enabled services via the use of a set of predefined forensic-related tasks. Zawoad et al. (2015) proposes the Open Cloud Forensics (OCF) model for reliable forensics where they consider the important role of the CSP in the investigation and also state *Continuous Forensics* in the cloud is required to facilitate the digital forensics procedures. Continuous Forensics, due to the volatile nature of data in the cloud, involves the continuous capture of electronically stored information (ESI) when the user interacts with the cloud service(s); and the translation of all ESI to verifiable ESI by the CSP to preserve their integrity. Such verifiable ESI is accessible to the investigator and can be verified by court authority. Figure 14 depicts the OCF model.

Similarly, Pichan et al. (2018) propose the implementation of CFLOG logging application which runs at the hypervisor level and which records logs of all users' activity on the server in user-separated log files like an audit trail. These logs could provide very useful forensic evidence and is logged transparently without the knowledge of the user as CFLOG runs at the hypervisor level. Users cannot interact or tamper with the logs, thus integrity of evidence is maintained. The implementation of CFLOG was tested on ownCloud, an open source cloud platform. However, integrating CFLOG in proprietary cloud platform solutions may not be possible.

Edington and Kishore (2017) also propose a proactive continuous forensic solution but which does not rely on the CSP and only involves capturing and logging data traffic between user and the cloud. The capture of cloud traffic is done by a centralized server outside the cloud. Existing network traffic monitoring and analysis tools such as E-Detective can be used to examine the traffic. However, network traffic may only provide a subset of evidence related to cybercrime in cloud based IoT systems. It might also be challenging to store all the network traffic.

Zawoad et al. (2013) proposes a mechanism for the CSP to securely capture and store logs such that the logs can be made available to forensic investigators, while preserving the privacy of cloud customers against cloud employee and external parties. Using a "Proof of Past Log (PPL)" mechanism, they also guarantee integrity

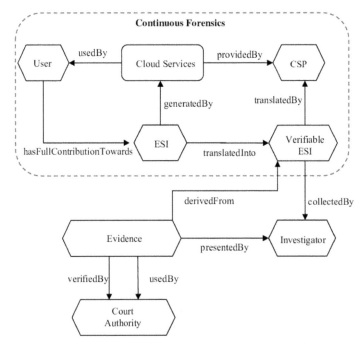

Figure 14: Open cloud forensics model (Zawoad et al. 2015).

of logs whereby the logs cannot be tampered "after-the-fact". Dykstra and Sherma (2013) describe the design, implementation and evaluation of FROST, a forensic tool for the OpenStack Infrastructure-as-a-Service (IaaS) cloud service which trusts the CSP but does not require interaction with the CSP to collect evidence. Liu et al. (2017) proposes a forensic enabled cloud whereby forensic tools are installed in the cloud environment, which logs activities from different layers and which was implemented on OpenStack. Such logs were then collected and analyzed by a prolog based forensic tool. With such log information, the tool can automate the correlation of evidence from both the clients and the CSP to construct attack steps and therefore re-create the attack scenarios on the cloud.

Kebande et al. (2016), Kebande et al. (2017a) propose a distributed agent based solution to proactively collect data in the cloud for making the cloud forensic ready. Such data can later be used by forensic investigators. The authors also propose a Cloud-Centric framework for isolating Big Data as Forensic Evidence from IoT Infrastructures (Kebande et al. 2017b).

7. Conclusion

CPS/IoT systems have a lot of potential to transform our society and the revolution has already begun with the increasing adoption of Industrial IoT, Smart Cities, Smart Homes Smart Healthcare and Smart Transportation solutions worldwide. IoT integrated with artificial intelligence (AI) and machine learning, cloud infrastructure, Big Data processing frameworks; and increased network agility will result in more intelligent, responsive and efficient systems and enable new opportunities for humankind. However, this also poses increased security risks of cyber attacks and cyber crime. In this chapter, the challenges of IoT forensics, which encompass Device Forensic, Network Forensics and Cloud Forensics, are discussed. New frameworks being proposed by researchers have been presented. It is clear that further research and development is needed for the field of IoT forensics to mature and offer wide range of tools, standards and processes for tackling forensic investigations in complex IoT environments.

References

Ab Rahman, N. H., Glisson, W. B., Yang, Y. and Choo, K. R. 2016. Forensic-by-design framework for cyber-physical cloud systems. In IEEE Cloud Computing 3(1): 50–59, Jan.-Feb. 2016. doi: 10.1109/MCC.2016.5.

Al-Masri, E., Bai, Y. and Li, J. 2018. A fog-based digital forensics investigation framework for IoT systems. 2018 IEEE International Conference on Smart Cloud (SmartCloud), New York, NY, pp. 196–201. doi: 10.1109/SmartCloud.2018.00040.

Al-Mhiqani, M. N., Ahmad, R., Yassin, W., Hassan, A., Abidin, Z. Z., Ali, N. S. and Abdulkareem, K. H. 2018. Cyber-security incidents: a review cases in cyber-physical systems. (IJACSA) International Journal of Advanced Computer Science and Applications 9(1): 499–508.

Ankara and Kocaeli. 2016. Major cyber-attack on Turkish Energy Ministry claimed. [Online] Available at: http://www.hurriyetdailynews.com/major-cyber-attack-on-turkish-energy-ministry-claimed. aspx?PageID=238&NID=107981&NewsCatID=348.

Ariffin, A., Slay, J. and Choo, K. -K. 2013. Data recovery from proprietary formatted CCTV hard disks digital forensics. pp. 213–223. *In*: Peterson, G. and Shenoi, S. (eds.). Advances in Digital Forensics

IX, Volume 410 of the series IFIP Advances in Information and Communication Technology. Springer, Berlin, Heidelberg.

Atlam, H. F., Alenezi, A., Alharthi, A., Walters, R. and Wills, G. 2017. Integration of cloud computing with internet of things: challenges and open issues. In Proceedings of the 2017 IEEE International Conference on Internet of Things (iThings) and IEEE Green Computing and Communications (GreenCom) and IEEE Cyber, Physical and Social Computing (CPSCom) and IEEE Smart Data (SmartData), Exeter, UK, 21–23 June 2017; pp. 670–675.

Awasthi, A., Read, H. O. L., Xynos, K. and Sutherland, I. 2018. Welcome pwn: Almond smart home hub forensics. Digital Investigation 26: S38–S46.

BBC News Technology. 2017. Ukraine power cut 'was cyber-attack', 11 January 2017, available at https://www.bbc.com/news/technology-38573074.

Boztas, A., Riethoven, R. J. and Roeloffs, M. 2015. Smart TV forensics: Digital traces on televisions. In the Journal of Digital Investigation, ISSN: 1742-2876, 12(S1): S72–S80, DOI10.1016/j.diin.2015.01.012.

Brotsis, S., Kolokotronis, N., Limniotis, K., Shiaeles, S., Kavallieros, D., Bellini, E. and Pavue, Clement. 2019. Blockchain solutions for forensic evidence preservation in IoT environments. To appear in IEEE Conference on Network Softwarization (IEEE NetSoft), 24–28 June 2019, Paris, France.

Chhabra, G. S., Singh, V. P. and Singh, M. 2018. Cyber forensics framework for big data analytics in IoT environment using machine learning. Multimedia Tools and Applications, pp. 1–20. https://doi.org/10.1007/s11042-018-6338-1.

Charette, R. N. 2018. Two Critical U.S. Dams at High Risk From Insider Cyber Threats: A new report by the Interior Department's Inspector General highlights several basic cybersecurity issues. IEEE Spectrum, 15 Jun 2018.

Clark, D. R., Meffert, C., Baggili, I. and Breitinger, F. 2017. DROP (DRone Open source Parser) your drone: Forensic analysis of the DJI Phantom III. Digital Investigation 22(Supplement, 2017): S3–S14, ISSN 1742-2876, https://doi.org/10.1016/j.diin.2017.06.013.

Davies, M., Read, H., Xynos, K. and Sutherland, I. 2015. Forensic analysis of a Sony PlayStation 4: A first look, Digital Investigation, 12(Supplement 1): S81–S89, ISSN 1742-2876, https://doi.org/10.1016/j.diin.2015.01.013.

Dignan, L. 2016. ZDNet, Dyn confirms Mirai botnet involved in distributed denial of service attack, October 26, 2016, available at https://www.zdnet.com/article/dyn-confirms-mirai-botnet-involved-in-distributed-denial-of-service-attack/.

Dykstra, J. and Sherman, A. T. 2013. Design and implementation of FROST: Digital forensic tools for the OpenStack cloud computing platform. Digital Investigation 10(Supplement, 2013): S87–S95, ISSN 1742-2876, https://doi.org/10.1016/j.diin.2013.06.010.

Edington, M. and Kishore, R. 2017. Forensics framework for cloud computing. Computers & Electrical Engineering 60: 193–205, ISSN 0045-7906, https://doi.org/10.1016/j.compeleceng.2017.02.006.

Edward, E. 2017. US supreme court to hear appeal in Microsoft warrant case, The IRISH TIMES, 2017. [Online]. Available: https://www.irishtimes.com/business/technology/us-supreme- court-to-hear-appeal-in-microsoft-warrant-case-1.3257825.

Etemadieh, A., Heres, C. and Hoang, K. 2017. Hacking Hardware with a $10 SD card reader. 2017, presentation at BlackHat USA.

Goudbeek, A., Choo, K. -K. R. and Le-Khac, N. -A. 2018. A forensic investigation framework for smart home environment. 17th IEEE International Conference on Trust, Security and Privacy in Computing and Communications/12th IEEE International Conference on Big Data Science and Engineering (TrustCom/BigDataSE), 1–3 Aug. 2018, New York, NY, USA, DOI: 10.1109/TrustCom/BigDataSE.2018.00201.

Greer, C., Burns, M., Wollman, D. and Griffor, E. 2019. Cyber-Physical Systems and Internet of Things, NIST Special Publication 1900-202, March 2019, https://doi.org/10.6028/NIST.SP.1900-202 available at https://nvlpubs.nist.gov/nistpubs/SpecialPublications/NIST.SP.1900-202.pdf.

Grispos, G., Storer, T. and Glisson, W. B. 2012. Calm before the storm: the challenges of cloud computing in digital forensics. International Journal of Digital Crime and Forensics 4(2): 28–48.

GrowthEnabler. 2017. GrowthEnablerIoT Market Pulse Report, Internet of Things (IoT): Discover Key Trends & Insights on Disruptive Technologies & IoT innovations, April 2017, available at https://growthenabler.com/flipbook/pdf/IOT%20Report.pdf.

Harbawi, M. and Varol, A. 2017. An improved digital evidence acquisition model for the Internet of Things forensic I: A theoretical framework. 2017 5th International Symposium on Digital Forensic and Security (ISDFS). doi:10.1109/isdfs.2017.7916508.

Hauser, C. 2017. In Connecticut Murder Case, a Fitbit Is a Silent Witness. The New York Times, 27 April 2017; www.nytimes.com/2017/04/27/nyregion/in-connecticut-murdercase-a-fitbit-is-a-silent-witness.html?mcubz=1.

Haque, S. A., Aziz, S. M. and Rahman, M. 2014. Review of cyber-physical system in healthcare. International Journal of Distributed Sensor Networks, https://doi.org/10.1155/2014/217415, April 27, 2014 Hindawi Publishing Corporation.

Horsman, G. 2016. Unmanned aerial vehicles: A preliminary analysis of forensic challenges. Digital Investigation 16: 1–11, ISSN 1742-2876, https://doi.org/10.1016/j.diin.2015.11.002.

Hossain, M. and Zawoad, S. 2017. Trust-IoV: A Trustworthy Forensic Investigation Framework for the Internet of Vehicles (IoV), IEEE International Congress on Internet of Things (ICIOT), 25–30 June 2017, Honolulu, HI, USA, DOI: 10.1109/IEEE.ICIOT.2017.13.

Hossain, M., Hasan, R. and Zawoad, S. 2018. Probe-IoT: A public digital ledger based forensic investigation framework for IoT. IEEE INFOCOM 2018 – IEEE Conference on Computer Communications Workshops (INFOCOM WKSHPS), Honolulu, HI, pp. 1–2. doi: 10.1109/INFCOMW.2018.8406875.

Hung, M. 2017. Leading the IoT, Gartner Insights on How to Lead in a Connected World, available at https://www.gartner.com/imagesrv/books/iot/iotEbook_digital.pdf.

ICS-CERT National Cybersecurity and Communications Integration Center (NCCIC)/Industrial Control Systems Cyber Emergency Response Team (ICS-CERT). 2016b. Alert (IR-ALERT-H-16-056-01), Cyber-Attack Against Ukrainian Critical Infrastructure, Original release date: February 25, 2016 | Last revised: August 23, 2018 available at https://ics-cert.us-cert.gov/alerts/IR-ALERT-H-16-056-01.

Industrial Control Systems Cyber Emergency Response Team (ICS-CERT). 2016a. Annual Assessment Report of 2016, NCCIC, U.S. Dept. Homeland Security, available at https://ics-cert.us-cert.gov/sites/default/files/Annual_Reports/FY2016_Industrial_Control_Systems_Assessment_Summary_Report_S508C.pdf.

ISO/IEC 27037:2012—Information technology—Security techniques—Guidelines for identification, collection, acquisition and preservation of digital evidence. https://www.iso27001security.com/html/27037.html.

Israel, T. O. 2016. Israel's Electric Authority hit by 'severe' cyber-attack. [Online] Available at: http://www.timesofisrael.com/steinitz-israels-electric-authority-hit-by-severe-cyber-attack/.

JeiYang, S., Choi, J. H., Kim, K. B. and Chang, T. 2015. New acquisition method based on firmware update protocols for Android smartphones. Digital Investigation 14(Supplement 1): pp. S68–S76, August 2015. https://doi.org/10.1016/j.diin.2015.05.008.

Jian, A., Xiaolin, G., Jianwei, Y., Yu, S. and Xin, H. 2015. Mobile crowd sensing for Internet of Things: a credible crowdsourcing model in mobile-sense service. IEEE International Conference on Multimedia Big Data, 20–22 April 2015, DOI: 10.1109/BigMM.2015.62, Conference Location: Beijing, China.

Kapersky. 2016. Kaspersky Lab Discovers Vulnerable Industrial Control Systems Likely Belonging to Large Organizations, July 11, 2016, available at https://usa.kaspersky.com/about/press-releases/2016_kaspersky-lab-discovers-vulnerable-industrial-control-systems-likely-belonging-to-large-organizations.

Kebande, V. R. and Ray, I. 2016. A generic digital forensic investigation framework for Internet of Things (IoT). IEEE 4th International Conference on Future Internet of Things and Cloud.

Kebande, V. R. and Venter, H. S. 2016. On digital forensic readiness in the cloud using a distributed agent-based solution: issues and challenges. Australian Journal of Forensic Sciences 50(2): 209–238. doi:10.1080/00450618.2016.1194473.

Kebande, V. R., Karie, N. M., Michael, A., Malapane, S. M. G. and Venter, H. S. 2017. How an IoT-enabled "smart refrigerator" can play a clandestine role in perpetuating cyber-crime. IST-Africa 2017 Conference Proceedings, ISBN: 978-1-905824-57-1.

Kebande, V. R. and Venter, H. S. 2017a. Novel digital forensic readiness technique in the cloud environment. Australian Journal of Forensic Sciences 50(5): 552–591. doi:10.1080/00450618.2 016.1267797.

Kebande, V. R., Karie, N. M. and Venter, H. S. 2017b. Cloud-Centric Framework for isolating Big data as forensic evidence from IoT infrastructures. 2017 1st International Conference on Next Generation Computing Applications (NextComp), Mauritius, pp. 54–60. doi: 10.1109/NEXTCOMP.2017.8016176.

Kebande, V. R., Karie, N. M., Michael, A., Malapane, S., Kigwana, I., Venter, H. S. and Wario, R. D. 2018. Towards an integrated digital forensic investigation framework for an IoT-based ecosystem. IEEE International Conference on Smart Internet of Things.

Khac, N. A., Jacobs, D., Nijhoff, J., Bertens, K. and Choo, K. K. R. 2018. Smart vehicle forensics: Challenges and case study. In Journal of Future Generation Computer Systems, https://doi.org/10.1016/j.future.2018.05.081.

Khan, S., Gani, A., Wahab, A. W. W., Iqbal, S., Abdelaziz, A., Mahdi, O. A., Abdallaahmed, A. I., shriz, M., Al-Mayouf, Y. R. B., Khan, Z., Ko, K., Khan, M. K. and Chang, V. 2016. Towards an applicability of current network forensics for cloud networks: A SWOT analysis. In IEEE Access 4: 9800–9820. doi: 10.1109/ACCESS.2016.2631543.

Kouwen, A., Scanlon, M., Kwang, K., Choo, R. and Le-Khac, N. -A. 2018. Digital forensic investigation of two-way radio communication equipment and services. Digital Investigation 26(Supplement, 2018): S77–S86, ISSN 1742-2876, https://doi.org/10.1016/j.diin.2018.04.007.

Koroniotis, N., Moustafa, N., Sitnikova, E. and Turnbull, B. 2019. Towards the development of realistic botnet dataset in the Internet of Things for network forensic analytics: Bot-IoT dataset. In Journal of Future Generation Computer Systems 100: 779–796.

Kumar, M. 2016. DDoS Attack Takes Down Central Heating System Amidst Winter in Finland. [Online] Available at: http://thehackernews.com/2016/11/heating-system-hacked.html.

Kumari, N. and Mohapatra, A. K. 2016. An insight into digital forensics branches and tools. Proceedings of the International Conference on Computational Techniques in Information and Communication Technologies.

Kushner, D. 2013. The real story of stuxnet. IEEE Spectrum 53(3): 48, 26 Feb 2013.

Larson, S. 2017. CNN, FDA confirms that St. Jude's cardiac devices can be hacked, January 9, 2017, available at https://money.cnn.com/2017/01/09/technology/fda-st-jude-cardiac-hack/.

Li, S., Choo, K. K. R., Sun, Q., Buchanan, W. J. and Cao, J. 2019a. IoT forensics: Amazon echo as a use case. IEEE Internet of Things Journal 6(4), Aug. 2019. DOI: 10.1109/JIOT.2019.2906946.

Li, S., Qin, T. and Min, G. 2019b. Blockchain-based digital forensics investigation framework in the Internet of Things and social systems. IEEE Transactions on Computational Social Systems, 1–9. doi:10.1109/tcss.2019.2927431.

Liu, C., Singhal, A. and Wijesekera, D. 2017. Identifying evidence for cloud forensic analysis. *In*: Peterson, G. and Shenoi, S. (eds.). Advances in Digital Forensics XIII. Digital Forensics 2017. IFIP Advances in Information and Communication Technology, vol. 511. Springer, Cham.

Losavio, M., Seigfried-Spellar, K. C. and Sloan III, J. J. 2016. Why digital forensics is not a profession and how it can become one. Criminal Justice Studies 29(2): 143–162.

Marty, R. 2011. Cloud application logging for forensics. In Proceedings of the ACM Symposium on Applied Computing, pp. 178–184.

Merlino, G., Arkoulis, S., Distefano, S., Papagianni, C., Puliafito, A. and Papavassiliou, S. 2016. Mobile crowdsensing as a service: A platform for applications on top of sensing Clouds. Future Generation Computer Systems, ISSN: 0167-739X, 56: 623–639, Elsevier BV.

National Institute of Standards and Technology (NIST). 2017. Information Technology Laboratory/ Software and Systems Division, Computer Forensics Tool Testing Program (CFTT), available at https://www.nist.gov/itl/ssd/software-quality-group/computer-forensics-tool-testing-program-cftt, last accessed 13.08.19.

Nickson, M. K. and Venter, H. S. 2015. Taxonomy of challenges for digital forensics. Journal Forensic Science 2015 Jul; 60(4): 885–893. doi: 10.1111/1556-4029.12809.

Nickson, M. K., Kebande, V. R., Venter, H. S. and Choo, K. -K. R. 2019. On the importance of standardising the process of generating digital forensic reports. Forensic Science International: Reports, ISSN: 2665-9107, 1: 100008, DOI10.1016/j.fsir.2019.100008.

Nieto, A., Rios, R. and Lopez, J. 2017. A methodology for privacy-aware IoT-forensics. IEEE Trustcom/ BigDataSE/ICESS, 1–4 Aug 2017, Sydney, NSW, Australia, DOI: 10.1109/Trustcom/BigDataSE/ ICESS.2017.293.

NIST, Cyber-Physical Systems Public Working Group. 2017, available at https://www.nist.gov/el/cyber-physical-systems.

Oriwoh, E., Jazani, D., Epiphaniou, G. and Sant, P. 2013. Internet of Things forensics: Challenges and approaches. 9th IEEE International Conference on Collaborative Computing: Networking, Applications and Worksharing (CollaborateCom 2013).

Osborne, C. 2018. Industroyer: An in-depth look at the culprit behind Ukraine's power grid blackout Malware which speaks the language of industrial machines is a danger to all of our critical services, April 30, 2018, https://www.zdnet.com/article/industroyer-an-in-depth-look-at-the-culprit-behind-ukraines-power-grid-blackout/.

Perumal, S., Norwawi, N. Md. and Raman, V. 2015. Internet of Things (IoT) digital forensic investigation model: top-down forensic approach methodology. 2015 Fifth International Conference on Digital Information Processing and Communications (ICDIPC), Sierre, Switzerland, 7–9 Oct. 2015, DOI: 10.1109/ICDIPC.2015.7323000.

Pichan, A., Lazarescu, M. and Soh, S. T. 2018. Towards a practical cloud forensics logging framework. Journal of Information Security and Applications 42: 18–28, ISSN 2214–2126, https://doi.org/10.1016/j.jisa.2018.07.008.

Positive Technologies, Industrial Control Systems. 2016. Report: Connected and Vulnerable, October 7, 2016, available at http://blog.ptsecurity.com/2016/10/industrial-control-systems-2016-report.html.

Quick, D. and Choo, K. K. R. 2016. Big forensic data reduction: digital forensic images and electronic evidence. Cluster Computing 19(2): 723–740. doi:10.1007/s10586-016-0553-1.

Quick, D. and Choo, K. K. R. 2018. IoT Device Forensics and Data Reduction. In IEEE Access 6: 47566–47574. doi: 10.1109/ACCESS.2018.2867466.

San Carlos, C. A. 2017. Check Point Joins Forces With LG To Secure Their Smart Home Devices, OCT 26 2017. [Online]. Available: https://www.checkpoint.com/press/2017/check-point-joins-forces-lg-secure-smart-home-devices/.

Sang-Hun, C. 2013. Computer Networks in South Korea Are Paralyzed in Cyberattacks, The New York Times, available at https://www.nytimes.com/2013/03/21/world/asia/south-korea-computer-network-crashes.html.

Sansurooah, K. 2006. Taxonomy of computer forensics methodologies and procedures for digital evidence seizure. Proceedings of the 4th Australian Digital Forensics Conference; 2006 Dec 4; Edith Cowan University, Perth, Western Australia. Perth, Western Australia: Edith Cowan University Publishers, 2006; 1–13.

Servida, F. and Casey, E. 2019. IoT forensic challenges and opportunities for digital traces. Digital Investigation 28: S22–S29.

Shin, C., Chandok, P., Ran Liu, R., Nielson, S. J. and Leschke, T. R. 2017. Potential forensic analysis of IoT data: An overview of the state-of-the-art and future possibilities. IEEE International Conference on Internet of Things (iThings) and IEEE Green Computing and Communications (GreenCom) and IEEE Cyber, Physical and Social Computing (CPSCom) and IEEE Smart Data (SmartData), 21–23 June 2017, Exeter, UK, DOI: 10.1109/iThings-GreenCom-CPSCom-SmartData.2017.182.

Simou, S., Kalloniatis, C., Gritzalis, S. and Katos, V. 2018. A framework for designing cloud forensic-enabled services (CFeS). Requirements Engineering. doi:10.1007/s00766-018-0289-y.

Sriram, R. 2013. Digital forensic research: current state-of-the-art. CSI Trans ICT 1(1): 91–114.

Statista. n.d. Size of the Internet of Things market worldwide in 2014 and 2020, by industry (in billion U.S. dollars).

Taylor, M., Haggerty, J., Gresty, D. and Lamb, D. 2011. Forensic investigation of cloud computing systems. Network Security 2011(3): 4–10, ISSN 1353-4858, https://doi.org/10.1016/S1353-4858(11)70024-1.

Vasile, S., Oswald, D. and Chothia, T. 2019. Breaking all the things—a systematic survey of firmware extraction techniques for IoT devices. *In*: Bilgin, B. and Fischer, J. B. (eds.). Smart Card Research and Advanced Applications. CARDIS 2018. Lecture Notes in Computer Science, vol. 11389. Springer, Cham.

Vincze, E. A. 2016. Challenges in digital forensics. Police Practice and Research 17(2): 183–194, DOI: 10.1080/15614263.2015.1128163.

Watson, S. and Dehghantanha, A. 2016. Digital forensics: the missing piece of the internet of things promise. Computer Fraud & Security 2016(6): 5–8.

Yaakobi, E. and Goldenberg, J. 2014. Social relationships and information dissemination in virtual social network systems: An attachment theory perspective. Comput. Hum. Behav. 38(September 2014): 127–135. DOI: http://dx.doi.org/10.1016/j.chb.2014.05.025.

Zawoad, S. and Hasan, R. 2015. FAIoT: Towards building a forensics aware eco system for the Internet of Things. 2015 IEEE International Conference on Services Computing. doi:10.1109/scc.2015.46.

Zawoad, S., Hasan, R. and Skjellum, A. 2015. OCF: An open cloud forensics model for reliable digital forensics. 2015 IEEE 8th International Conference on Cloud Computing, New York, NY, pp. 437–444. doi: 10.1109/CLOUD.2015.65.

Zawoad, S., Kumar Dutta, A. and Ragib, R. 2013. SecLaaS: Secure logging-as-a-service for cloud forensics. ASIA CCS 2013 – Proceedings of the 8th ACM SIGSAC Symposium on Information, Computer and Communications Security. 10.1145/2484313.2484342.

Zatyko, K. 2007. Commentary: Defining digital forensics. Forensic Magazine, 2 January 2007, www.forensicmag.com/articles/2007/01/commentary-defining-digital-forensics.

8

Social Media Crime Investigation and Forensic Analysis

Manish Kumar

1. Introduction

Social media does not require any introduction. Billions of users are active on social media platform and each user spends significant time on it. No doubt social media has brought people together and the world is more connected, however with time social media has evolved as disruptive technology. The massive number of active users generate an abundance of personal information on the social media platforms, which makes it heaven for cybercrime and anitsocial activities.

The exponential growth in social media platforms has gone to the level where it is no more under the control of few actors or organizations. It has become the most easily accessible platform for the public to share their views, thoughts and opinions. However anonymity and the difficulty in vetting content, make it easy for propagandists to establish flash narratives and influence dialogue.

The mammoth amount of personal data generated on social media is collected and analysed by many organizations and individuals for various purposes. This data and information are considered more precious than gold or diamonds. As processed data and information gives intelligence. It can be used for building the society and can also be used to destroy society. Social media platform are witnessing both these scenarios. Before social media, intelligence-gathering was a tough job and required a vast human network. It was not only a costly effort but also a risky job. Today it can be done remotely, just with the help of few computers and by scouring data from social media platforms at minimal cost and almost at no risk (Baccarella et al. 2020).

The impact and influence of the social media is so strong that around the world many countries have dedicated teams for policing social media platforms.

Assistant Professor, Department of Master of Computer Applications, M S Ramaiah Institute of Technology, Bangalore – 54, India.
Email: manishkumarjsr@yahoo.com

Some countries are even reluctant to give complete freedom for social media use. Though there are concerns raised by many individuals and organizations for freedom of speech and uncensored use of social media platforms, however when national security is at stake, no country would compromise.

The Islamic State in Iraq and Levant (ISIS) and Islamic State (IS) is known for committing a blood bath, mass killing and public executions. ISIS used social media platforma to mobilize 40,000 foreign nationals from 110 countries to join their group. ISIS had a pool of potential support through social media platforms around the world. ISIS heavily used social media platform to radicalize young and innocent minds to join their group.

ISIS's strategic use of social media in not new and unique. Al-Qaeda and Arabian Peninsula (AQAP) has also used social media for more than a decade to spread online propaganda and to circulate their digital magazine which inspired the Boston Marathon bombers in 2010. The Taliban has also made strategic use of social media for antisocial activities. Taliban had its own Telegram channel in multiple languages including Pashto, Persian and Turkish. The Taliban's demonstration of governance ability in its propaganda has been critical in attracting fighters and projecting itself as a legitimate governing entity, distinguishing it from the vast majority of other violent extremist groups.

How social media influenced the voters in 2016 U.S. presidential election is no longer a secret. It was the Facebook and Twitter ad campaign which helped the Donald Trump to win the election. As quoted by BBC "A Facebook executive has claimed the company was "responsible" for Donald Trump being elected as U.S. president". The opinion piece is emblematic of concerns about the threat that social media poses to democracy by corrupting citizens' perceptions of political reality. It is not only the Facebook executive's claims but a more shocking incident was when the Cambridge Analytica Scandal erupted in March 2018. It emerged that the firm had misused personal data from millions of Facebook profile without their consent and used it for political advertising purposes. Facebook was hit with a $5bn (£3.8bn) fine in July 2019 following an investigation by The Federal Trade Commission (FTC).

2. Types of Social Networking Platforms

There are so many different types of social media platforms available in the market (Figure 1). Each platform has unique features which attract the users and bring them together on the platforms to socialize. Social media platforms can be categorized based on their features and services. Some common categories are as follows:-

- **Social Networks:** Social networks are one of the most popular and commonly used platforms. Normally people use it to be connected with friends, family and colleagues. However, it is also popularly used for business purposes and connecting with the clients and customers. Ever since the rise of smartphones and mobile internet, it has transformed every aspects of life. Peoples are using it in many creative ways to share their moments of life. Facebook, Twitter, WhatsApp and Linkedin are some of the well-known services used for social networking.

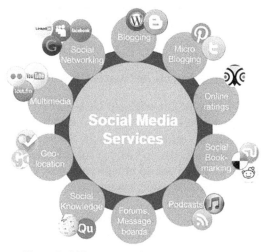

Figure 1: Different types of social media platforms.

- **Media Sharing Networks:** Media sharing platform is used by the users for sharing Photos, and Videos. It is not only used by the common users to share their moments of life with their friends and family but heavily used by corporates for their brand promotions. YouTube, Instagram, Snapchat, etc. are some of the most well-known services in this category.

- **Discussion Forums:** It's one of the oldest type of platform commonly used for knowledge sharing, discussion forum, market research, etc. There are various discussion forums available on specific domains, subject matter and topics (e.g., Reddit, Quora, Digg, etc.). Not specific but such platforms are commonly used by students, academics, and technical experts.

- **Consumer Review Networks:** These platforms are specifically used by the consumers to express their experience and opinions about specific brand, product and services. Now a days it is also used by the users and consumers to share their travel and stay experiences. Yelp, Zomato, TripAdvisor are popular services known for consumer review.

- **Blogging and Publishing Networks:** Blogging and publishing sites give an open platform to the people to share their knowledge experience and thoughts in a free and fearless manner. Blogging and Microblogging platforms are popular among writers who are also called as bloggers. WordPress, Tumblr, Medium, etc. are well known blogging and publishing platform.

- **Sharing Economy Networks:** These platforms are generally used by the users for selling, buying, advertising, etc. (e.g., Airbnb, Task rabbit, etc.). It's not a substitution for e-commerce platforms but provide a similar features at a very micro level for individual users.

- **Anonymous Social Networks:** Such platforms are used by people to communicate anonymously. Though these platforms were meant for protecting user's identity from unknown people, it is increasingly used for unsocial activities. Whisper, Secret, Yik Yak are few popular services used for anonymous social networking.

3. Cyber Crime Using Social Network Platforms

Any technology which is very powerful can be misused and can be devastating for society. Every technology has advantages and disadvantages and the internet and social media also do. No doubt that the social media has brought tremendous changes in our day-to-day life, but no one can rule out that it has also made our life very vulnerable. Society is made-up of individual people and any system which can physiologically influence the public sentiments, their thoughts and feelings can virtually control the society.

Social media platforms are misused for various type of cybercrimes. It's not only used for committing cybercrime but also used as an instrument to commit traditional crimes. It is really up-to the creativity and imagination of the cybercriminal, how they use social media platform for illicit purposes. Some of the common social media cybercrimes are classified as:-

- **Reconnaissance:** Social media platform is treasure of information about individuals. Knowingly or unknowingly social media user's share many personal information on social network, i.e., location details, like and dislikes, friend and family details. Sometime they also disclose their sensitive information like date of birth, personal contact numbers, email address etc. Reconnaissance is type of attack in which the attacker passively collects and analyses the personal information of victims and plan a targeted attack. It's very difficult to detect such kind of attack.

- **Fake Profiles/Identity Theft:** The most difficult task in social media network is to ascertain the authenticity of the user profile. Fake social media profile is one of the most common issues in social media network. Cybercriminals normally mimic the profile of legitimate users. Cybercriminal use these fake profile in various creative way to attack the victim. Generally cybercriminals create the fake accounts of celebrities, politicians, CEO or CFO of organizations who have a big circle of friends and followers. Using the fake profile attacker to try to become close with people and exploit them in various ways.

- **Social Engineering Attack:** Social engineering is the art of exploiting human psychology. Normally in social engineering, attackers psychologically manipulate the victim to divulge their confidential information or sensitive data. For example instead of hacking someone's bank account, an attacker may pose as bank employee and call the victim over phone. He may convince the victim that it's a routine audit process and gather sensitive information from him like his ATM Card details, ATM Pin, date of expiry etc. After collecting this information, it's easy for the attacker to do various transactions. There are various modus-operandi used by attackers such as fake email, malicious web link, SMS, etc. To craft such an attack, generally the attacker collects every minute details about their target from social media platform. Such attacks are very successful and most common on social media. Except for awareness among users, there are no other countermeasures for such attack.

- **Fake News:** The dark side of social media is its misuse for fake publicity, propaganda, campaign and news. The feed shared on the social media spreads like wildfire and by the time someone ascertains its authenticity, it has already dented many things. Knowing the impact of social media feeds on millions of users and how its spread, cybercriminals use it as a remote weapon. It is heavily used during election campaign to influence the user's sentiments. There are various tools and professional services available for manipulating and spreading the fake news and propaganda on social media network targeting to specific group or community.

- **Malicious Content:** Many times an attacker lures the victim to click on particular web link. These link take the users on third-party website or download malicious content on the users system or smartphone. Once the system or smartphone is compromised, it is sufficient for the attacker to compromise the user's social media account and takeover control.

In today's scenario, social networking is not only used for attacking individuals, but also used against country, government, corporate, religion, caste and community (Krishna et al. 2019). It is not wrong to say that social media services are getting used as a cyber weapon. It has tremendous power to create unrest in the society.

3.1 Social Media as a Cyber Weapon

With the powerful use of social media, an actor can win the war before it even begins by weakening the trust in national institutions and consensus. The concern for security was raised after occurrences and impacts of social media user accounts being hacked and the economic loss it caused to the national security. Understanding the grave threat to national security many nations have guidelines to secure social media use. Social media applications such as Twitter, Facebook and WhatsApp are banned at government workplaces.

The well-coordinated, coherent and carefully managed social campaign has great effectiveness to influence the people. Many nations are using social media as cyber-weapons to target their enemy countries. In recent years there are series of incidents were it was found that social media platforms were misused for social, political and economic gain. They normally spread fake news, fabricated messages, hack private communications and release it publically. Some countries have professional organizations doing this as a full time job on contract.

4. Social Media Forensics

Not only cybercrime but even in traditional crime, social media is one of the vital sources of evidence. As mentioned earlier, sometimes social media platforms are used for anti-national activities. It is used strategically against country, religion, political party and reputed organizations to defame and create un-rest in the society.

Exponential growth in social media crime and its misuse for committing traditional crime has increased the demand for digital forensics (Arshad et al. 2019).

Social network forensics is application of digital forensics. However, the approach of investigation is slightly different. In social network forensics, speed of the investigation is very important. Social media generates a huge amount of data and metadata, which makes the job of investigator little complex as a minor mistake may divert the whole investigation. The focus is more on extracting the evidence from social media platforms like Facebook, Twitter, Whatsapp, Linkedin, etc. Social media artefacts can be retrieved from computers, laptops, smartphones and sometime through network analysis. The evidence collected from social network platform plays important role to trace the cybercriminals and its conviction in the court of law.

Basically, from the investigator's point of view, social network forensics will be a question of finding where the evidence lies and collecting it in a forensically sound manner without violating any laws. Investigator's need to follow a standard approach for forensics analysis.

4.1 Social Networking Apps & Mobile Devices

Social media investigation discussions would be incomplete without the discussion of smartphone forensics. Exponential growth and development in smartphone technology has made it a favourite platform for social media. As of 2018 the average user spends 136 minutes per day on social media which was 135 minutes in the year 2017. The number of social media users are expected to number around 3.02 billion by 2021. It's clear with the facts and figures that forensics investigators doing social media forensics will most likely encounter the smartphone as a source of evidence. However, smartphone forensics poses some unique challenges.

4.1.1 Challenges of Social Networking Forensic Analysis on Mobile Devices

Mobile forensics is different from computer forensics and presents unique challenges to forensic examiners. Mobile devices can store and access data across multiple devices and storage media. As the mobile data is volatile, it can be quickly deleted. It can also be accessed remotely and hence extreme precaution is required for the preservation of data.

Law enforcement agencies and forensic examiners face many critical issues to obtain digital evidence from mobile devices. Some of the major challenges are as follows:-

- **Hardware differences:** Market is flooded with mobile phones of various different makes and models. New models emerge very frequently. These phones are have different specification running on different types of customize operating systems.

- **Mobile operating systems:** There are various mobile OS available in market among which only a few OS are popular and used in most of the mobile devices. Forensic tools and examiners should be capable to examine all types of mobile OS and devices, which increase the challenges. Though forensics tools and software support well known mobile OS and handsets, sometimes it may not support customized OS and a new handset with modified hardware and firmware.

- **Mobile platform security features:** Most of the modern mobile phone have in-built advanced security features to protect the user data and privacy.
  - Biometric Lock (Fingerprint)
  - Pattern Lock
  - Password
  - PIN, PUK
  - PIN and Password for Apps
  - Data Encryption

4.2 Digital Forensic Process

Digital forensics and investigation is now a matured filed and has standardized process. The major steps of digital forensics as shown in Figure 2 is generally applicable in all types of cybercrimes investigation and well suited for social media forensics also with slightly different approach (Huber et al. 2011).

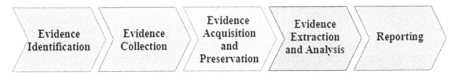

Figure 2: Digital forensics process.

4.2.1 Evidence Identification

First and foremost thing for the investigator is to understand "how" and "where" social media information is stored and how to retrieve such information. In today's connected world when every gadget and device are interconnected, it makes the job of investigator's complex to identify the exact source of evidence (Newman 2018). SNS is a distributed service provided over internet and the evidences are distributed, volatile and discontinuous in nature. In order to investigate any case involving SNS, investigators need to access the suspect's internet history, session details, emails, downloaded contents, cookies, etc.

In a general scenario, investigators raid the crime scene. As a standard practice they search and seize the potential source of evidence from the crime scene. However, it may not be always possible for the investigating officer to physically visit the crime scene. Most of the time investigators only know the link or URL of the social media account which is used for committing the crime. In such case there is no physical seizure of any gadgets or equipment. The whole investigation has to begin only with the SNS account detail or URL.

4.2.2 Evidence Collection

Evidence collection is the process of seizing a potential source of evidence from a crime scene. In case the investigator has the opportunity to visit the crime scene, he may find many potential sources of evidence to seize. Traditionally, the social media services are accessed through an Internet Browser or smartphone apps. Hence the potential source of information may be any device, e.g., Desktop, Laptop, Tablets, etc. It is important to maintain chain of custody while seizing the device. Chain of Custody basically records the sequence of events beginning from seizure of evidence, transfer, analysis and its disposition in chronological order. Every minute details of the crime scene and device details need to be recorded while collecting the evidence.

In many scenarios evidence needs to be collected manually by visiting the website, taking a screenshot, etc. Investigator may need to store the raw HTML file and take a printout. The raw HTML file needs to be preserved in forensically sound manner. However it is important to understand that storing a web page in raw HTML form may not store all the important metadata. Hence forensics tool may be required to store and preserve it. These tools also support establishing the authenticity of the evidence at any stage during the trail in court. Authenticity of any evidence is most important during the trial in court.

4.2.3 Evidence Acquisition and Preservation

Once the source of evidence is identified, the next step is evidence acquisition form the source device in forensically sound manner. Various specialized tools are available in the market to extract the social media artefacts from the device.

There are basically two types of data acquisitions:-

- **Live Acquisition:** If the device is found in running (switched ON) state, then the examiner needs to do live acquisition. Most of the digital gadgets have Primary Memory (RAM) and Secondary Memory (External Storage). Any gadget seized in running state, may have crucial evidence in primary memory. Primary memory are volatile in nature, once the gadgets are switched off, all the information will be lost. SNS artefacts are most likely to be present in primary memory. Hence it is important to do the data acquisition from primary memory. There are various open source as well as professional software available which can dump the data from running memory.

- **Offline Acquisition:** This method require system to be powered down and the storage media to be removed from the system. Specialized hardware and tools are available in the market which forensically create the image copy of the storage device. The entire process of data acquisition ensure that integrity of the evidence is maintained. Offline acquisition is comparatively easier than live acquisition.

Evidence acquisition from smartphone needs a different approach. Hardware architecture of smartphones are slightly different from laptop and desktop. It is important to understand the smartphone's Internal and External memory structure. The operating system and pre-installed apps are stored in the internal memory of the smartphone. External memory is called as extended or expandable memory, where user generally keeps images, videos or some other important files. Some moveable apps can also be installed on external memory, if supported by smartphone operating system. Several high-end smartphones also support cloud storage to meet the increased storage demand of users (Yusoff et al. 2017). The smartphones data acquisition is generally categorised in two categories:-

- **Logical Acquisition:** In this method the extraction tools communicate with device and try to extract the data. Logical extraction is a quick and easy method however, deleted files and data cannot be recovered using logical extraction. Logical extraction is also difficult if the device is locked or password protected. Some of the live data, e.g., call records, apps data, password of active social media like Twitter, Facebook can be retrieved using logical acquisition.

- **Physical Acquisition:** It collects all the data of device in bit-by-bit format. It's like cloning of the storage media. In addition to the logical extraction, physical extraction can help to retrieve deleted files, messages, pics, videos, GPS location tags, etc.

As per standard forensics practice, the forensics examiner should never do any analysis directly on the seized device or on the primary evidence. The examiner should always make a copy of the evidence file (secondary evidence). The analysis and examination shall be carried out on the secondary evidence.

4.2.4 Evidence Extraction and Analysis

Evidence extraction and analysis is a challenging task as the potential data related to SNS may be scattered in various form like network log, cookies, internet history etc. Additionally, suspects may also try to remove the evidence using anti-forensics techniques to obstruct the investigation process. Once the data is retrieved from target device, it can be analysed using forensics tools (Cusack and Son 2020). There are specialized tools available in the market, which are helpful to extract social media artefacts from the image file (forensics image file of the suspect device). Some of the standard tools used for social media analysis are shown in Table 1.

4.3 Social Media Metadata

In many cases it is possible that the investigators do not get access to the computer or devices used for social media crime. Physical access of the crime scene and gadgets are possible only when the criminal is in custody or the investigator has the warrant for search and seizure. However, that may not be the scenario all the time, hence the investigation has to proceed with the link and URI used in unsocial activity on SNS (Taylor et al. 2014).

The URI and social medial post's link contains much metadata. Metadata is a data about data. It provides additional information about the social media evidence. Generally metadata is hidden from the user and need to be analysed.

Table 1: Social media forensic tools.

Product name	Host operating system	Supported social media platforms
Belkasoft Evidence Center	*Windows*	*Facebook* *Flickr* *Foursquare* *Google+* *Instagram* *LinkedIn* *MySpace* *Pinterest* *Skype* *Telegram* *Tumblr* *Twitter* *Vkontakte*
BlackLight	*Windows* *Mac OS*	*Facebook* *Twitter* *LinkedIn* *Foursquare*
Internet Evidence Finder (IEF)	*Windows* *Linux* *Mac OS*	*Facebook* *Twitter* *LinkedIn* *MySpace* *Google+* *Foursquare* *Flickr*
Magnet AXIOM	*Windows*	*Facebook* *Twitter* *LinkedIn* *MySpace* *Google+* *Flickr*
UFED Cloud Analyzer	*Windows*	*Facebook* *Twitter* *LinkedIn* *Google+* *Skype* *Telegram* *Vkontakte* *Instagram* *OKCupid*

Twitter posts contain a plethora of metadata such as a tweet's unique ID, creation date, reply user id, geolocation (if enabled), timezone and many more as shown in Table 2 (X1 Twitter 2020). This metadata plays a significant role for the investigator. Similarly Facebook users are also assigned with a unique user ID which is hidden from the users. Any post or share on Facebook contains metadata like User ID, Sent Time, Message ID, etc. as shown in Table 3 (X1 Facebook 2020).

Table 2: Twitter metadata.

Metadata field	Description
created_at	UTC timestamp for tweet creation
user_id	The ID of the user of a tweet
Handle	User's screen name (different from user name)
retweet_id	The post ID of a retweet
retweet_user	The username of the user who retweeted
Reply	Indicates if this tweet is a reply
direct_message	Indicates if this tweet is a direct message
Hashtags	List of all hashtags in the tweet
Description	Up to 160 characters describing the tweet
geo_enabled	If the user has enabled geo-location (optional)
Place	Geo-location from where user tweeted from
Coordinates	Geo-location coordinates from where tweet is sent
in_reply_to_user_id	Unique id for the user that replied
profile_image_url	Location to a user's avatar file
recipient_id	Unique id of direct message recipient
recipient_screen_name	Display name of direct message receiver
screen_name	Display name for a user
sender_id	Unique id of direct message sender
Source	Application used to Tweet or direct message (i.e., from an iPhone or specific Twitter app)
time_zone	A user's time zone
utc_offset	Time between user's time zone and UTC time
follow_request_sent	Indicates request to follow the user
Truncated	If the post is truncated due to excessive length

4.4 Support From Social Media Service Providers

Having a handful of metadata information, the next step for the investigative agency is to collect evidence and further information from SNS service providers. Law enforcement agency should follow the standard procedure to collect information from service provider. Most of the SNS service providers has a dedicated legal team which provide the support to the law enforcement round the clock. While approaching the service providers the law enforcement agency must follow instructions provided by individual social media service providers.

4.5 Jurisdictional Issues

Jurisdiction is one of the most common and complex issues in social media forensics. Internet is not restricted to any specific geographical boundary whereas law is specific to geographical boundary and territory. Services provided through SNS are accessible

Table 3: Facebook metadata.

Metadata field	Description
Uri	Unified resource identifier of the subject item
fb_item_type	Identifies item as Wallitem, Newsitem, Photo, etc.
parent_itemnum	Parent item number-sub item are tracked to parent
thread_id	Unique identifier of a message thread
recipients	All recipients of a message listed by name
recipients_id	All recipients of a message listed by user id
album_id	Unique id number of a photo or video item
post_id	Unique id number of a wall post
application	Application used to post to Facebook (i.e., from an iPhone or social media client)
user_img	url where user profile image is located
user_id	Unique id of the poster/author of a Facebook item
account_id	Unique id of a user's account
user_name	Display name of poster/author of a Facebook item
created_time	When a post or message was created
updated_time	When a post or message was revised/updated
To	Name of user whom a wall post is directed to
to_id	Unique id of user whom a wall post is directed to
Link	url of any included links
comments_num	Number of comments to a post
picture_url	url where picture is located

globally. The problem with social media investigation is that evidence are stored on cloud based platform located in foreign territory often in USA. The conventional policing method of search and seizure, simply do not apply in this circumstances. Most of the countries have "mutual assistance agreement" or "bilateral agreement". Under the bilateral agreement of treaty the law enforcement agency is able to seek the required information for investigation. It may also seek evidentiary data along with proof of authenticity, if require for prosecution.

While approaching the service provider for any support or evidence, the investigators should be extremely careful in drafting their legal documents. The legal documents should satisfy all the requirements as mentioned by the individual services providers. Many time service providers reject the request just because the legal verbiage is incorrect or it does not contain the desired text (Brunty and Helenek 2016).

4.5.1 Service Provider's Terms of Service (ToS)

Every SNS service provider has its own Terms of Service (ToS). Terms of service are the legal agreement between users and service providers. The terms of service not only affect the users but also include the limitation that what information may be collected and can be shared by the service provider to the external agency. Generally the term of services are written in favour of service provider and restrain what an outside investigator can effectively do.

Many time SNS service providers impose restrictions on the external agency from collecting any information from their websites by using any manual or automated tools without prior permission (by-means of a privacy policy). It's important to understand that in-case of any criminal investigation, if the investigator violate any terms of service, the offender's defense may try to use this as an opportunity to discredit the evidence. Hence, it is important for the investigator to have a thorough understanding of legal terms and conditions posed by service provider before initiating the investigation. Some of the major guidelines, terms and conditions by popular social media service providers are discussed below:-

i. ***Twitter***: Twitter does not disclose non-public information about the users to law enforcement agencies except in a case with valid court order through legal process. The entire process is cumbersome and time taking process, however Twitter does have emergency disclosure. The law enforcement agency can submit an emergency disclosure request through Twitter's legal request submission site. The law enforcement agency must include the following information while requesting the account information (Help.twitter.com 2020).

- Include the Twitter @username and URL of the subject Twitter account in question (e.g., https://twitter.com/twittersafety (@twittersafety) or an account's unique, public user identification number or UID).
- And/or include the valid Periscope username and URL (e.g., @twittersafety and https://periscope.tv/twittersafety).
- Provide details about what specific information is requested (e.g., basic subscriber information) and its relationship to your investigation;
  - ○ **NOTE:** Please ensure that the information you seek is not publicly available (e.g., Tweets that are not protected).
- Include a **valid official email address** (e.g., name@agency.gov)
- Be issued on law enforcement letterhead.

ii. ***Facebook***: Facebook discloses the information to the law enforcement agency as per the terms of service and applicable law. Law enforcement agency need to have Mutual Legal Assistance Treaty or letter rogatory to compel the disclosure. Facebook need following basic minimum information for processing the request (Safety Center 2020).

- The name of the issuing authority and agent, email address from a law-enforcement domain, and direct contact phone number.
- The email address, phone number (+XXXXXXXXXX), user ID number (http://www.facebook.com/profile.php?id=1000000XXXXXXXX) or username (http://www.facebook.com/username) of the Facebook profile.

iii. ***Instagram***: Instagram stores various types of information for different time periods (Help.instagram.com 2020). All requests must be made with particularity, including the specific data categories requested and date limitations for the request, as well as:

- The name of the issuing authority and agent, email address from a law enforcement domain, and a direct contact phone number.

- The username of the Instagram account in question on the relevant date and details regarding specific information requested and its relationship to your investigation. Usernames are not static and they are unable to process requests that do not include the relevant date combined with the username.

iv. *WhatsApp*: Whatsapp discloses account records solely in accordance with their terms of service and applicable law. Additionally, they assess whether requests are consistent with internationally recognized standards including human rights, due process, and the rule of law. A Mutual Legal Assistance Treaty request or letter rogatory may be required to compel the disclosure of the contents of an account (WhatsApp.com, 2020). All requests must identify requested records with particularity and include the following:

- The name of the issuing authority, badge or ID number of responsible agent, email address from a law enforcement domain and direct contact phone number

- The WhatsApp account number, including any applicable country codes

v. *Youtube*: Youtube is one of the popular platform for sharing video content. Many time the platform is misused for sharing derogatory videos. Youtube follow legal procedure and need court order for any complain under trademark, defamation, counterfeit and other legal complaints. The law enforcement agency need to provide video link (URL) for the investigation (Support.google.com 2020).

There are many social media platforms available on internet and almost all of them support the law enforcement agency in case of any legal complaint or cybercrime investigation. However the law enforcement agency should be aware that SNS service providers maintain the data and logs for specific time period. It's based on country specific law and organizational policy. Legal procedure is cumbersome and takes its own time. Overall, if the entire process exceeds the maximum time period of data retention by the service provider, law enforcement agency may not be able to get any evidential information. Hence the law enforcement agency should approach as early as possible. As a precautionary measure, the law enforcement agency can give an early request for data retention for the suspected accounts.

4.6 Reporting

Reporting is the last stage of the investigation. The examiner need to present the facts found in analysis in context to the given case. The investigator may need to support his analysis with the supporting documents received from SNS service provider (email communication or specific report received). The report is the final outcome of the whole investigation which has to be presented in the court. Hence the report should be very clear and precise. Authenticity of the report is most important.

5. Conclusion

In conclusion, there are many tools available in the market which are capable to extract and examine the social media artefacts from various electronic gadgets. However, the evidence collected from electronic gadgets may not be sufficient for the social media investigations. Support from the social media service providers to the law enforcement agencies is most vital. There is no global cyber law. Complex jurisdiction issue, mutual assistance agreement or bilateral agreement are some of the major obstacles in investigation. Fake profiles, highly encrypted and anonymous communication are some of the major cause of concern. Preserving the individual privacy without compromising the national security is a strategic decision which country need to take. The threats created by social media platform are serious and there are no simple technological solution. It can be addressed only with the support of policy, legal and technology framework.

References

Arshad, H., Aman Jantan, A. and Omolara, E. 2019. Evidence collection and forensics on social networks: research challenges and directions. Digital Investigation 28: 126–38. https://doi.org/10.1016/j. diin.2019.02.001.

Baccarella, C. V., Wagner, T. F., Kietzmann, J. H. and Mccarthy, I. P. 2018. Social media? Its serious! Understanding the dark side of social media. European Management Journal 36(4): 431–38. https://doi.org/10.1016/j.emj.2018.07.002.

Brunty and Helenek, K. 2016. Social Media Investigation for Law Enforcement. London: Routledge.

Cusack, B. and Son, J. 2020. Evidence examination tools for social networks. Research Online. Accessed February 18, 2020. https://ro.ecu.edu.au/adf/109/.

Guidelines for Law Enforcement. Twitter. 2020. Twitter. Accessed February 10, 2020. https://help.twitter. com/en/rules-and-policies/twitter-law-enforcement-support.

Huber, M., Mulazzani, M., Leithner, M., Schrittwieser, S., Gilbert Wondracek, S. G. and Weippl. 2011. Social snapshots: digital forensics for online social networks. Social snapshots | Proceedings of the 27th Annual Computer Security Applications Conference, December 1, 2011. https://dl.acm. org/doi/10.1145/2076732.2076748.

Information for Law Enforcement Authorities. 2020. Safety Center. Accessed February 10, 2020. https:// www.facebook.com/safety/groups/law/guidelines/.

Instagram Help Center. 2020. Information for Law Enforcement | Instagram Help Center. Accessed February 12, 2020. https://help.instagram.com/494561080557017.

Key Facebook Metadata Fields Lawyers and EDiscovery Professionals Need to Be Aware Of. 2011. X1, October 11, 2011. https://www.x1.com/2011/10/11/key-facebook-metadata-fields-lawyers-and-ediscovery-professionals-need-to-be-aware-of/.

Key Twitter Metadata Fields Lawyers and EDiscovery Professionals Need to Be Aware Of. 2011.X1, October 6, 2011. https://www.x1.com/2011/10/06/key-twitter-metadata-fields-lawyers-and-ediscovery-professionals-need-to-be-aware-of/.

Krishna, P. V., Gurumoorthy, S. and Obaidat, M. S. 2019. Social Network Forensics, Cyber Security, and Machine Learning. Singapore: Springer Singapore.

Legal Support Contact Information - YouTube Help. Google. Google. Accessed February 15, 2020. https://support.google.com/youtube/answer/6154232?hl=en.

Newman, M. C. 2018. Evidence in social networks. The Nature and Use of Ecotoxicological Evidence, 2018, 219–43. https://doi.org/10.1016/b978-0-12-809642-0.00008-x.

Taylor, M., Haggerty, J., Gresty, D., Almond, P. and Berry, T. 2014. Forensic investigation of social networking applications. Network Security. Elsevier Advanced Technology, November 9, 2014. https://www.sciencedirect.com/science/article/pii/S1353485814701126.

WhatsApp FAQ - Information for Law Enforcement Authorities. WhatsApp.com. Accessed February 20, 2020. https://faq.whatsapp.com/en/general/26000050.

Yusoff, M. N., Dehghantanha, A. and Mahmod, R. 2017. Forensic investigation of social media and instant messaging services in firefox OS. Contemporary Digital Forensic Investigations of Cloud and Mobile Applications, 41–62. https://doi.org/10.1016/b978-0-12-805303-4.00004-6.

Part 3
Cyber Security

9

Bayesian Networks and Cyber-Crime Investigations

Richard E Overill[1,]* and *Kam-Pui Chow*[2]

1. Introduction

This chapter discusses the use of Bayesian networks (BNs) in analysing and understanding cyber-crimes from a digital forensics perspective. The next section introduces Bayes theorem and the notion of conditional probability, followed by a description of the construction and operation of Bayesian networks. The following sections demonstrate the application of Bayesian networks to a number of actual cyber-crimes from the Hong Kong Special Administrative Region, illustrating the various quantitative measures, such as posterior probabilities and likelihood ratios, that can be obtained from them. The sensitivity of these measures to variations in the parameters associated with the Bayesian networks is also discussed, and their utility in constructing economically near-optimal triage schemes is emphasised. In the final section, the contributions that Bayesian network analysis can offer to both the digital forensic investigation process and the juridical legal process are summarised.

2. Bayes' Theorem and Bayesian Networks

Bayesian methods are based on the conditional probability theorem of Revd. Thomas Bayes in his renowned posthumously published essay (Bayes 1763) and have recently been cited as one approach to gaining quantitative traction in conveying degrees of (un)certainty in digital forensic results (Casey 2018). Bayesian networks (BNs) were developed by Judea Pearl and are used to construct probabilistic inference and reasoning models (Pearl 1982, 1988). A BN is defined as a directed acyclic graph (DAG) with nodes and arcs. Nodes represent variables, events or evidence. An arc between two nodes represents a conditional dependency between the nodes. Arcs

---
[1] King's College London.
[2] University of Hong Kong.
* Corresponding author: richard.overill@kcl.ac.uk

are unidirectional and feedback loops are not permitted. Because of this feature, it is straightforward to identify a parent-child relationship or the probability dependency between two nodes.

A Bayesian network operates on conditional probabilities. For example, if the occurrence of some evidence E is dependent on a hypothesis H, the joint probability that both H and E occurred is given by:

$$\Pr(H,E) = \Pr(H).\Pr(E|H)$$

According to the multiplicative law of probabilities, which expresses commutativity, if H is relevant for E, then E is also relevant for H. The corresponding joint probability expression is given by:

$$\Pr(H,E) = \Pr(H).\Pr(E|H) = \Pr(E).\Pr(H|E)$$

Hence:

$$\Pr(E|H) = \Pr(E).\Pr(H|E) / \Pr(H)$$

which is a form of the celebrated Bayes' Theorem. From a statistical point of view, it denotes the conditional probability of E if H is true. This is also referred as the likelihood of E given H. It denotes the degree of belief that E will occur given a situation where H is true. $\Pr(H|E)$ is the posterior probability, i.e., the probability that when E is detected H has actually occurred. $\Pr(H)$ denotes the prior probability of H at a stage where the evidence is not yet presented. $\Pr(E)$ is the prior probability of E, which is sometimes referred to as a normalizing constant. Therefore, the above expression can be formalized as:

likelihood = posterior probability × normalizing constant/hypothesis prior probability

Since the likelihood is proportional to the posterior probability, a larger posterior probability denotes a higher likelihood. In the evidentiary context, it also means that the greater the evidence supporting the hypothesis, the more likely that the hypothesis is true.

For a hypothesis (or proposition, or claim) H, with a single mutually exclusive and exhaustive alternative $\bar{H}$, and recovered evidence E, Bayes Theorem can be conveniently expressed as:

$$\frac{\Pr(H\,|\,E)}{\Pr(\bar{H}\,|\,E)} = \frac{\Pr(H)}{\Pr(\bar{H})} \cdot \frac{\Pr(E\,|\,H)}{\Pr(E\,|\,\bar{H})}$$

where the left-hand side quotient represents the posterior odds ratio, and on the right-hand side the first quotient represents the prior odds ratio while the second quotient represents the likelihood ratio. This simple expression can be generalised in a straightforward manner to situations involving multiple mutually exclusive and exhaustive alternative hypotheses.

A Bayesian network has three elementary connections between its nodes that represent three different types of probability distributions (Figure 1). For a serial connection, if B's evidential state is unknown, then A and C are dependent on each other. In other words, there is an evidential influence between A and C if the evidential state of B is unknown. However, if B's state is known, then A and C are independent of each other; this means that A and C are conditionally independent of each other

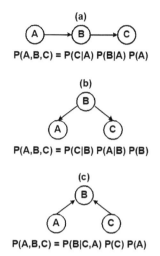

(a)

P(A,B,C) = P(C|A) P(B|A) P(A)

(b)

P(A,B,C) = P(C|B) P(A|B) P(B)

(c)

P(A,B,C) = P(B|C,A) P(C) P(A)

Figure 1: The three elementary connections in Bayesian networks.

given B. In a diverging connection, the same conditional independence is observed for A and C, i.e., if B's state is known, then A and C are independent. In a converging connection, if B's state is unknown, then A and C are independent. In other words, unless the state of B is known, A and C can influence each other.

These three elementary connections represent the different ways in which evidence may be transmitted through a Bayesian network variable. Figure 1 illustrates the three elementary Bayesian network connections.

3. Cyber-crime Investigations

3.1 Illicit BitTorrent Uploading

One of the main capabilities of computer technology is the sharing of information between different computers through computer networks, such as private network or the Internet. The meaning of information sharing does not limit to sharing of files, it also includes the providing of web contents to a large number of computers, fostering of videos to various client computers simultaneously, etc. One popular file sharing tool is BitTorrent (BT) which was developed by Cohen (2003).

In order to sharing out a file by using BT network, the owner of the file (or known as the "initial" uploader) has to perform a series of computer operations. These operations are indeed the basis of the digital traces that a digital forensic analyst would look for. It is therefore necessary to understand the operations in uploader or downloader. The operation of a BT network is as follows:

a) An uploader who wants to share data, for example, a motion picture, must firstly store the digitized format of the motion picture at a computer (i.e., the seeder computer);

b) The uploader thereafter has to create a file with the extension.torrent. The.torrent file stores information about the URL (i.e., the web address) of the tracker servers (the number of tracker server can be one or more), the location of files stored in the seeder computer (this can be an indication to identify the seeder computer), creation date of the.torrent file, hash values of the files, etc. Tracker servers are responsible for helping downloaders find each other, in particular the "seeder" (i.e., the seeder computer). It is not the responsibility of tracker servers to keep track of file contents at each peers;

c) The uploader must then find a way to publish the created.torrent file to enable downloaders to locate the seeder computer and to download the file. Usually, the.torrent file is published by way of newsgroup messages;

d) Aside from placing the.torrent file on newsgroups, the uploader has to activate the created.torrent file (or sometimes called seeding). By such, the uploader has to connect the seeder computer with the tracker server through the torrent file. The tracker server, when connected, will examine the information contained in the.torrent file and will communicate with the connecting party. When the tracker server knows the seeder computer has already stored with the questioned files in 100%. The tracker server will regard the computer as a "seeder" of the BT network. Indeed, for the actual downloading to take place in a BT network, it is required to have at least one peer that already has the whole file for others to download. At this stage, the tracker server will ledger the IP address of the seeder for subsequent downloader;

e) The remaining parts are activities conducted by downloader. Suppose there is a computer user A, who wants to download the motion picture. Downloader A has to locate the.torrent file from, for instance, newsgroup forums and then download it to his/her computer;

f) Thereafter, downloader A has to activate the.torrent file. By such, A's computers will call or activate related BitTorrent program and establish connections with the tracker servers according to the information contained in the.torrent file. After establishing connections, the tracker servers will return IP addresses of peers that have been connected earlier. If A's computer is the first downloading peer, then the returned IP address would be the IP address of the initial seeder (i.e., the IP address of the seeder computer);

g) After making connections, the tracker servers will retrieve download status and corresponding percentage of downloaded data from A's computer. The BitTorrent program at A's computer will then establish connections according to the peers' IP address returned by the tracker servers (if A is the 1st comer, then it will connect the initial seeder, i.e., the seeder computer);

h) The actual downloading process will then take place at this stage. Meanwhile, suppose there is another user B, who wants to get the same motion picture. B has to locate and download the.torrent file first. B also needs to activate the.torrent file in order to communicate with the tracker servers;

i) After receiving peers' information (IP addresses of existing peers, download percentage, etc.) from the tracker servers, the BitTorrent program residing at B's computer would then establish connections with the seeder and computer A by their IP addresses;

j) Thereafter, data segments of targeted files will be downloaded both from the seeder and A. A main principle in BT downloading is that data segments downloaded to A may not be the same as those downloaded to B. Therefore, B may also contribute its downloaded segments to A for those A does not have. Therefore, the more peers appear in the network, the faster the seeder finishes files uploading. In other words, the overall uploading bandwidth of the network is escalated when the number of peers joining the BT network increases.

There was a criminal case concerning online distribution of 3 pirated movies using BitTorrent. It took place in May 1995 in Hong Kong. According to the Reasons for Verdict (2005), defendant of the case was alleged using his own computer to distribute pirated movie to others through the Internet using the BitTorrent program. It is ruled that the defendant was in possession of the optical discs of the movies. To achieve the distribution act, the defendant copied the movies from the optical discs onto his computer. He then used the BitTorrent program to create three torrent files from the movie files. Torrent file contains meta-date of the source file (i.e., the movie file) and the URL of the Tracker server. It can facilitate other Internet users to join the Peer-to-Peer network.

To make it available for other users, the defendant sent the torrent files to various newsgroup forums. He thereafter activated the created torrent files on his computer, which rendered his computer connected to the Tracker server. When connected, the Tracker server would query the computer with regard to the meta contents of the torrent files. The Tracker server would then return a peer list showing existing IP addresses on the network and the percentage of the target file existing on each peer machine.

Since the defendant's computer had complete copies of the movies, hence the Tracker server would label it as seeder computer. Finally, the defendant maintained the connection between the Tracker server and his computer so that other peers could download the movies from his computer.

One of the first attempts to apply a Bayesian network quantitatively to the analysis of an actual digital forensic investigation was made by Chow and co-workers using a Bayesian network model of an illicit peer-to-peer (BitTorrent) uploading case from the Hong Kong S.A.R. (Kwan et al. 2008). The prior probabilities were taken to be strictly non-informative and the requisite conditional probabilities (likelihoods) were elicited from a survey of 31 domain experts. This model yielded a posterior probability of *ca.* 92.5% in favour of the hypothesis that an illicit upload had indeed occurred given that all 18 anticipated items of digital evidence were recovered. A credible alternative hypothesis was not available for this case against which to compare the result. However, it nevertheless corresponds to a Likelihood Ratio of *ca.* 12.3 in favour of the prosecution hypothesis. In subsequent studies, the sensitivity of this result to the absence of one (*ca.* 0.08%), two (2.0%) or more items of digital evidence was found to be consistently small, while its sensitivity to uncertainties in the conditional probability (likelihood) values populating the nodes of the Bayesian network was also inconsiderable at *ca.* 0.25% (Overill et al. 2010). The Bayesian network for this case was subsequently refined and simplified by the group (Tse et al. 2012). Figure 2 shows the connections for the BitTorrent Bayesian network.

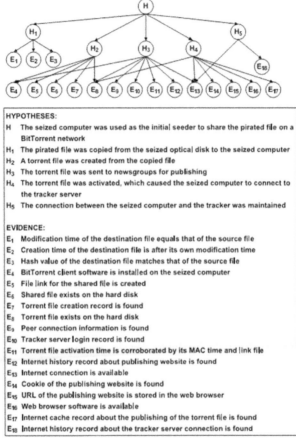

Figure 2: The BitTorrent Bayesian network.

3.2 Internet Auction Fraud

Internet auction fraud has become a major threat. According to the report (2008) of the Internet Crime Complaint Center, the median dollar loss per complaint of Internet fraud was USD 931 in 2008 in the USA and the total dollar loss was USD 264.60 million. During 2008, there were 275,284 received complaints in the USA, which includes auction fraud, non-delivery, and credit/debit card fraud, computer intrusions, spam, and child pornography. Internet auction fraud was the most reported offense, which comprised 25.5% of all complaints and covered 16.3% of the reported total dollar loss. The average median dollar loss per Internet auction fraud complaint is USD 610.

Sakurai and Yokoo (2003) concluded that remaining anonymous was a factor in Internet fraud and that the existence of indivisible bids caused difficulty in matching supply and demand. This was because a seller or a buyer might submit a false-name-bid by pretending to be a potential buyer or seller. In this way they may be able to manipulate the supply-and-demand chain. Chae et al. (2007) confirmed the findings of Sakurai and Yokoo and concluded that online auction fraud was successful through the information asymmetry and anonymity problems.

According to the study of Ku et al. (2007), fraud may happen to either the buyer or the seller, but the buyer is more easily targeted as a victim than a seller. Due to the nature of the Internet auction, it was found that 89.0% of all seller-buyer pairs conducted just one transaction during the time period of the study. At most, there were four transactions between a seller-buyer pair. This means that the repeated transaction rate of the same seller-buyer pair is lower than 2% (Ku et al. 2007). This transaction rate is an indication of whether or not the transactions between a sell-buyer pair are normal. If the transaction rate is significantly higher than 2%, it indicates that the transactions between a seller-buy pair might be suspicious, for example they may be shilling or shielding (Ku et al. 2007).

As observed by Kobayashi and Ito (2008), a common trick in Internet auction fraud was for the fraudsters to pretend to carry out honest dealings in the early period of using the auction, but once they became trusted they committed fraud. Having studied the behavior of fraudsters in Internet fraud, Ochaeta (2008) concluded that these criminals had tried to establish a good enough reputation prior to their imminent fraudulent acts, which in result, rendered their reputation building process different from that of legitimate users. Ochaeta (2008) found that these fraudsters attempted to gain as much one-time profit as possible as quickly as practicable. If their reputation fabrication process can be discovered, the fraudsters can be identified (Ochaeta 2008). The patterns used by these fraudsters to build their reputations are:

a) selling or buying numerous cheap items from users with a good reputation;

b) selling or buying moderate value or expensive items from accomplices; and

c) the process usually takes place over a short period of time.

In order to build up a reputation over a short period of time, most Internet auction fraudsters tend to sell a lot of low priced or cheap products. These acts take place at the beginning of their fraudulent auction lives. Simultaneously, fraudsters also try to bid inexpensive items from users with good reputation scores. This is done for the purpose of establishing a favorable reputation score through numerous legitimate transactions.

278 cases in Hong Kong were statistically examined in order to reveal the characteristics of Internet auction fraud regarding fake goods. The cases were complaints lodged to the Hong Kong Customs & Excise Department on selling of fake goods on Internet auction sites. The Customs & Excise Department is the prime law enforcement agency in Hong Kong responsible for the protection of intellectual property rights. In these 278 cases, we noted the following characteristics for fraudsters selling counterfeit or faked goods on Internet auction sites:

a) The fake goods were sold at unreasonably low costs at about only 10% of legitimate products;

b) About two-thirds of them (180 out of 278) offered to sell those goods within 7 days of setting up their accounts;

c) They have multiple auction accounts that do not carry high trust values or reputation scores of 8 or more out of 10;

d) They are short lived (less than 10 days) and tend to switch to other auction accounts before expiry of the auction period;

e) Many varieties of items (more than 5) belonging to different categories are sold, e.g., a mixture of watches, mobile phone, footwear, sportswear, etc.

From 20 typical cases of internet auction fraud prosecuted in the Hong Kong S.A.R., Bayesian networks for both the prosecution and the defence cases were created and the likelihood ratio (LR) of the two alternative explanations for the existence of the recovered digital evidence was computed to be 164,000 in favour of the prosecution hypothesis (Kwan et al. 2010). This finding may be interpreted as providing "very strong support" for the prosecution's hypothesis (ENSFI 2015). The conditional probabilities required for the BN were sourced from a survey of the members of the Hong Kong Customs & Excise digital investigation team involved in the prosecutions. While LRs are generally regarded as the preferred way to present forensic findings when at least two mutually exclusive and exhaustive hypotheses are available, it should nevertheless also be mentioned that there has been considerable debate regarding the possible (mis)interpretation of LRs potentially resulting in misleading conclusions being drawn (SciJus 2017).

Because there were no detailed judgments on these 20 prosecuted cases, interviews with specialists in this field were conducted in order to identify the forensic hypotheses and related digital evidence for online auction frauds. According to Cleman and Winkler (1987), five experts are sufficient for the aforementioned purposes. Therefore, three digital forensic examiners from the Computer Forensic Laboratory of the Hong Kong Customs & Excise Department were interviewed. The experts have performed numerous forensic examinations to online auction fraud cases. In addition, two digital crime investigators from the Intellectual Property Investigation Bureau of the Hong Kong Customs & Excise Department were also selected and interviewed. The selected investigators are chartered to perform criminal investigations to online auction fraud cases, in particular selling of counterfeit goods by online auction sites. From the interviews and discussions with the selected experts, the following three forensic hypotheses for online auction crime were recognised. These hypotheses are:

1. Uploading of auction related material (e.g., images or descriptions of the items) has been performed;
2. Manipulation of the corresponding auction item (e.g., price adjustment) has taken place;
3. Communication between the seller and the buyer related to the auctioned fake item (e.g., email, instant messaging) has occurred.

These three sub-hypotheses, which substantiate the overall prosecution hypothesis that an online auction fraud crime has been committed in the 20 prosecuted cases, are supported by 13 distinct evidential traces, again obtained from the responsible digital forensic examiners and digital crime investigators, as shown in the graphical representation given in Figure 3.

This investigation model does not of itself substantiate the whole prosecution case. The auctioned item also has to be procured physically by the investigator and to be examined by the trademark owner in order to ascertain whether or not the item is counterfeit in nature.

In order to evaluate the relevance of the digital evidential traces, another set of hypotheses and digital evidence representing the defense scenario has also been

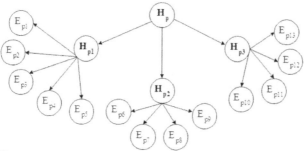

Hypotheses

H_p : The seized computer has been used as transaction tool for the auction of the fake item

H_{p1} : Uploading of auction material related to the fake item has been performed

H_{p2} : Manipulation of the corresponding auction item has taken place

H_{p3} :Communication between the seller and the buyer on the fake auction item has occurred

Evidence

E_{p1} : Material of the auctioned fake item (e.g. image file, text files, etc.) was found on the seized computer

E_{p2} : Seller's account login record was retrieved from auction site

E_{p3} : Meta-data of file found on the seized computer matched with that found on the auction site

E_{p4} : IP address assigned to the seized computer matched with that which performed the data transfer

E_{p5} : Internet history cached contents for transferring the auctioned fake item material was found on the seized computer

E_{p6} : Seller's account login record was retrieved from auction site

E_{p7} : IP address assigned to the seized computer matched with that logged into the auction site

E_{p8} : Editing of an auction item has occurred (e.g. price adjustment) on the auction site

E_{p9} : Enhanced material of an auction item (e.g. image file, text file, etc.) was found on the seized computer

E_{p10} : Messages from auction site related to an auction item were found on the seized computer

E_{p11} : Messages to/from the buyer related to an auction item were found on the seized computer

E_{p12} : Address book containing covert investigator's email account was found on the seized computer

E_{p13} : IP address assigned to the seized computer matched with that which performed the email communication

Figure 3: Graphical representation for prosecution hypotheses and related evidential traces.

established. Although the root hypotheses of the two models appear to be the same, they are in fact different due to the two different sets of supporting sub-hypotheses representing the prosecution and defense scenarios respectively. In both models, the same set of evidential traces is used. Figure 4 presents the defense's hypotheses and their associated evidential traces.

Although the forensic hypotheses and related digital evidence were identified, it is always difficult for digital forensic examiner and digital crime investigators to express their knowledge and beliefs in probabilistic values to the recognized entities. To this end, the probabilities elicitation model proposed by Boondao (2008) is adopted to elicit probabilities from the experts. Indeed, the Boondao (2008) model was stemmed from the Keeney and von Winterfeldt (1991) approach, which was based on the Bayesian theory of probability and decision analytic models that involved techniques for eliciting and using expert judgments. A process which consists of six steps has to be applied in order to put Boondao (2008) model into practice. These steps are:

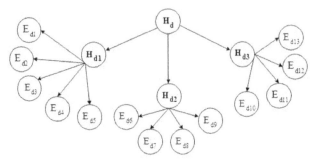

Hypotheses

H_d : The seized computer has been used as transaction tool for the auction of the fake item

H_{d1} : Auction material related to the fake item was downloaded from the auction site

H_{d2} : Manipulation of a non-fake auction item has taken place

H_{d3} :Communication between the seller and the buyer on a non-fake auction item has occurred

Evidence

E_{d1} : Material of the auctioned fake item (e.g. image file, text files, etc.) was found on the seized computer

E_{d2} : Seller's account login record was retrieved from auction site

E_{d3} : Meta-data of file found on the seized computer matched with that found on the auction site

E_{d4} : IP address assigned to the seized computer matched with that which performed the data transfer

E_{d5} : Internet history cached contents for transferring the auctioned fake item material was found on the seized computer

E_{d6} : Seller's account login record was retrieved from auction site

E_{d7} : IP address assigned to the seized computer matched with that logged into the auction site

E_{d8} : Editing of an auction item has occurred (e.g. price adjustment) on the auction site

E_{d9} : Enhanced material of an auction item (e.g. image file, text file, etc.) was found on the seized computer

E_{d10} : Messages from auction site related to an auction item were found on the seized computer

E_{d11} : Messages to/from the buyer related to an auction item were found on the seized computer

E_{d12} : Address book containing covert investigator's email account was found on the seized computer

E_{d13} : IP address assigned to the seized computer matched with that which performed the email communication

Figure 4: Graphical representation for prosecution hypotheses and related evidential traces.

1. Identification and selection of the issues relating to the case. This is achieved through a broad review on the online auction fraud cases. Opinions from investigators who are engaging in this field are also considered.

2. Selection of experts. In the current case which involves selling of counterfeit goods on online auction sites, three digital forensic examiners and two digital crime investigators from the Hong Kong Customs & Excise Department were selected. These experts are either digital forensic examiners or digital crime investigators responsible for the forensic analyses and investigations regarding selling counterfeit goods by online auction sites.

3. Identification of forensic hypotheses and supporting evidence for both the prosecution and defense scenarios. In this process, interviews and discussions are conducted with the selected experts in order to define the forensic hypotheses and their relating evidence, which are going to be elicited. A detailed description on this part is given in Section 3.4.1.

4. Preparing for elicitation. After identifying the hypotheses and evidence that are required to be elicited, the selected experts are given seminar in concepts of probability assessment and elicitation methods.

5. Performing the elicitation. Interviews with the experts are conducted. From the interviews, the probabilistic values and the conditional probability tables for the hypotheses and evidence are constructed.

6. Analysis of the elicitation. After the assignment of probabilities by individual experts, the elicitations are analysed in order to obtain comparable probability distributions over the relevant event or quantity for each expert. To achieve this, each expert's probability distributions are aggregated and then taking the average of overall distributions.

After the elicitation of probability distributions for the forensic hypotheses and related evidence, it is time to construct the Bayesian networks for the prosecution and defense cases.

3.3 Yahoo! Email Leak

Bascuas (2008) gave a brief summary on the Yahoo! Case. Alone in his office in Changsha, Hunan, late on the night of April 20, 2004, Chinese journalist Shi Tao sent an e-mail using his personal Yahoo! China account to a Taiwanese colleague in New York City. The e-mail summarized a government document warning against disruptive commemorations on the upcoming fifteenth anniversary of the Tiananmen Square massacre and directing the media to discourage such demonstrations. Two days later, the Beijing State Security Bureau demanded Yahoo! Holdings (Hong Kong) Limited to produce identifying information, login times, and e-mail contents for the account Mr. Shi had used. The notice stated that the information pertained to an investigation into the provision of state secrets to foreign entities. Yahoo! Holdings (Hong Kong) Limited complied the demand. Seven months later, state police arrested Mr. Shi on a street near his new home in Taiyuan, Shanxi. They transported him 667 miles south to Changsha, where he was imprisoned. About a month later, China charged Mr. Shi with the crime of "providing state secrets to foreign entities." At his trial on March 11, 2005, Mr. Shi did not contest the charge, but argued that his disclosure did not involve "special serious circumstances," a contention the court rejected. The court imposed a sentence of ten years in prison because Mr. Shi admitted his guilt and because his crime did not cause serious harm. Mr. Shi is scheduled to be released from Chishan Prison on November 24, 2014.

Months after, Shi Tao's authorized representative in Hong Kong lodged a complaint to the Privacy Commissioner of the Office of Privacy Commissioner for Personal Data. That complaint alleged that Yahoo! Hong Kong has breached the Hong Kong Personal Data (Privacy) Ordinance by disclosing subscriber's personal data to the Chinese authorities. The Privacy Commissioner commenced an investigation. In the Office of the Privacy Commissioner for Personal Data (2007) the Commissioner concludes that an IP address on its own does not constitute personal data. He takes the view that an IP address is a specific machine address assigned by the ISP to the user's computer and is therefore unique to a specific computer. Therefore, an IP address *per se* does not meet the definition of personal data. The Commissioner further concludes that no safe conclusion can be drawn that the corresponding user information of that IP address belongs to a living individual as opposed to a corporate or unincorporated body or relates to a real as opposed to a fictitious individual. Accordingly, an IP address combined with the corresponding user information also does not meet the definition of personal data. Although an IP address is not viewed as personal data, it is one of the reasons for the conviction (First Instance Reasons for Verdict of the Changsha Intermediate People's Court of Hunan Province 2005).

The information provided by Yahoo! Holdings (Hong Kong) Limited to the Beijing State Security Bureau are: user registration information, IP log-in information and certain email contents (Office of the Privacy Commissioner for Personal Data 2007). In the United States, neither the Constitution nor any federal law prevents the government from obtaining subscriber information and emails from an Internet company, just as China obtained Shi Tao's records from Yahoo! (Bascuas 2008).

The Changsha Intermediate People's Court of Hunan Province concluded that between approximately 7:00 p.m. on 20 April 2004 and approximately 2:00 a.m. the following morning, Shi Tao used his computer in his employer's office to send from his personal email account (huoyan-1989@yahoo.com.cn) some notes to the email account of Hong Zhesheng (caryhung@aol.com). Shi Tao secretly made those notes regarding the summary of the main contents of a top-secret document issued by the China government. Hong Zhesheng is one of the founders of the "Asia Democracy Foundation" located in New York, USA. He is also the editor-in-chief of the foreign web site "Democracy Forum" and the electronic publication "Democracy News." Shi Tao gave "198964" as the alias of the person who provided the document. He asked Hong Zhesheng to find a way to distribute it as quickly as possible without using Shi Tao's name (First Instance Reasons for Verdict of the Changsha Intermediate People's Court of Hunan Province 2005). When Shi Tao's file was sent to Hong Zhesheng's email account, various events took place. Figure 5 and Table 1 illustrate the relationships and linkages between different entities for the web-based email transmission in the Yahoo! case.

In a criminal case, the prosecution is required to prove the criminal's activities beyond reasonable doubt. For digital forensic analysis, the examiner is required to

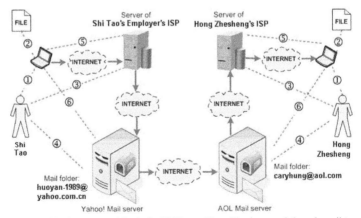

Figure 5: Relationships between entities in the Shi Tao to Hong Zhesheng web-based email transmission.

Table 1: Descriptions of the linkages between entities of email transmission shown in Figure 6.3.

① Shi Tao (Hong Zhesheng) controls the computer.
② The attached file exists on Shi Tao's (Hong Zhesheng's) computer.
③ Shi Tao's employer's (Hong Zhesheng's) ISP subscription record.
④ Shi Tao's (Hong Zhesheng's) Yahoo! (AOL) email account registration record.
⑤ The computer connects to the ISP.
⑥ The Web browser program displays Yahoo! (AOL) email web page.

retrieve digital evidence in order to reconstruct the series of activities showing that Shi Tao has or has not performed the activities in sending the email in question. These activities are:

1. Shi Tao was able to gain access to a computer, which was connected to the Internet.

2. A copy of the electronic file was stored in the computer.

3. In order to obtain Internet access, Shi Tao established a connection between his computer and the Internet Service Provider (ISP). In fact he used the dial-up account subscribed by his employer. The ISP checked the validity and authenticity of Shi Tao's employer's account, and then assigned an Internet Protocol (IP) address to Shi Tao's computer. Shi Tao's computer then recorded the assigned IP address and used it for subsequent Internet access. Internet data originated from or destined to Shi Tao's computer would go through the ISP's computer.

4. Shi Tao launched the Web browsing program. In order to connect to the email server of Yahoo! mail, Shi Tao input the Uniform Resource Locator (URL) or the web address of Yahoo! email in the Web browser program.

5. The Web browser program then sent an HTTP request to the Yahoo! email server. When the requested web page was retrieved, it was displayed by the Web browser program.

6. In order to login his email account, Shi Tao input the corresponding user name and password. According to the email subscription details, the Yahoo! mail server authenticated Shi Tao and allowed him to log in to his email folder.

7. Shi Tao composed the email, attached the file and input Hong Zhesheng's AOL email account. He then "clicked" the "send" button to send out the email together with the file as the attachment. Since Shi Tao used Web browser program to compile the email. The content of the email might be cached in Shi Tao's computer.

8. Yahoo! mail server then stored the email, including the attachment, and placed it into the message queue for sending it to Hong Zhesheng's AOL email server via SMTP.

In order to construct a Bayesian network to model this case, the prior probabilities were taken to be strictly non-informative and the conditional probabilities (likelihoods) were elicited by questioning a domain expert. The structure of the resulting Bayesian network comprised a root hypothesis node associated with 6 sub-hypothesis nodes, which in turn were linked to a total of 14 evidential (leaf) nodes (Kwan et al. 2011). With every anticipated item of digital evidence successfully recovered the posterior probability in favour of the prosecution hypothesis was *ca.*

97.2%. While a credible alternative hypothesis was not available for the case against which to compare this result, it does nevertheless correspond to a Likelihood Ratio of *ca.* 34.7 in favour of the prosecution's hypothesis, Furthermore, both single-parameter and multi-parameter sensitivity analyses of the Bayesian network resulted in minimal perturbations to that value (Kwan et al. 2011, Overill et al. 2012).

4. Cost-effective Investigation Models

In addition to providing quantitative estimates of the plausibility of alternative hypotheses (e.g., explanations proposed by the prosecution or defence sides) regarding how the recovered digital evidence came into existence, Bayesian networks also have the potentiality to expedite the digital investigation process itself by offering quantitative estimates of the importance (weight or probative value) of individual items of digital evidence in a particular criminal investigation.

The probative value of an individual item of digital evidence reflects the degree to which the presence of that item of evidence, if recovered, contributes to the overall plausibility of the hypothesis concerning the processes that created all of the recovered digital evidence. Perhaps the simplest method to achieve this is to take the difference in the posterior probabilities of the Bayesian network for the hypothesis in the presence and in the absence of that item of evidence (Overill and Chow 2018). A second method is to generate the so-called Tornado diagram for the Bayesian network, which shows the ordered range of variation in posterior probability due to each evidential item with respect to all the remaining items (Agena 2016). Another, still more sophisticated, approach is to use information theory: the Kullback–Leibler divergence of the Shannon entropy gives the information gain as a measure of the difference between the probability distributions for the Bayesian network with (P) and without (Q) that item of evidence:

$$D_{KL}(P \parallel Q) = \sum_i P_i \log \frac{P_i}{Q_i}$$

These three approaches lead to somewhat different orderings for the evidential weights of the BitTorrent case mentioned above (Schneps et al. 2018).

In digital forensic investigations it is commonly the case that the individual items of digital evidence may, at least to a first approximation, be considered conditionally independent of one another. Knowing the relative importance of each individual item of digital evidence in an investigation can then enable an efficient digital investigation scheme to be devised in which the most highly probative evidential items are searched for first, in order, relegating the items of lesser importance until later. If one or more of the anticipated items of high importance are not recovered the search may be de-prioritised or even abandoned; conversely, if all of the anticipated items of high importance are found then it may not be considered necessary to search for those items of lowest importance as the overall plausibility of the investigative hypothesis would not be sensibly improved by doing so.

Such investigative schemas can be termed cost-effective if additional information is available regarding the cost (in terms of fungible resources such as investigator time, equipment usage, etc.) of locating and recovering each item of evidence

(Overill et al. 2009); it is then possible to invoke basic concepts from the domain of economics such as return on investment (RoI), or conversely cost-benefit ratio (CBR), to rank the items of evidence in order of descending RoI or, equivalently, ascending CBR, to produce a near cost-optimal investigation strategy (Overill 2013).

5. Summary and Future Work

The use of BNs to quantify the plausibility of hypotheses relating to the creation of recovered digital evidential traces has been described and illustrated with actual examples of real world criminal cases from the Hong Kong S.A.R. In additional, the application of BNs to quantify the relative weights or strengths of individual evidential items in a particular investigation, using any one of several methods, leading to a cost-effective investigation strategy, has been outlined.

In terms of future research, comparative studies of the divergence of various more general forms of entropy, for example, the family of Sharma–Mittal entropies (Crupi et al. 2018) applied to the quantification of evidential weight or strength would be well motivated.

It is also worthwhile to note that the application of BNs has recently been extended to the much wider, but nevertheless related, context of the proliferation of software as a weapon (Silomon 2019).

References

Agena Ltd. 2016. AgenaRisk 7.0 User Manual, pp. 99–102.

Bascuas, R. J. 2008. Property and probable cause: the fourth amendment's principled protection of privacy. Rutgers Law Review 60: 575–645.

Bayes, T. 1763. An essay towards solving a problem in the doctrine of chances. Phil. Trans. Roy. Soc. Lond. 53: 370–418.

Casey, E. 2018. Clearly conveying digital forensic results. Digit. Invest. 24: 1–3.

Chae, M., Shim, S., Cho, H. and Lee, B. 2010. Empirical analysis of online auction fraud: credit card phantom transactions. Expert Systems with Applications 37: 2991–2999.

Clemen, R. T. and Winkler, R. L. 1987. Calibrating and combining precipitation forecasts. pp. 97–110. *In*: Viertl, R. (ed.). International Symposium on Probability and Bayesian Statistics. Springer-Verlag USA.

Cohen, B. 2003. Incentives build robustness in BitTorrent. pp. 68–72. *In*: Proceedings of the 1st Workshop on Economics of Peer-to-Peer Systems, Berkeley, CA, USA. Available online at: https://www.bittorrent.org/bittorrentecon.pdf.

Crupi, V., Nelson, J. D., Meder, B., Cevolani, G. and Tentori, K. 2018. Generalized information theory meets human cognition: introducing a unified framework to model uncertainty and information search. Cog. Sci. 42: 1410–1456.

ENSFI. 2015. ENFSI guideline for evaluative reporting in forensic science v3.0, p.17. Available online at: http://enfsi.eu/wp-content/uploads/2016/09/m1_guideline.pdf.

First Instance Reasons for Verdict. 2005. Changsha Intermediate People's Court of Hunan Province, Reasons for Verdict, First Trial Case No. 29, Changsha Intermediate Criminal Division One Court, Changsha, China. Available online at: HYPERLINK "www.pcpd.org.hk%20/english/publications/files/Yahoo_annex.pdf" www.pcpd.org.hk /english/publications/files/Yahoo_annex.pdf.

Keeney, R. L. and von Winterfeldt, D. 1991. Eliciting probabilities from experts in complex technical problems. IEEE Trans. Engg. Mgmt. 3: 191–201.

Kobayashi, M. and Ito, T. 2008. A transactional relationship visualization system in internet auctions. Studies in Comput. Intell. 110: 87–99.

Ku, Y., Chen, Y. and Chiu, C. 2007. A proposed data mining approach for internet auction fraud detection. pp. 238–243. *In*: Yang, C. C. et al. (eds.). Proceedings of the Pacific Asia Workshop on Intelligence and Security Informatics (PAISI 2007). Chengdu, China. Springer-Verlag, Berlin Heidelberg.

Kwan, M., Chow, K. P., Law, F. and Lai, P. 2008. Reasoning about evidence using Bayesian networks. Advances in Digital Forensics IV, Ch. 22: 275–289, Springer.

Kwan, M., Overill, R., Chow, K. -P., Silomon, J., Tse, H., Law, F. and Lai, P. 2010. Evaluation of evidence in internet auction fraud investigations. Advances in Digital Forensics VI, Ch. 7: 95–106, Springer.

Kwan, M., Overill, R., Chow, K. -P., Tse, H., Law, F. and Lai, P. 2011, Sensitivity analysis of digital forensic reasoning in Bayesian network models. Advances in Digital Forensics VII, pp. 213–244, Springer.

Ochaeta, K. 2008. Fraud detection for internet auctions: a data mining approach, Ph.D. Thesis, College of Technology Management, National Tsing-Hua University, Hsinchu, Taiwan.

Office of the Privacy Commissioner for Personal Data. 2007. The Disclosure of Email Subscriber's Personal Data by Email Service Provider to PRC Law Enforcement Agency, in report published under Section 48(2) of the Personal Data (Privacy) Ordinance RO7-3619, Hong Kong. Available online at: HYPERLINK "http://www.pcpd.org.uk/english/publications/files/Yahoo_e.pdf" www.pcpd.org.uk/english/publications/files/Yahoo_e.pdf.

Overill, R. E., Kwan, Y. K., Chow, K. P., Lai, K. Y. and Law, Y. W. 2009. A cost-effective digital forensics investigation model. pp. 193–202. *In*: Peterson, G. L. and Shenoi, S. (eds.). Advances in Digital Forensics V. Springer Verlag, Berlin Heidelberg, Germany.

Overill, R. E., Silomon, J. A. M., Kwan, M. Y. K., Chow, K. P., Law, F. Y. W. and Lai, P. K. Y. 2010. Sensitivity analysis of a Bayesian network for reasoning about digital forensic evidence. 4th International Workshop on Forensics for Future Generation Communication Environments, in Proc. 3rd International Conference on Human-Centric Computing, Cebu, Philippines, pp. 228–232, IEEE Press.

Overill, R. E., Zhang, E. P. and Chow, K. P. 2012. Multi-parameter sensitivity analysis of a Bayesian network from a digital forensic investigation. Proc. ADFSL Conference on Digital Forensics, Security and Law, Richmond, Virginia, USA.

Overill, R. E. 2013. Digital forensonomics—the economics of digital forensics. *In*: Blackwell, C. (ed.). Proceedings of the 2nd International Workshop on Cyberpatterns (Cyberpatterns 2013). Abingdon, UK.

Overill, R. E. and Chow, K. P. 2018. Measuring evidential weight in digital forensic investigations: a role for Bayesian networks in digital forensic triage. Advances in Digital Forensics XIV, pp. 3–10, Springer.

Pearl. J. 1982. Reverend Bayes on inference engines: a distributed hierarchical approach. Proc. Natl. Conf. on A.I. (AAAI'82), pp. 133–136. Available online at: https://aaai.org/Papers/AAAI/1982/AAAI82-032.pdf.

Pearl, J. 1988. Probabilistic Reasoning in Intelligent Systems, Morgan Kaufmann.

Reasons for Verdict. 2005. Magistrates' Court at Tuen Mun, Hong Kong Special Administrative Region v. Chan Nai Ming, TMCC 1268/2005, Hong Kong, China. Available online at: HYPERLINK "http://www.hklii.hk/hk/jud/en/hksc/2005/TMCC001268A%202005.html" www.hklii.hk/hk/jud/en/hksc/2005/TMCC001268A 2005.html.

Sakurai, Y. and Yokoo, M. 2003. A false-name-proof double auction protocol for arbitrary evaluation values. pp. 329–336. *In*: Rosenschein, J. S. et al. (eds.). Proceedings of the 2nd International Joint Conference on Autonomous Agents and Multiagent Systems (AAMAS'03). Melbourne, Australia. ACM Press.

SciJus. 2017. Science & Justice Special Virtual Issue: Measuring and Reporting the Precision of Forensic Likelihood Ratios. Available online at: https://www.sciencedirect.com/journal/science-and-justice/special-issue/102F0FGVD03.

Schneps, L., Overill, R. and Lagnado, D. 2018. Ranking the impact of different tests on a hypothesis in a Bayesian network. Entropy 20(11): 856–870.

Silomon, J. 2019. A Bayesian network approach to the proliferation of software as a weapon. pp. 377–387. In Proc. Intl. Conf. on Cyber Warfare & Security, Reading: Academic Conferences International Ltd.

Tse, H., Chow, K. P. and Kwan, M. 2012. Reasoning about evidence using Bayesian networks. pp. 99–113. *In*: Peterson, G. L. and Shenoi, S. (eds.). Advances in Digital Forensics XII. Springer Berlin Heidelberg New York.

10

The Future of Democracy in a Cyber-Security Framework

Marios Panagiotis Efthymiopoulos[1,]* and *Kleanthis Kyriakidis*[2]

1. Introduction: Democracy, Cyber-Security and the Covid-19 Global Pandemic

The year 2020 will be remembered in human history as the year of the first 21st century global pandemic, or simply "the year of the Coronavirus". Yet, global pandemics, are not new. Humanity has insofar faced numerous pandemics, that annihilated hundreds of millions of people. Such pandemics include among them the bubonic plague during the 14th century. It eliminated one third or even half of the European population and livestock alike. In the 20th century we witnessed an equally destructive one, the 1918 Spanish influenza, which killed more than 20 million people or, according to other estimations, as much as 50 million through its second wave. Such numbers supersede by far the 26 million victims of the Great War. An estimation—global population wise—is that 5% of mankind perished (Coppola 2011; Green 2008). Other pandemics include the Zika, SARS, HIV, and Ebola viruses, which however hold a relatively small spread, compared to the current Covid-19 pandemic in 2020. Frank Snowden very cleverly dubbed the two latter, in a book published just months before the Covid-19 outbreak, "dress rehearsals for the Twenty-First Century" (Snowden 2019).

Nevertheless, no pandemic preceding to the Covid-19 ever necessitated such drastic measures as the ones taken within 2020, some of which have now been deemed threatening to our democracies. Two of the main reasons for our false sense of invincibility are the relatively fast containment of pandemics for a century and the

---

[1] Associate Professor of International Security and Strategy, College of Security and Global Studies, American University in the Emirates.

[2] Assistant Professor of Security Studies, College of Security and Global Studies, American University in the Emirates.
Email: kleanthis.kyriakidis@aue.ae

* Corresponding author: marios.panagiotis@aue.ae

enormous progress of medical science. It is true that in the 20th century the enormous progress in the field of medicine in tandem with the technological advancement was reassuring. Our society became more and more open, diverse and global, leading to a vast amount of borderless opportunities, so no one could anticipate a possible pandemic that would bring things to a standstill. This pandemic proved to us that we are far yet from being, at least in a medical sense, invincible.

This pandemic has obviously caused a global social disruption. Not far after the formal announcement of the pandemic, measures that were taken, brought our market economies to a halt. Measures that were taken were drastic, to say the least: from banning of events, banning of public gatherings, domestic movement restrictions to full curfews, closure of educational institutions from primary to tertiary education, non-essential shops closure to general lockdowns, and international but also local movement restrictions with passenger flights mostly restricted worldwide, created an incomparable landscape.

This new environment is dominated by three significant factors: (1) Limitations to the physical contact, utilities and services provided by an open market economy. (2) Increase of the utility and usefulness of our technology sectors. (3) Increased vulnerability from the extended personal or public use of the utilities and services provided by the world wide web.

Never before have so many people 'upscaled and updated themselves' onto the opportunities delivered by the use of the internet. Great numbers of people suddenly must work online, socialize online and conduct online transactions. Many took refuge in online communication to counter social distancing. This fact created fertile ground for malefactors of all kinds. Consequently, it has raised concerns pertaining to issues related with cyber-security in terms of national or collective security and therefore, democracy (Efthymiopoulos 2019).

This chapter examines and analyses the future of democracy within the framework of cyber-space. It argues for the importance and requirement of cyber-security. It addresses the fine balance between the risk of a possible authoritarianism and the necessity of civil protection. It addresses the absolute need of increased cyber-security within the framework of a new working and operating virtual environment. However, it limits its scope to sound information and scientific research with regards to the future of our society in order to avoid an Orwellian scenario of mass surveillance, vast violations of privacy, and extreme repression to "deviant" behaviors (Orwell 1949).

The chapter answers crucial questions and ethical dilemmas concerning the future of our democracy:

- Are the measures taken out of necessity or out of choice?
- What are the alternatives when taking a measure that evidently restricts personal freedoms and limits democracy?
- Are moral and social norms concerning race, sex, and especially faith addressed?
- What are the long-term socioeconomic consequences of the measures taken?
- Is it legitimate for our leaders to make decisions that affect democratic institutions?

- Is the world wide web and the internet the "new normal" in our professional and social life?
- Should cyber-security be the new online methodology for social protection?

The chapter views elements from a holistic approach. The chapter targets policymakers with recommendations in each subchapter concerning democracy and cyber-security in a Post-CoVid-19 era.

As a disclosure note, the current chapter is delivered by two authors whose interest is purely academic and scientific. All work presented hence forth, is in no direct or indirect representation or association with any private or public entity, government institution or organization. These are personal scientific outcomes of the writers and can only be treated as per pure personal scientific and academic research interest.

2. Democracy 2.0

A comprehensive insight into the term democracy and its components is a prerequisite to any discussion for the future of democracy. The term consists of a synthesis of two Greek words, since democracy, as a political system, was born in Ancient Greece. The first word is "demos", which means people and the second word is "kratos", which means "power". Sometimes this word is falsely translated as "rule". Hence, democracy is the political system where people have the power, not the system that people rule, because at all times, there were elected representatives of the people that ruled. Needless to say that in a democracy, the rulers depend on and act according to people's desires and actual needs while there are mechanisms to safeguard that people have the power, like elections, referenda, and the like.[1]

Furthermore, in a democratic society, people have certain rights but also specific obligations. Frequently the obligations, restrict some freedoms in order to safeguard the rights of others, and this is where there has been much debate as regards the governments' reactions to CoVid-19. Regarding citizens' rights, democracy should protect individuals' civil, but even more profoundly, human rights. Usually, when referring to human rights, our point of reference is the United Nations Universal Declaration of Human Rights (UDHR), a groundbreaking document adopted by the United Nations General Assembly (UNGA) in Paris on December 10, 1948 (United Nations 1948). The most fundamental of the aforementioned rights are described in Article 3, which reads, "Everyone has the right to life, liberty and security of person". Nevertheless, most of the democratically elected governments, during the pandemic, in order to protect the lives of the vulnerable violated the following rights:

- Article 12: "No one shall be subjected to arbitrary interference with his *privacy...*"
- Article 13: "Everyone has the right to *freedom of movement* and residence within the borders of each state. Everyone has the right to leave any country, including his own, and to return to his country".

---

[1] Ancient Athens was close to "direct democracy" through its Assembly that would really decide about the main issues for the city-state; however, day-to-day decisions were taken by the Council, the Magistrates, the Generals and the Municipal officials. See Osborne (1985). Demos: The Discovery of Classical Attika. Cambridge University Press.

- Article 20: "Everyone has the right to *freedom of peaceful assembly* and association…"
- Article 23: "Everyone has the *right to work…*"

2.1 Restricting Freedoms

The core issue regarding democracy is that during and after the Covid-19 pandemic, at least until humankind finds an effective vaccine, individual freedoms are likely to continue to be restricted in various ways. As such, we are to notice in the foreseeable future a more "surveillance democracy" (Zuboff 2019), based mostly on human security. Surveillance will be augmented; hence the right of privacy will be devalued. The right to work has already waned, with literally armies of young unemployed people, in an era that we had already been witnessing the rise of the "Precariat" class, a term coined by Guy Standing which refers to young people living in a globalized world full of insecurity, without welfare, unemployed or underemployed with low wages, who live in a precarious way and it obviously alludes to the famous proletariat class (Standing 2011).

Concerning the restrictions to the freedom of assembly and the freedom of movement, that were made by elected governments with the support of the vast majority of the population. However, it is highly contested that even democratic elected leaders with the backing of public opinion have the right to limit the aforementioned freedoms. It is worth highlighting that the freedoms of movement and of assembly, along with the right to free speech, are the first to be targeted in totalitarian regimes. Hence, we need to assess the requirement for such undemocratic measures. There is no doubt that a significant percentage of citizens' lack of self-restraint and common sense led to the measures as an absolute necessity, even if some "illiberal democracies" used them as a pretext for stark violations.

What is more disturbing is the uncertainty as regards the duration of the limitations on our freedoms. Many people wonder: "But, for how long?", "When will the rights of people be fully reinstated?", "Will the fear of a second wave of the pandemic allow governments to keep the aforementioned restrictions in perpetuity?" Unfortunately, the answer is "as long as it takes". We need to highlight that even countries that, in the beginning, rejected any restrictive policies or tried to reinstate some rights, had to retreat and apply harsh measures. In the US alone, the death toll of Covid-19 at the time of this writing has surpassed the death toll of World War I and, as a calamity, ranks only 3rd after the American Civil War and World War II.[2] Desperate times require desperate measures, and ultimately, the old dilemma "security vs. democracy"[3] grows to be even more challenging when it

---

[2] It is really interesting to note that the Vietnam War, which haunted the American consciousness and collective memory for decades had a death toll of less than 60,000 American soldiers, while World War I a bit more than 115.000. World War II with 400,000 dead and the American Civil War with 650,000 are still much worse than the CoVid-19. Data vary from different sources and the ones dues here are based on different sources and gathered in Wikipedia. See https://en.wikipedia.org/wiki/United_States_ military_casualties_of_war.

[3] All Debate Clubs and practitioners have addressed the question "is freedom more important than security". As an example see https://www.debate.org/opinions/is-freedom-more-important-than-security.

becomes "safety vs. democracy". The answer to this dilemma in general cannot be a straightforward positive or negative one, as the variables of the common good and public safety need to be taken into serious consideration. Nonetheless, nowadays and as long as Covid-19 is globally on the rise, safety prevails.

2.2 Hybrid Regimes

The rise of populist regimes with totalitarian tendencies, worldwide, has been identified as a trend, long before the spread of the Covid-19, but nowadays it is further exacerbated. According to the 25th annual Freedom House "Nations In Transit" Report released on May 6, 2020, there has been a dramatic democratic breakdown in countries such as Poland and Hungary, and this was not due to Covid-19. Actually, from the seventeen countries in Central and South-eastern Europe monitored in the aforementioned report, democracy has been eroded in ten. Four member states of the European Union, i.e., Croatia, Bulgaria, Romania, and Poland, are considered "semi-consolidated democracies" and Hungary, which is also an EU member state, is characterized as "hybrid regime" (Csaky 2020). The leadership of these countries had already deviated from the democratic processes to quell any remaining checks on their power, and the post Covid-19 Corona virus era presents a golden opportunity for further encroachment on democracy. Apparently, the ongoing pandemic has facilitated and accelerated the attacks on democratic institutions. It is an undeniable fact that in recent times representative democracy is faltering and cracking while emerging societal tensions are a symptom of a broader systemic crisis. The growing political dissatisfaction and "democratic fatigue" (Van Reybrouck 2016; Bauman 2007)[4] have triggered but simultaneously been incited by rapidly escalating populism and extremism.

2.3 Role of Social Media

The catalyst for the aforementioned "democratic fatigue" is social media. Social media influences people by convincing them that participation in the democratic processes is a farce,that the political parties are nothing but corrupt elite institutions and that decisions are not really taken by the elected officials. Other times we witness interventions through social media that become instruments of propaganda and disruption. For instance, Congressional hearings in the aftermath of the American elections of 2016 would strive to determine the scope and the extent of Twitter bots, Facebook data manipulation, Russian trolls, like the Internet Research Agency, a notorious "troll farm's" influence on the outcome of the elections. Social media are

---

[4] David van Reybrouck argues that democracies around the world increasingly suffer from the "Democratic Fatigue Syndrome (DFS)" which as a "disorder…has not yet been fully described", but its symptoms include apathy, low voter turnout, declining political party membership, governmental inefficacy, political paralysis, fear of electoral failure, lack of competent new politicians, "compulsive self-promotion, chronic electoral fever, exhausting media stress, distrust, indifference and other persisting paroxysms" See Van Reybrouck (2016), Against Elections: The Case for Democracy, Random House, p. 16. Zygmunt Bauman argues that we live in an era of corrosion of citizenship and rise of individualism. See Bauman (2007). Liquid Times: Living in an Age of Uncertainty, Polity Press.

deemed an unprecedented colossal danger to democracy for a plethora of reasons, especially in the CoVid-19 era, when people restricted due to shelter in-home measures are likely to depend more on them in order to be "informed".

Moreover, social media has grown in power so much as to present an imminent threat of destruction to the State as a malevolent provocateur with the gift of the gab that can whip the hoi polloi into an irrational frenzied spiral of ideologically preposterous self-destruction (Shearer and Matsa 2019; Boukes 2019).[5] It is worth highlighting that there is a significant difference between conventional mass media and social media, as well as the past and the present news dissemination landscape since the advent of the latter. In the past, newspapers, TV channels and radio stations had to abide by a code of ethics and specific rules regarding libel, slander, and propaganda. Moreover, they employed professional journalists and gave space to renowned intellectuals to offer their expert opinion. Political discussions and debates on TV and the radio, as well as newspaper columns, and articles were all done by professionals whose reputation was at stake. Ergo, the means of fake news, smear campaigns, and propaganda tactics were minimal in democratic societies.

In contrast, every individual, in the era of social media dominance, irrespective of their academic background and expertise or most usually the lack of those, is able to become their own media publisher and most importantly, to found groups with enormous following through their Twitter, Facebook, and other social media accounts, and therein lies the problem. They exploit the omnipotence of social media, which shirks from their institutional duty of gatekeeping, hiding behind Section 230 of the US Communications Decency Act (CDA) of 1996.[6] Since the most prominent online services are based in the United States, this American Law has practically quasi-universal appeal and provides a safe haven for websites/platforms that promote controversial or political speech based on fake news.[7]

2.4 Covid-19 and Infodemic

Having examined the Social Media landscape and the threat they pose to democracy, we need to underline that the Covid-19 pandemic led to a global epidemic of

---

[5] According to a PEW Research in 2018, about two-thirds of U.S. adults (68%), mostly for the sake of convenience, keep up with current affairs via social media sites, with about four in ten (43%) of them to depend mostly on Facebook. YouTube comes second with 21% followed by Twitter at 12%. However, despite a significant percentage (57%) expressing scepticism regarding the accuracy of the news on social media, it is a cause of concern that 36% social media news consumers, overly underestimate the influence of those news sources in their understanding of current events while another 15% feel that it has helped them more than confusing them. See Shearer and Matsa (2019). News Use Across Social Media Platforms 2018, Pew Research Centre.

[6] Section 230 (C) (1) reads as follows: "No provider or user of an interactive computer service shall be treated as the publisher or speaker of any information provided by another information content provider". See https://www.law.cornell.edu/uscode/text/47/230 . In effect online intermediaries that host or republish speech are protected against a range of laws that might otherwise be used to hold them legally responsible for what others say and do. The protected intermediaries include not only regular Internet Service Providers (ISPs), but also any online service that publishes third-party content.

[7] Undeniably social media has played a pivotal role in the success of grassroots movements such as the "Twitter Revolution" in Moldova and the Iranian Green Movement in 2009, the so-called "Arab Spring" in many Arab countries in 2011 and the "Orange Revolution" in Ukraine in 2013. Hence, we should not underestimate the crucial role of social media in those uprisings. Nevertheless, they have also been used for nefarious purposes as well endangering democracy.

misinformation, spreading precipitously through social media platforms and other outlets, posing a grave danger for global public health. The Ethiopian, World Health Organization Director-General, Dr. Tedros Adhanom Ghebreyesus, highlighted that "We're not just fighting an epidemic; we're fighting an infodemic... But the difference now with social media is that this phenomenon is amplified, it goes faster and further, like the viruses that travel with people and go faster and further... What is at stake during an outbreak is making sure people will do the right thing to control the disease or to mitigate its impact. So it is not only information to make sure people are informed; it is also making sure people are informed to act appropriately" (Zarocostas 2020).

In this milieu, it is almost impossible for the layperson to distinguish which of the information available is valid and which is fake, especially in the era of advanced technological capabilities enabling the creation of deepfakes. Cyber-security could help, as long as fake news are not spread by the government itself. Thus, the critical question during the infodemic is, "who will protect us from the protectors"? The answer lies in the individuals' sense of personal responsibility as they need to check the credibility of the sources of information they rely on and to compare and contrast news feeds by a plethora of sources of information. In the case of failed governments, populist leaders or hybrid regimes, citizens need to exercise caution and take everything with a pinch of salt regarding the validity of information disseminated by government-controlled sources of information.

3. The Importance of Cyber-Space and Cyber-Security in the Future of Democracy

Cyber-space is an important virtual formation entrenched in our modern society. Cyber-space is a catalyst towards societal progress. It is a tool offered through technology innovation. It is an integrative tool at the service of among others, our national and international system of democracy. Today we cannot live without the usefulness and utilization of cyber-space.

Throughout the first two decades of the 21st century we have enabled through cyber-space, methods to bring our global societies closer to one another. We have managed to concentrate and upload many government and private services to the virtual world of the internet. And in doing so we facilitate our way of life but also a better way to conduct business and trade. And this is what is offered in cyber-space: unlimited options with unlimited space, virtual and geographical. With the development of the internet and the world wide web, we have managed to 'bend time and distance'. We have managed to bring true technological advancement, growth and innovation that is now characterising our 21st century society.

Cyber-space may be today the most important market asset and can be said that it is the single most important commodity. While the world has 'gone digital', in infrastructure, methods of conducting business, social and professional awareness, education, we have also become dependent on it. New generations are now integrated into a system that we call the 'matrix' from a young age, and our young generation cannot do without.

Our societies and governments, our democracies, as much as they have come together in the post-Cold War, which characterized the second half of the 20th century, have found 'refuge' in something new, a new 'platform' they can invest in, a place where all would be equal in the benefit of making a profit or with which platform our new digital society would come together. In the 21st century, societies have become both interdependent and dependent on each other. Information flow and knowledge transfer travel fast, in milliseconds (Ross 2016). Trade is now completely simplified through various software cyber-based platforms that generate billions and as well employ a new generation cyber-based employees and human capital that has grown into the positive effects of technology. Operational decisions are taken in live cooperation from where-ever the location as the internet has ameliorated communication methods. While our actions are therefore more digitally operated, so is also our system of governance and rule (Schwab 2018).

Cyber-space and the extended utilization of the world wide web and the internet itself, has enabled us to facilitate our lives. It has enabled us to include our 'culture map' (Meyer 2015). The proper use of cyber-space could also enable our democracies to expand onto a more inclusive and more direct rule of democracy itself. Where a simple user through the utilization of the social media can have as much as a direct contact and impact in the decision-making processes of our democracies.

A few decades ago, we would only dream to have an email account or to somehow be in contact with people through the internet. Today we can read online, upload writings and historical documents. We can exchange information and we can write what we call as emails to each other as means of written online correspondence. We can increase our knowledge efficiency and manage knowledge distribution from the simple use of the internet, and platforms that are utilizing the internet and cyber-space to operate upon. We communicate in and through official channels between governments through emails and the internet itself.

While technology is becoming today more diverse and more embedded in our everyday life, so is our way we conduct business and communicate in a post Covid-19 period. We can therefore assume that the creation and utilization of cyber-space is a true technological revolution that has already taken place. It is a reflective characteristic of our 21st century. It is reflective as it provides us with the ample choices that are provided to us through the extensive utilization of the digital world and beyond.

3.1 Regulation and Cyber-Space

Cyber-space is currently nationally, legally and operationally, regulated by each country. Which means that our national governments, do indeed hold control of the virtual national space. Yet cyber-space does not limit itself only in one country or one market. It does not have national borders (Weiss and Rorden 2019). You can see, visit or operate through cyber-space virtually everywhere being either in the centre of the city of the capital or the town or being somewhere remotely with access to electricity and the world of the internet.

Our National Telecommunication agencies are the regulators of our own cyber-space. They are also the 'door keepers' the ones who allow for the influx of information that comes in, and therefore what we know of as downloads and the out flux of information, what we know as the uploads onto the internet or otherwise known as the world wide web.

However, the world wide web as foresaid does not limit itself to one area, city or country (Meyer 2015). We can all have 'access' to the "glory" and opportunities of the internet provided, with which we now conduct our business from. It is upon the universality of regulatory methodology presumably to be adopted by the members of the United Nations that one should start on. As and although we do believe that the internet and the world wide web provides us with unlimited options, yet malevolent deeds have taken place in the world of cyber-space. Where malicious attacks and threats do call for each country and international organizations or cooperative sides to take part into what is called method of cyber-security or defence.

4. Cyber-Security in 2020

Cyber-security stands out as a digital strategy and policy of protection against current and emerging threats and challenges over cyber-space. Cyber-security is a most complex phenomenon. It has become a science that is now taught at schools, institutions and universities. Cyber-security is also operated by companies, organizations, and governments in the name of protection of national public and private infrastructure but also personal belongings. Cyber-security is of strategic value. It constantly develops implemented methods and actions of security against any malicious and non-malicious attacks or hacking activities (Carayannis et al. 2018). While threats and emerging challenges loom in our conventional world so do they in the world of cyber-space. As such, asymmetrical and hybrid threats are existential. And methods are required to constantly battle the obvious.

In the framework of national and international security countries and governments seek to create, develop, enhance, or constantly apply, a cyber-security and defence mechanism. A sound and constantly adaptable protection method, for all and any kind of possible threats; whether these are infrastructural or personal.

4.1 The Characteristics of Cyber-Security and its Resilience

Cyber-security does not limit itself to traditional forms of security. And rightly so, as it deals with events taking place in cyber-space. Cyber-security has become a quite important and absolute tool of protection. As we foresaid, while our society progresses into a new digital world, so does our security. While our lives are now integrated into a collective cyber-matrix so is our collective security personal and collective apparatus.

In the 21st century, cyber-space has enabled us to come closer to one another. It makes up part of one of the most important single technological innovations that characterises this century. However, Cyber-security emerges as a most important policy and tool to defend and protect cyber-space. It requires a global and local regulatory and application status and framework. Writing on topics such as security in cyber-space, requires sound theoretical and practical capacity knowledge of all possible current security threats through the internet itself. Even more so the fact that we are getting more and more interconnected day by day (Carayannis et al. 2018).

Cyber-security is a strategy that requires resilience to the objective of securing against threats and challenges. Cyber-security is a field of operational defensive capacity in nature that operates in defensive measures against malevolent attacks or threats. Cyber-security can become a pivotal policy framework for technological security and business continuity. A multinational cooperative approach could enhance elements of pluralism in Democracy; it will help boost interconnectedness and will boost security efforts to meet all security threats symmetrical and asymmetrical.

National governments resolute is based on security and defence strategies. More so when cyber-space is involved. Democracies rely on national cyber-security protection policies and application methods; how cooperation can and will be achieved; how information agility is advanced. What current and future tools we may use to technological advance new forms of mechanisms.

In 2020 and beyond, the world is more e-interconnected than ever. In this new world, we seek sound and robust solutions to "secure all lines of communication". There is an increasing need to adopt and adapt to new methodologies and new ideas that may as well increase the level of security, as insecurity measures increase, while technology progresses, while cyber-space becomes an integrative element of our democracies and our democracies rule and operate through them (Zuboff 2019). New methods and actions for cyber-protection continue and will continue to emerge, to be examined, analyzed and applied. Existing threats will continue to emerge, now and in the future.

Cyber-Security reflects human security as well as human capital and abilities. Increase technological information and knowledge, innovation, strategy and operations at all levels of defense, national and global but also through international organizations (Efthymiopoulos 2016).

In security operations, "future war-like operations"… and other related measures … "will be held in far more complicated than the current one, military operational environments, where battles will be dealt at multiple levels and multiple dimensions" (Efthymiopoulos 2009). In turn, in "military and police missions we will continue to require agile and networked, well-trained and well-led forces" (Efthymiopoulos 2014). More so, knowledge efficiency and knowledge based democratic rules that we explore below.

5. Knowledge Democracy

David Campbell and Elias Carayannis, conceded to the notion of 'knowledge democracy' and 'cyber-democracy' (Carayannis et al. 2014). They claimed that the notion is reflective in practice, in democracies with an advanced level of what we may call 'an enhanced and cooperative rule of law': One that allows for true methods of growth, production, knowledge innovation and application to take place. Knowledge democracy "excels" on innovation and carries the effects of sustainable development (Carayannis et al. 2018). In our modern cyber-space based society, knowledge democracy has become an advanced tool for current and future growth and ultimately a method in bringing us together under a 'global cyber-roof'. The very essence of a global e-society.

Knowledge democracy is a growth/advancement tool. In a cyber-space democratic rule as in a traditional democracy, progress comes with constant upscale of production, regulation, operation, true creativity in all sectors and innovation for the future. By doing so, in cyber-space, we all benefit of global innovation at the same time. We equally and universally grow by moving forward our democracies.

Nowadays, knowledge democracy is also about ethics. It helps establish the framework for progress. In this case it helps to establish the ethical uses and tools for growth and development of our society through cyber-space. For, true development and growth to take place, we need to push forward through a tangible process of progress: To develop.

The future of our democracies, that is also part of the title of our chapter, depends on principles, notions and morality and methods of action. On how we regulate and operate daily in cyber-space. Whether and how we innovate and how we share amongst each other the outcomes of our creation with our global cyber-society.

In the near future, our democracies will be completely digitized. They will be operating at a 100% capacity through cyber-space. With an absence of a physical presence. Knowingly, for it to succeed we need to establish sound sustainable pragmatic methods strategies and policies for cyber-space. It is the manifestation of the future of democracy in cyber-space that makes knowledge democracy meaningful. Innovation will be for the long run and always at the forefront of cyber-space. A cyber-space that transcends traditional and national boundaries. Where public space is now our global cyber-space.

While cyber-space is public to access it from whatever remote area we are located at, will nonetheless need to be constructively and operationally globally regulated. It should be governed universally in similar ways, places and platforms. In where all our societies converge and agree to, even more enhanced rules, regulations and methods of operation and security among others than what is achieved by the year 2020.

Cyber-space, as stated prior, needs to be protected. Its good-willing operation and the future of the internet or web-based formats, applications and other software/ hardware methods, rest in the framework of protection and defence against current and emerging threats and challenges against unregulated, unlawful and malicious operations, ways, attacks and hybrid non-asymmetrical challenges. Cyber-security is and will always be the best terminology for operations in protection of cyber-space. It will be the only term to define a form of action against any unlawful, unregulated way in cyber-space.

While we enhance our cyber-security methodology and while we innovate in the way we conduct protective or policing operations in cyber-space, there is a great deal of true architecture to take place that will shape the future of our 4th Industrial revolution and our 5th Technological revolution.

The 4th Industrial revolution, a term coined by Klaus Schwab of the World Economic Forum (Schwab 2016), can only the beginning of something far greater and far more convergent with our physical life and presence in cyber-space. Cyber-space does not only regulate the future, but shapes the future. Knowledge democracy does not only innovate the future but shapes the future, as well. Within the framework of technology, we have not seen a great innovation to date (2020), but the creation of the world wide web. We are still to see the future of our global democracy in a complete law-based, economic-based, politically-scaled arrangement cyber-space, regulated and cyber-security protected.

In our future cyber-democracy, there will be a new architecture. We shall see the phenomenon of a truly global society taking shape virtually but with a more -physical presence method- (augmented reality), while the internet and cyber-space brings us virtually closer through a character. This means that new and embedded technology will be created (Wall 2011). Cyber-spaced and based technologies such as cybernetics, robotics, artificial intelligence, cloud based technology, augmented reality, bid data and the internet of things, among others, will allow cyber-space to converge with physical space, to take a new shape and form that will be a true innovation.

While, we become more and more dependent on technology, we become digitally more dependent. However, in our conventional life we become more socially distant from each other. And we also need to take care of this. While we have made a great achievement, that is to bend time and space, we need to be careful that we do not forget our real world. Although our cyber-world seems to be more interesting, while more diverse with options and opportunities it can also become more capitalist than ever before (Collier 2018).

In our future democracy, in a cyber-security framework, two major elements will be characterizing our global digitized democracy. (1) Knowledge democracy (2) Surveillance and security (Zuboff 2019). Both elements will develop further our cyber-system of governance. Cyber governance will certainly be regulated, while global in nature of services and in applicability, use and innovation.

6. The Efficiency, Efficacy, and Effectiveness in Applying E-governance and Enhancing Internet Governance

Undoubtedly, in the foreseeable future, e-governance will become more prevalent, but there will also be an urgent need to enhance internet governance, i.e., the development of norms, rules, and processes to regulate the Internet. Cyber-governance or e-governance will be an improved form of governance in terms of efficiency and efficacy. Nevertheless, we need to investigate its effectiveness. Usually, we use these words interchangeably, but someone may be very efficient, but due to lack of efficacy or setting the wrong goals to be ineffective. On the other hand, someone else can be effective but wasteful regarding resources, which renders them inefficient. It is a matter of semantics as efficacy is related to the capacity/capabilities to produce the desired effect, and internet/high tech, as already discussed, gives as a wide range of new capabilities. Hence, efficacy is a given. Efficiency is related to effort, time, and procedures. It is about doing the correct or wrong things optimally. Yet again, it is evident that the use of high technology minimizes any waste and the future e-governance will be more efficient. However, the measure of achieving one's goals is related to effectiveness. 'Grosso modo', the same rules apply for our effort to predict the ability of the internet governance to fulfill its potential. With cyber-security, we will have the tools, the capabilities to achieve the task and do that efficiently. But will we be effective?

Effectiveness in both cases has to do with doing the right things rather than doing the things right; hence it is a leadership quality more than a managerial one, but of course, the aim is to "do the right things right" (Stack 2016). The challenge for the e-governance, as described exceptionally by Jeremy Pitt, Ada Diaconescu and Josiah Ober, is "to design self-governing socio-technical systems, which are democratically founded and constituted 'ab origine', and have a concept of digital citizenship that is correlated with civic participation in processes of self-determination" (Pitt et al. 2019). High technology cannot be sufficient on its own, because effectiveness has a moral component, and the cyber-space has no inherent values. In Cyber-Democracy effectiveness will depend on the creation of "human-centred design and iterative software development techniques—what some in the field are starting to call 'Human-Centred Policymaking.'" (Sinai et al. 2020).

The effectiveness of enhancing Internet governance largely depends on our moral and ethical standards, rules, customs, and traditions. However, these are not universally accepted, although cyber-space is global. Ergo, for some, cyber-space is considered a global opportunity while for others a global threat. There is a consensus that the same rights that people enjoy in their everyday life must also be protected in cyber-space. However, it has become apparent that people around the world do not have either the same rights or even a common notion of what these rights should be. This is why, ideally, the Internet governance should be on a genuinely supranational level. Not national, not regional, not even intergovernmental. It will be at the forefront of the conflict between globalization, regionalization, and fragmentation. Internet governance should be among our foremost aims, a component of strengthening universal institutions like the political, security, or judicial ones. We already described how social media, which are practically under American jurisdiction, are unregulated or at best self-regulated. Even though most criminal activities are conducted through the dark or deep web, frequently, the mainstream Internet is misused and abused, and it allows or even instigates crimes. Hate speech against communities or professions (journalism and law enforcement are the first that come to mind), criminally deviant behaviour like paedophilia and terrorist group recruitment are among the leading examples of the dire consequences of the unregulated Internet. Most of the aforementioned crimes have already been described in the Budapest Convention on Cybercrime, initiated by the Council of Europe, which was signed and ratified by 64 countries, including the US, Australia, Canada, and Japan (Council of Europe 2001). Forgery, fraud, child pornography, were included in the Convention, while crimes related to hate speech, xenophobia, and racism were included in its first Additional Protocol. Nonetheless, there are uncharted areas with much more room for interpretation of what constitutes a crime, from digital gambling to different copyright laws and ownership of information or data.

Admittedly, the concept of a universal internet governance is intricate and surely requires many safety valves and features that would guarantee its integrity and citizens' safety. Both individual countries' initiatives, like the French initiative, "Paris Call for Trust and Security in Cyberspace," launched by President Emmanuel Macron on November 12, 2018, and most importantly multi-lateral efforts like the United Nations Internet Governance Forum (UNIGF)'s outcomes include principles to that effect. The latter is an inter-agency, inter-governmental and multi-stakeholder group that confers each year, since 2006, and discusses the problems and the possible solution in cyber-space. Almost always, the cyber-security is the primary concern, but we can identify new concerns like the complexities of internet infrastructure, the internet of Things, the Darknet (a dark subsidiary of the internet) and utilization of the internet by aging populations, the Deepfakes, the Digital Identity and Sovereignty, and the Surveillance Capitalism (i.e., collection of personal/private data by commercial entities for marketing purposes), which were introduced in 2019 (UNIGF 2019). Nonetheless, along with identifying crimes and challenges and despite the worldwide agreement as regards some sort of Internet governance, in both sides of the Atlantic, there is also much apprehension concerning privacy, which we predict that for security and safety issues (like the Covid-19 pandemic) will go unheeded. Until very recently, the EU tried to ensure the maximum privacy for its citizens via the European General Data Protection Regulation (EGDPR). In fact, even this meticulous regulation has flaws because someone's personal data can raise privacy considerations as regards other persons' data, when the latter is indirectly involved (Karaboga 2018).

Even if we identify the issues to be dealt with, and there is co-operation as regards the definition of cyber-crimes, a universally applicable International Law on cyber-space should become an integral part of Internet Governance. Nevertheless, even after that step, which is considered utopian at the moment, there should also be a minimum consensus as regards the penalties for the individuals, companies, or even States that infringe this law. From the aforementioned analysis, we conclude that both the future Cyber-Democracy, e-governance, and the Internet governance will be more efficient. Still, their effectiveness depends on the human leadership factor, which, although it is the main determinant of cyber-democracy's success, it is actually highly contested.

7. The Effects of a Future Cyber-Democracy

Our analysis leads to the conclusion that a fundamental change in mentality, rules, and norms, in what we have coined "future cyber-democracy" is essential. In a future cyber-democracy, we should expect to have limited privacy but increased surveillance (Zuboff 2019) for security reasons. As it became evident with Covid-19, surveillance played a crucial role in the counter-pandemic measures. Isobel Hamilton illustrated this quite accurately in her article entitled "Compulsory selfies and contact-tracing: Authorities everywhere are using smartphones to track the coronavirus, and it's part of a massive increase in global surveillance" (Hamilton 2020). The new norm resembles the Orwellian dystopia of a Big Brother in many aspects. Furthermore, the constant threat of criminal activity in cyberspace has created a quandary for laypeople. Given that hackers and cybercriminals breach individuals' privacy for their nefarious purposes, people see no alternative but to concede to concessions regarding their privacy willingly. Individuals expect governments to protect them from any harm in cyber-space as in physical space, but efficient cyber-security entails relinquishing, partially, one's right to privacy. Hence, the prominent characteristic of the future Cyber-Democracy is enhanced surveillance with potentially detrimental effects on our privacy.

The future cyber-democracy most likely will have several characteristics of a hybrid regime regarding the limitation of citizens' freedoms. The regulation of social media would be another characteristic of those regimes. Because of the aforementioned "infodemic" and the prevalence of the fake news, governments have decided, and this is a trend that is here to stay long after the Covid-19 pandemic is history, to be more vigilant and intervene regarding the mostly unregulated Internet and especially the social media. When we previously discussed the influence of social media, we highlighted that they curb democracy.[8] Nevertheless, it is challenging to differentiate proper regulation (which can be self-regulation, co-regulation, and lastly, legal regulation) and outright censorship. What is a foregone conclusion, though, is that social media will not remain unregulated or self-regulated. Therefore, there is a genuine concern regarding legal overregulation or even absolute control in the name of democracy and the protection of public interest. The Covid-19 crisis simply accelerated the governmental response in liberal democracies. In a very noteworthy research of 21 liberal democracies Andreas Busch, Patrick Theiner, and Yana Breindl found out that the Internet was practically unregulated before 2004. In contrast, there is some form of regulation in all countries in 2012 (Busch et al. 2018). It is expected that social media will follow.[9]

The regulation of social media will lead us to a cyber-democracy, where the freedom of speech will be 'de-facto controlled or limited'. Some might argue that this will happen for a valid reason, like public health. For instance, during the pandemic, there were several cases of fearmongering with people spreading conspiracy theories, via social media, that the virus does not even exist, and thus there is no cause for concern, while the whole situation is a global social experiment. People, though, without critical thinking skills and limited background knowledge, are susceptible to conspiracy theories and fearmongering. As a result, a gullible person may not only disregard the government's guidelines and restrictive measures but even revolt against them. In the end, they are either dead or even worse asymptomatic carriers of

---

[8] The best description concerning the negative influence of social media in the creation of the so-called "post-truth" with fake news and democratic erosion is given by Gabriele Cosentino: "Social media platforms, by allowing sensational, polarizing and misleading content to overshadow more cautious, objective and lucid discussions, by creating a precompetitive attention economy that rewards virality over veracity and by skirting their responsibility as carriers of problematic or dangerous content, are further contributing to the erosion of rational and democratic public discussion and consensual political reality". See Cosentino (2020). Social Media and the Post-Truth World Order: The Global Dynamics of Disinformation, Palgrave/MacMillan, p.140.

[9] At the time of the writing the President of the US, Donald Trump, was about to announce an executive order concerning the regulation of the social media. See Hamerman and Conger (2020). Trump Prepares Order to Limit Social Media Companies' Protections, The New York Times, May, 28. Available online https://www.nytimes.com/2020/05/28/us/politics/trump-executive-order-social-media.html. Last accessed on May, 28, 2020.

the virus and thus responsible for the death of other people. Such scenarios raise the question of whether the particular individual is the sole culprit or should the initiator of the rumour be punished as well. Even more so in the case of a rumour getting viral via a social network shouldn't the platform held accountable as well, facing criminal charges?

On the other hand, in an "illiberal democracy",[10] a government with less democratic sensitivities might go after ordinary people or even journalists for "spreading false rumours". It is a given that the first case is to be avoided but preventing the second one presents serious challenges pertaining to the exploitation of legislation regulating free speech. The future of cyber-democracy largely depends on our ability to walk the thin line between absolute free speech and controlled free speech, even if this sounds like an oxymoron.

Future cyber-democracy should not infringe on personal liberties, especially the freedom of association and the freedom of movement. People who put up with widespread surveillance and measures such as shelter in-home will be indignant if all restrictions are not lifted in full when the pandemic is over. However, freedom of movement or association in the future cyber-democracy does not signify guaranteed privacy. It is common knowledge that via smartphones and GPS, all our movements and associations can be monitored. Moreover, the social score system that is already used in China with the help of face recognition technology and artificial intelligence is a cause for concern. We should also take into account the fact that personal data is a commodity in cyberspace, making third parties such as governments and private companies cognizant of individuals' purchases, finances, preferences, passions, vices, and virtues. A full profile is readily available, and we are genuinely helpless because, in cyber-democracy, everything is done via the Internet. Nonetheless, the freedom of speech, association, and movement, even under surveillance, is what differentiates the Cyber-Democracy from a high-tech Totalitarianism.

The quality of governance depends on citizens' civic education. Our future largely depends on our education, the most important of the industries of the future (Ross 2016). The trend is to focus on the specialization of education based on hard science and high technology sectors. The famous STEM (Science, Technology, Engineering and Mathematics) is on the rise, while humanities and social sciences are in decline and this is a dangerous trend for the future cyber-democracy. Our future education will be a "cyber" education, from remote to distance learning, and with educators playing a different role, the role of a coach and mentor. Already any information can literally be found via the Internet, so the educators are not the sole knowledge keepers. Their main task is to check and filter the available data weeding out unscientific data, outright lies, deepfakes, and propaganda through semi-true statements, hate speech and extremism. The next step is for the educators to explain how their students can use a methodology to convert the filtered data to proper information. Obviously, the transformation from information to knowledge depends on individuals' sense of personal responsibility. However, if we focus in the future

---

[10] Examples of illiberal democracies today include Russia, Turkey and Hungary. See Glassman (2019). The Future of Democracy, Springer, pp. 128–132.

only on hard science, we might lose much more than just knowledge. If in the future, we teach the values of liberal democracy, we will have a true cyber-democracy. The values of Ancient Greek Democracy, Renaissance, and Enlightenment must be the basis of our future democracy (Glassman 2019). Else, illiberal democracies will prevail. Our cyber-space world will become much more totalitarian, populist, and authoritarian as our societies will move towards a unified global digital governance.

8. Conclusion

This chapter adopted a holistic approach pertaining to Cyber-Security and Cyber-Democracy. The chapter targeted questions for policymakers on the future of democracy in a new cyber-space environment and world. It examined and analyzed the future of democracy, the perils, and the prospects, within the framework of cyber-space. It argued for the importance and necessity of cyber-security in a future cyber-democracy. It addresses various aspects, theories, and considerations: between the progress of technology and the fine balance between the risk of limited freedoms to increase of surveillance cyber-authoritarianism and the important necessity of civil protection in cyber-space.

More importantly, the chapter addressed the absolute necessity of cyber-security in a post Covid-19 world, within the framework of a new working and operating virtual environment. It answered crucial questions and ethical dilemmas with regards to the future of our cyber-democracy that we have yet to define in the very near future. In this future we must make sure to protect civil rights but also safeguard individual's privacy and our culture map. Last but not least, we have determined that the future education is of paramount importance. On the one hand, it will certainly be specialized in order to render the market even more technologically agile and resilient in a unified, global and virtual market economy. On the other hand and most importantly, it should be an education based on values, humanities and classics, else we run the risk to end up with high-technology subjects instead of cyber-citizens and out system to be a high technology totalitarian dystopia instead of the Cyber-Democracy that we deserve.

References

Bauman, Z. 2007. Liquid Times: Living in an Age of Uncertainty, Polity Press. Cambridge, UK.

Boukes, M. 2019. Social network sites and acquiring current affairs knowledge: The impact of Twitter and Facebook usage on learning about the news. Journal of Information Technology and Politics 16: 36–5.

Busch, A., Theiner, P. and Breindl, Y. 2018. Internet censorship in liberal democracies: learning from autocracies? pp. 11–28. In: Schwanholz, J., Graham, T. and Stoll, P. -T. (eds.). Managing Democracy in the Digital Age: Internet Regulation, Social Media Use, and Online Civic Engagement. Springer. New York, USA.

Carayannis, E., Campbell, D. and Efthymiopoulos, M. P. (eds.). 2014. Cyber-Development, Cyber-Democracy and Cyber-Defense. Springer. New York, USA.

Carayannis, E., Campbell, D. and Efthymiopoulos, M. P. (eds.). 2018. Handbook of Cyber-Development, Cyber-Democracy and Cyber-Defense. Springer. New York, USA.

Csaky, Z. 2020. Dropping the Democratic Façade, Nations in Transit Report. Freedom House. Washington, USA.

Coppola, D. 2011. Introduction to International Disaster Management. Butterworth-Heinemann Elsevier. Singapore.

Cosentino, G. 2020. Social Media and the Post-Truth World Order: The Global Dynamics of Disinformation, Palgrave/MacMillan. London, UK.

Collier, Paul. 2018. The Future of Capitalism, Harper Collings. New York, USA.

Council of Europe. 2001. Budapest Convention on Cybercrime Available online through the CoE site, [Last accessed on May 28, 2020]. https://www.coe.int/en/web/conventions/full-list/-/conventions/rms/0900001680081561.

Efthymiopoulos, M. P. 2008. NATO in the 21st Century: The Need for A Renewed Strategic Concept and the ever Lasting NATO-Russia Relations. Sakkoulas Press. Thessaloniki-Athens, Greece.

Efthymiopoulos, M. P. 2009. NATO's security operations in electronic warfare: the policy of cyber-defence and the alliance new strategic concept. Journal of Information Warfare 8: 3.

Efthymiopoulos, M. P. 2014. NATO's cyber-defence: a methodology for smart defence. pp. 303–319. *In*: Carayannis, E., Campbell, D. and Efthymiopoulos, M. P. (eds.). Cyber-Development, Cyber-Democracy and Cyber-Defence. Springer. New York, USA.

Efthymiopoulos, M. P. 2016. NATO Smart Defence and Cyber-Resilience. Karamanlis Chair of International Affairs-Fletcher School of Law and Diplomacy-.Boston. USA 1: 16. Monography.

Efthymiopoulos, M. P. 2019. A cyber-security framework for development, defense and innovation at NATO. Journal of Innovation and Entrepreneurship 8: 12. https://doi.org/10.1186/s13731-019-0105-z.

Glassman, R. 2019. The Future of Democracy. Springer. New York, USA.

Green, R. 2008. Global Perspectives: Pandemics. Cherry Lake Publishing. Ann Arbor, USA.

Hamerman, M. and Conger, K. 2020. Trump Prepares Order to Limit Social Media Companies' Protections. The New York Times: May, 28. Available online https://www.nytimes.com/2020/05/28/us/politics/trump-executive-order-social-media.html. Last accessed on May, 28, 2020.

Hamilton, I. A. 2020. Compulsory selfies and contact-tracing: Authorities everywhere are using smartphones to track the coronavirus, and it's part of a massive increase in global surveillance. Business Insider: 14 April. Available online https://www.businessinsider.com/countries-tracking-citizens-phones-coronavirus-2020-3. Last accessed May, 28, 2020.

Karaboga, M. 2018. The emergence and analysis of European data protection regulation. *In*: Schwanholz, J., Graham, T. and Stoll, P. T. (eds.). Managing Democracy in the Digital Age: Internet Regulation, Social Media Use, and Online Civic Engagement. Springer. New York, USA.

Meyer, E. 2015. The Culture Map. New York: Perseus Group Public Affairs. New York, USA.

Orwell, G. 1949. Nineteen Eighty-Four. Various Publishers. London, UK.

Osborne, R. 1985. Demos: The Discovery of Classical Attika. Cambridge University Press. Cambridge, UK.

Pitt, J., Diaconescu, A. and Ober, J. 2019. Knowledge management for democratic governance of socio-technical systems. *In*: Contucci, P., Omicini, A., Pianini, D. and Sirbu, A. (eds.). The Future of Digital Democracy: An Interdisciplinary Approach. Springer. New York, USA.

Ross, A. 2016. The Industries of the Future. Simon & Schuster. London, UK.

Schwab, K. 2018. Shaping the Future of the Fourth Industrial Revolution. Penguin Random House. New York, USA.

Shearer, E. and Matsa, K. E. 2019. News Use Across Social Media Platforms 2018, Pew Research Centre. London, UK.

Sinai, N., Leftwich, D. and McGuire, B. 2020. Policymaking Can Learn from Human-Centered Design and Agile Software Development. Harvard Belfer Center Paper. Boston, USA.

Sithigh, D. M. and Siems, M. 2019. The Chinese Social Credit System: A model for other countries? Working Papers, LAW 2019/01. European University Institute. Florence, Italy.

Snowden, F. 2019. Epidemics and Society: From the Black Death to the Present. Yale University Press. Yale, USA.

Stack, L. 2016. Doing the Right Things Right: How the Effective Executive Spends Time, Berrett-Koehler Publishers. San Francisco, USA.

Standing, G. 2011. The Precariat: The New Dangerous Class, Bloomsbury Academic. New York. USA.

United Nations Organization. 1948. Universal Declaration of Human Rights (UDHR). Available on line through the United Nation Organization [Last accessed on May 28, 2020]. https://www.un.org/en/universal-declaration-human-rights/index.html.

UN Internet Governance Forum. 2019. Available online through the official site. [Last accessed on May 28, 2020]. https://www.intgovforum.org/multilingual/content/igf-2019.

Van Reybrouck, D. 2016, Against Elections: The Case for Democracy. Random House. New York. USA.

Wall, M. 2011. What the Next 50 Years Hold for Human Spaceflight. Space.com. 12 April. [Accessed 10 April 2020. https://www.space.com/11364-human-space-exploration-future-50-years-spaceflight.html.

Weiss, T. G. and Wilkinson, R. 2019. Rethinking Global Governance. Polity. Cambridge, UK.

World Economic Forum. 2016. The Fourth Industrial Revolution. The World Economic Forum. Geneva, Switzerland.

Zarocostas, J. 2020. How to Fight an Infodemic, Elsevier The Lancet 395: 10225 p676. https://doi.org/10.1016/S0140-6736(20)30461-X.

Zuboff, S. 2019. The Age of Surveillance Capitalism. Profile books. London, UK.

11

Is it a Cyber Security Strategy for Social Development?

Anthony C Ijeh

1. Introduction

The terms "cyber security" and "cyberspace" are not used by all countries. However, the extent of most strategies generally covers all computer information systems, networks and critical information infrastructures that are not connected to the Internet (OECD 2020). Strategy narratives vary across countries with differing key objectives and concepts, however a general agreement on the need for a more holistic approach to cybersecurity policy making has been agreed. Holistic in this context, means the inclusion of facets such as economic, social, educational, legal, law enforcement, technical, diplomatic, military, and intelligence as well as stakeholders inside the government, throughout the society and foreign partners.

Nigeria, in its ambition to embrace the United Nations 17 Sustainable Development Goals (SDG's) has committed to create a better, fairer, country which by 2030 addresses the following critical issues; poverty (SDG-1), an inclusive economy (SDG-8), health and well-being (SDG-3), education (SDG-4), gender equality (SDG-5), enabling environment of peace and security (SDG-16) and partnerships (SDG-17). In the 2020 Voluntary National Review (VNR), Nigeria highlighted the institutional mechanisms it has put in place to achieve effective implementation of SDGs across the country (OSSAP 2020).

To support Nigeria's ambition the Office of the National Security Adviser (ONSA) has developed a cybersecurity framework and policy (ONSA 2014a). The ONSA recognises that cyberspace has far reaching implications, making it imperative to examine its cyber security strategy, capacity, and the threats faced. The objectives and scope of the cybersecurity strategy Act are to provide an effective legal framework for the prohibition, prevention, detection, prosecution, and punishment of

DASCROSE Limited, England, United Kingdom.
Email: enquiry@dascrose.com

cybercrimes in Nigeria. It also enhances cybersecurity and the protection of computer systems and networks, electronic communications, data, and computer programs in Nigeria. The provisions of the Act are enforced by law enforcement agencies in Nigeria to the extent of the agency's statutory powers (CSA 2011).

Nigeria cooperates with other countries in cyber defence to address cyber insecurity and even though there has been no single framework outlining the ultimate format of cooperation among the countries on cyber security is the recently endorsed UN-Wide Framework on Cyber security and Cybercrime that is widely referenced (Gelvanovska 2013).

Defending the cyberspace of a developing nation needs an understanding of how Information Communication Technology (ICT) is being used and how it is expected to be used. It is for this reason that the perceived benefits of ICT deployment need to be understood to set the motivation for implementing cyberspace defence (Weber 2018). Understanding the benefits and motivation of ICT deployment, define the objective of the cyberspace defence strategy (Osho and Onoja 2015).

According to Bidemi (2018) the benefits and motivation of ICT deployment in Nigeria have been to boost the economy, foster development and alleviate poverty, however the paper concludes that cyberspace access and utilisation must be effectively controlled against abuse with focus on productive engagements such as education, political engagement, economic development, local science and technological inventions amongst others.

This was emphasized by Targert (2010) as a route to evaluate performance by determining if the benefits were protected. OECD (2012) also emphasized the correlation between the benefits and motivation of ICT deployment, initially in its 2002 security guidelines which, following review, resulted in the Recommendation on Digital Security Risk Management for Economic and Social Prosperity and United Nations 2030 Sustainable Development Goals (OECD 2015). These are not enough on their own as to measure the successful implementation of the strategic objectives of any cybersecurity strategy, dedicated institutions for ensuring its successful roll out must also be identified (Daskin 2019).

Economic and social development is essentially a national undertaking, with the state having a critical role in this task. No other institution can replace this role as the history of Europe, North America, East Asia, China, and similar states has demonstrated (Sarbo 2013). Good governance, peace, stability, and security are necessary prerequisites for social and economic progress to take place in any society over a sustained period of time, and only a legitimate and effective state can provide the framework for that to happen. For many African states without the restructuring of the economic, political, and social space that accommodates most of society their legitimacy will continue to rest on international systems that have no local content (Sarbo 2013).

After the introduction in Section 1, the rest of the chapter is structured as follows: Section 2 discusses the goals of the study and presents the methodology used in achieving them. Section 3 looks at the benefits and motivation for Nigeria's cyber space strategy. Section 4 appraises the capacity of Nigeria's cyber space strategy to support social development and the effects cybercrime has on it. Section 5 looks at

Nigeria's cyber space security strategy. Section 6 discusses the impact of Nigeria's cyberspace strategy on social development. Section 7 presents a summary of the chapter and Section 8 recommends future work to be done.

2. Methodology

The goal of this study is to ascertain if the current Cyber Security Strategy of Nigeria supports social development. The methodology used involved reviewing cyber security strategies of other developing countries and global institutions such as the World Bank and United Nations which encourage the use of cyber space for social development. During the study the Nigerian Cyber Security Bill (2011), Nigerian Cyber Security Policy (2014a), Nigerian Cyber Security Strategy (2014b), Action Plan for the Implementation of the Nigerian Cyber Security Strategy (2017), 2nd Voluntary National Review (2020), the National Digital Economy Policy and Strategy 2020–2030: For a Digital Nigeria (2020) and the Nigerian Communications Commission, Strategic Management Plan (2020) were used to explore the supporting structure in place for social development in Nigeria.

3. Cyber Space Strategy Benefits and Motivation

ONSA (2014b) defined Nigeria's Cyberspace as an interdependent network of critical and non-critical national information infrastructures, convergence of interconnected information and communication resources using information and communication technologies. In the report it states that Nigeria's Cyberspace encompassed all forms of digital engagements, interactions, socialisations, and transactional activities; contents, contacts and resources deployed through interconnected networks.

Cyberspace has become highly instrumental for socio-economic development, however, it is not enough for citizens to have access to cyberspace but rather emphasis should be placed on the ability of people to effectively and legitimately utilise their access for the overall well-being of themselves, and society. The proliferation of Information and Communication Technologies (ICT) provides a better opportunity to enhance democracy and citizen participation in governance in Africa and other parts of the world. In this vein, digital technology has expanded the breadth of possibilities for people to enjoy freedoms of expression and association that serves as an enabler for enjoying the right of access to information (Bidemi 2018).

Motivation for the Nigerian Cyberspace Strategy came about in recognition of the existing domains of land, Sea, Air and Space with cyberspace being recognised as the fifth for driving other pillars such as economic development and social interactions, etc. (ONSA 2014b). The aim of the Nigerian Cyberspace Strategy is to provide a cohesive roadmap, initiatives, and implementation mechanism for achieving the national vision on cyber security (ONSA 2014b). Until the establishment of the Nigerian Communications Commission (NCC), Nigeria's journey in cyberspace had been without a planned strategy, and with the growth in users with access, cyber-crime grew at a proportional rate (Mbanaso et al. 2015). It is also in part because the NCC's last strategic plan expired in 2018 (NCC 2020).

The Vision of having a Nigerian Cyberspace Strategy is one that provides a safe, secured, vibrant, resilient, and trusted community that provide opportunities for its citizenry, safeguards national assets and interests, promotes peaceful interactions and proactive engagement in cyberspace for nationals (ONSA 2014b). Legislation that supports a cyber space strategy usually enables the implementation of the mission and vision and prevents non-state and state actors from disrupting them. This is partly because legislation follows a well-planned and structured cyber space strategy (Lin and Zegart 2017).

The prosperity envisioned by creation of the Nigerian Cyberspace Strategy includes platforms and opportunities for securing and growing the nation's economy. This is because every citizen that is connected to the Nigerian cyberspace through the internet becomes empowered by unhindered access to the digital economy. It is also envisioned that Nigerian cyber space will have massive capacity to bridge gaps in mobility, commerce, innovations, education, poverty reduction, and economic empowerment (ONSA 2014b). The strategy aims to nurture and build confidence in the use of Nigerian cyberspace to enable the socio-economic well-being of its citizenry, thereby infusing high level of confidence and trust in its digital economy. It asserts that it will provide after implementation a resilient digital economy, stimulating innovations, wholesome engagement, development, and inflow of foreign direct investment. The emergence of the Nigerian cybercitizen and the growth and penetration rates of Nigeria's Internet usage are important indicators of the encouraging healthy growth of Nigerian cyberspace (Mbanaso et al. 2015). Whilst the cyberspace strategies of developing countries recognise the benefits of a connected world they need to facilitate their cybersecurity capacity through bilateral and multilateral organizations so that they have the means to protect their digital infrastructure, strengthen their global networks, and build closer partnerships in the consensus for open, interoperable, secure, and reliable networks (Obama 2011).

To engage with all industries, sector specific plans which highlight levels of performance, objectives, and feedback to a coordinating agency of government have been created. These sectors include: communication, government facilities, manufacturing, dams, defence, chemical, power and energy, commercial facilities, financial services, food and agriculture, emergency services, transportation systems, public health and healthcare, water and waste-water systems an information technology.

4. Cyberspace Strategy and Social Development

Despite the growing access to cyberspace and proliferation in the use of social media, the opportunities abound for socioeconomic development have not been widely harnessed by the youths who are predominant users of cyberspace to advance learning, economics and other productive activities. The foregoing and other factors account for widespread poverty and poor economic growth in Nigeria. This situation thus suggests a critical evaluation of the difference between general access to cyberspace and its actual utilisation. This is true because, access to cyberspace without proper utilisation and regulations can result in cyberspace abuse which could result in cyber-fraud, illegal gambling, cyber-prostitution, cyber terrorism, and other non-productive activities. The consequential effect of the foregoing would hinder opportunities for self-development, economic growth and further encourage widespread poverty in Nigeria (Bidemi 2018).

According to the NCC in their Strategic Management Plan, NCC (2020) accelerating access to digital technologies spurs innovation, efficiency, and productivity, and brings about choice and opportunities for greater growth and inclusion. Their report shows that many Nigerian citizens and businesses remain excluded from the digital ecosystem because of limited access to broadband and non-availability of adequate devices (mobile devices and computers) to fully utilize the Internet. The report argues that to meet the Governments' 2030 aspirations of greater access to the digital economy and meet the bold objective of creating 100 million jobs in Nigeria, the country needs to increase investment in infrastructure and create an enabling regulatory environment for the digital economy to grow. The NCC recommends in the report that the Nigerian Government undertakes radical reforms that bring about improved skills and a more competitive digital job market, supports public-private partnerships to stimulate and sustain demand for the use of digital platforms, and improves the current business climate to boost more investment opportunities (NCC 2020).

The NCC supports the correlation between advancement in digital economy and economic growth and its role in facilitating the development of the digital economy in Nigeria which it considers a key planning issue (NCC 2020). The department of New Media and Information Security NMIS (2016) in its report supported the creation of a National Development Plan for a large-scale investment project to develop the infrastructure of a country. The report advocates for central planning and monitoring on a national level and implementation on a micro, local level in which goals should focus on the development of economic infrastructure, education, social welfare, science, and innovation are implemented (NMIS 2016).

The NCC states that its vision is to digitally transform the economy of Nigeria into a leading global economy providing quality life and digital opportunities for all her citizens. Its mission is to build a nation where every citizen, business and institution can utilize readily accessible digital technologies for improving themselves and developing the national economy (NCC 2020). The environment however needs to be conducive as war and government corruption can have a negative impact on economies. During conflict, there is a distortion of economic activities and corruption can increase the cost of business transactions and scare away foreign investors (NMIS 2016). As Nigeria's critical infrastructure continues to connect to computers and information networks, nations will rely on these networks for essential service delivery. Therefore, cyberspace has become a driving force for productivity and development, which makes the protection of Critical Information Infrastructure a national security responsibility requiring government, public and private sector to collaborate and synergise (ONSA 2017). The recently published FMCDE (2020) will enable Nigeria to take advantage of opportunities in the global digital economy. It promises to position Nigeria as an early adopter of digital technology, and it gives Nigeria a good opportunity to become major participants in the growing global

Figure 1: Pillars of the digital economy policy and strategy document (FMCDE 2020).

digital economy. The Digital Economy Policy and Strategy document (see Figure 1) is based on the 8 pillars for the acceleration of the National Digital Economy for a Digital Nigeria (FMCDE 2020).

Pillar #2 provides policy backing for massive training of Nigerians from all works of life to enable them to obtain digital literacy skills. The training programmes will be expected to culminate in globally recognized certifications (FMCDE 2020).

Pillar #6 advocates the importance of cybersecurity and other standards, frameworks and guidelines that encourage citizens to go digital. Many Nigerians do not have confidence in online services, especially when they relate to financial transactions because of the perception that they are unsafe online. With identity being digitized and tied to biometrics, initiatives like the National Identity Number (NIN), Biometric Verification Number (BVN), Voter IDs and SIM-card registration details can provide channels for identifying citizens to facilitate credible transactions, considering its great benefits (FMCDE 2020).

Pillar #7 focuses on tying the development of the digital economy to indices of well-being in the lives of the ordinary citizens. Digital and financial inclusion are some of the issues that this pillar seeks to address. The Digital Society and Emerging Technology pillar will map the development of the digital economy to the attainment of 7 of the Sustainable Development Goals (SDGs) that are most relevant to the digital economy, namely: (1) Poverty Eradication; (2) Good Health and Well-being; (3) Quality Education; (4) Decent Work and Economic Growth; (5) Industry, Innovation, and Infrastructure; (6) Reducing

Inequality; and (7) Sustainable Cities and Communities. Emerging technologies can enable the nation to attain these goals. As such, an emerging technology programme will be introduced in the country (FMCDE 2020).

Pillar #8 aims to identify jobs that are currently being outsourced and support the repatriation of these jobs to digitally skilled Nigerians. Promoting and adopting indigenous content will enable Nigeria to benefit from the increasingly global digital technology market. It will also help to conserve foreign exchange for the country and boost exports. The activities in this pillar will ensure that "Made in Nigeria" digital economy products are of globally accepted quality. The pillar will also seek to make Nigeria a global outsourcing destination for digital jobs (FMCDE 2020).

4.1 Cyberspace and Cyber Crime

The cost of cyber crime to a society can be both qualitative and non-qualitative. There are the financial losses to individuals and organizations (figures rarely made public), as well as the sizable expense of security software and personnel to protect against possible digital incursions. Then there is the damage to brand image should a country be the unfortunate victim of online crimes (NMIS 2016).

In meeting the Government goal of ensuring a secure cyberspace for Nigeria, Section 41 (b) of the cyber crime (Prohibition, Prevention, etc.) Act, 2015 mandates the Office of the National Security Adviser (ONSA) to "ensure formulation and effective implementation of a comprehensive National Cyber Security Strategy and a National Cybersecurity Policy for Nigeria". In furtherance of this mandate, ONSA has developed an Action for implementing the National Cybersecurity Strategy. This is with a view to enable government to effectively utilize the numerous potentials inherent in the cyberspace while mitigating the effects of cyber crime and improving safety and security of Nigerians (ONSA 2017)

Many attacks on Nigeria's cyberspace in 2020 have moved from big organisations to seemingly unlikely targets, especially companies who are of the notion that they are not prone to cyber-attacks or do not have enough resources to attract any attack (Aladenusi 2020). The main targets for cyber-attackers have been cloud-based systems, user mobile devices, internet-of-things, and small and medium enterprises as well as organisations in the non-financial sector (Aladenusi 2020).

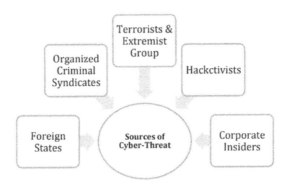

Figure 2: Sources of cyber threat (ONSA 2014b).

The widespread use of cyberspace through social media has created opportunities and space for many people in Nigeria to interact and express their opinion on the issues bordering on socio-economic and the political situation within their environment (Oloyede and Elega 2019). Despite the opportunities offered by cyberspace access in terms of socialisation, enhanced learning opportunities, communication, entertainment, political participation, and economic development, it also poses serious challenges to socio-cultural identity, security, democracy stability and youth productivity (Bidemi 2018). In the case of Nigeria, widespread of poverty has become more evident due to increased cyber abuse by youth, who constitute the majority in the country. Thus, it is argued that cyberspace for non-productive activities such as online sport betting, cyber prostitution, cyber frauds, cyber violence, and related cyber crimes hinder government capacity to alleviate poverty, and additionally, such activities damage the country's image and prevent access to national socio-economic and political opportunities (Bidemi 2018).

Establishing the appropriate legal infrastructure is an integral component of a national cyber security strategy. The related mandate of ITU about capacity building was emphasized by Resolution 130 (Rev. Guadalajara 2010) of the ITU Plenipotentiary Conference, on strengthening the role of ITU in building confidence and security in the use of information and communication technologies (Gercke 2011). The first of the seven strategic goals of the ITU Global Cyber Security Agenda (GCA), call for the elaboration of strategies for the development of cyber crime legislation that are globally applicable and interoperable with existing national and regional legislative measures, as well as able to address the approach to organizing national cyber security efforts under ITU-D Study Group 1 Question 22/1 (Gercke 2012).

Securing cyberspace is a Herculean and complicated task. The creation of a technological, commercial, and social environment in which commerce and civic transactions are promoted and encouraged, while criminal and terrorist activities are discouraged and prevented faces numerous challenges and obstacles. The barriers to effective cyber security are rooted both in the technological composition of cyberspace and in the political, cultural, societal, and legal differences that hinder international cooperation in general (Levin 2012).

The international nature of cyberspace is, in and of itself, a challenge to effective cyber security. Since cyberspace is, in essence, a nexus of networks of computers that are physically located in many different countries and legal jurisdictions, no one country can dictate or control interactions in cyberspace. Countries therefore attempt to enter into international agreements, either bilateral or multilateral, in an effort to regulate cyberspace and coordinate cyber security, but these attempts are often guided by other interests and affiliations, which do not always correspond with the most effective responses to cybercrime (Levin 2012).

Nigeria as part of the nations classified under developing countries has benefited immensely from Foreign Direct Investments since the mid 1990's. It goes without saying that the country's economy in recent times have had advancements in Information and Communications Technology which can be seen in every facet of its industries. This growth has also attracted innumerable crimes which have directly and otherwise affected the influx of Foreign Direct Investments, especially in the form of cyber crime (NMIS 2016).

Taking an in-depth analysis of the said subject matter, it is apt and of utmost interest to pose some questions that will enable us shed additional light for posterity sake. Has the increase in cyber crime reduced the rate of Foreign Direct Investments? Is there a direct correlation between cyber crime and the reduction in FDI in Nigeria particularly in recent times? Can we say that the negative impact of cyber crime has in-turn decelerated National Development? This project is underpinned on the conceptual analysis of cyber crimes' adverse effect on FDIs. It goes further to establish a nexus between cyber crime and technological advancement with a view to contextualise the answers in lieu of the objectives and appraise the situation. The issue of cyber crime and its antagonistic impact on the Nigerian economy is alarming and has increasingly become disheartening. To this extent, the government must become proactive and focused on the continuous fight to curb the menace and mitigate its effect on the citizenry. For Nigeria to serve as a fertile ground for economic breakthrough, it must be built in a crime free society. But an ideal economy is virtually impossible. As technology upsurges, so also is the cyber crime rate on the rise. Cyber criminals will always keep at pace with any technological advancement. It is true that technology gives rise to cyber crime, we could live with it or we can do something momentous about it (NMIS 2016).

5. Nigeria's Cyber Security Strategy

To comprehend better the global and regional needs of an effective cyber security strategy that supports social development, the current and future defence projections, are required for a holistic approach which also takes into account, innovation, entrepreneurship, geostrategic and geo-economic challenges (Efthymiopoulos 2019; Ijeh et al. 2009; Ijeh 2011). The last decade has seen behaviour in cyberspace veering in a direction that much of cyber security literature has not. Whereas much of the academic and policy communities have focused on cyber war, the actual behaviour of actors has been of a far more nuanced and different nature. The fundamental nature of cyberspace rests on a structure of interconnectedness and a condition of constant contact. Once recognised, that structural environment requires us to study cyber means not as enablers of war, although they be, but more critically as the strategic alternative to it (Harnett and Smeets 2020). It is worth noting that forward defence is only one among several policies that can be termed active defence or indeed cyber deterrence (Healey 2019).

The realization that cyber forces are in constant contact is certainly correct and persistent engagement is a reasonable response. But the power of the theory rests heavily on the nature of engagement between participants, so much so that there is only one response, a technologically determined dominant strategy: defending forward in close contact with adversaries to intercept and halt their operations with few restraints (Healey 2019).

Nations around the world recognize cyber security as a critical issue for public policy. They are concerned that their adversaries could conduct cyberattacks against their interests—damaging their military forces, their economies, and their political processes. Thus, their cyber security efforts have been devoted largely to protecting important information technology systems and networks against such attacks. Recognizing this point, the Oxford Dictionary added in 2013 a new word to its lexicon—it defined cyber security as "the state of being protected against the criminal or unauthorized use of electronic data, or the measures taken to achieve this." But a nation can also conduct cyberattacks against other nations as deliberate instruments of policy, and many nations around the world are also exploring the use of offensive cyber operations in such a manner (Lin and Zegart 2017).

On cyber security, the Federal Government of Nigeria has recognised the importance of cyber security and has introduced several initiatives. In 2004, the Nigerian Cybercrime Working Group (NCWG) was established, a 15-member committee drawn from government and the private sector to look into the legal and institutional framework for addressing cyber crime in Nigeria. The Committee developed the first Bill on Cyber crime and Critical Information Infrastructure Protection, which was conveyed to the National Assembly, although sponsored by a private individual. However, the Bill suffered an inexplicable setback. In 2011, a National Committee was set up by the National Security Adviser charged with the responsibility to harmonise the various cyber security bills pending in the National Assembly. The draft cyber security 2011 Bill was finally signed into law in 2015. The National Cyber security Policy and Strategy was launched in March 2015. Some federal government institutions are confronting cyber-criminality aligned with their constitutional mandates (Mbanaso et al. 2015).

Cyber security has become a complex and fast-moving security challenge in the age of Information Communication and Technology (ICT). As the dependence on ICT is deepening across the globe, cyberthreats appear likely to penetrate every nook and corner of national economies and infrastructure; indeed, the growing dependence on computers and Internet based networking has been accompanied by increased cyberattack incidents around the world, targeting individuals, businesses, and governments. Meanwhile, ICT is increasingly being seen by some governments as both a strategic asset to be exploited for the purposes of national security and as a battlefield where strategic conflicts can be fought. Indeed, the ever-growing interdependence of the digital sphere, across borders, has provoked the emergence of cybersecurity as a major component of national security strategies 10 in states across the globe and countries like India are not delaying in their adoption of strategies but following their example (Parmar 2018).

Senol and Karakuha 2020, presented a new national cyber security strategy (NCSS) covering the deterrence perspective from creation to implementation. With the aim of responding to and ensuring cyber security effectively, studies on which pathways should be followed and what methods should be used to develop, create, and implement a NCSS are being conducted in Turkey, as in all countries. In addition, this approach, which has been put forward for effective implementation of cyber security by ensuring better management, control, and supervision, can be easily used by all other countries.

The World Bank has asked developing countries to build up their local technological capabilities by increasing research and development expenditures accompanied by institutional reform and designing new policy making institutions (Arroio 2012). The World Bank has made clear that transfer of technology from developed countries is not an alternative to the development of local science. The World Bank described as difficult, for a country without local science, technology and innovation capacity and particularly without the trained people required to know what useful technology exists elsewhere, to understand it, select it, absorb, adapt and operate, repair, and then, generate new knowledge (Arroio 2012). The main argument for adopting technologies from developed countries as an alternative to local science is the ability to leapfrog across several stages of development and faster implementation (Ndulu et al. 2007). However, policy documents, directives and mission statements of leading international cooperation Organizations, multilateral development institutions and Official Development Assistance agencies usually refer to the role of local science in development and the promotion of capabilities for sustainable social development (Arroio 2012).

For Nigeria, there exists a digital divide within the country, as seen from the survey conducted (Mbanaso et al. 2015). Some Federal Ministries and states have a Stage Two online presence, while the LGAs are generally yet to commence e-governance. Most tertiary institutions have established a web presence, while very few secondary schools have keyed in. Similarly, in the business sector, most multinationals and banks are enjoying the benefits of e-business, while microfinance institutions are lagging behind. With economic and social activities increasingly moving to the Internet, cyberspace has become the platform for innovations, enterprises, social networking, criminality, and war. Nigeria and some other West African countries have started moving towards an increased online presence. It is vital for Nigeria and other sub-Saharan African countries to learn from global best practice and collaborate to develop a harmonised framework with necessary defence against cyber-criminality and cyber-warfare (Mbanaso et al. 2015).

Nigeria like most other countries recognizes the importance of cyber security and is actively involved in the implementation of the Global Cyber Security Agenda and has taken concrete steps to secure its cyber space. In December 2014 Nigeria published its National Cyber Security Strategy which clearly mapped out Nigeria's National Cyber Security Vision and the strategies for achieving this vision. Furthermore, in May 2015 the President of the Federal Republic of Nigeria signed into law the Nigeria Cybercrime (Prohibition, Prevention, etc.) Act. The Act provides an effective, unified, and comprehensive legal, regulatory, and institutional framework for the prohibition, prevention, detection, prosecution, and punishment of cybercrimes in Nigeria. The Act also ensures the protection of critical national information infrastructure and promotes Cyber Security and the protection of computer systems and networks, electronic communications, data and computer programs, intellectual property, and privacy rights.

6. Discussion

Nigeria is a developing nation with a growing population with access to cyber space. To secure its information and critical infrastructure, the Nigerian Senate was presented a cybersecurity bill in 2011, which it passed in 2014 and whose stakeholders implemented in 2017 through the office of the National Security

Adviser. To meet its bilateral and multilateral transaction obligations Nigeria uses the UN-Wide Framework on Cyber Security and Cyber Crime. The perceived benefits of Information and Communication Technology (ICT) deployment need to be clearly understood to set the motivation for any Cyber Security Strategy and it is these benefits that determine its focus. Social development is a national undertaking, with the state having a critical role in this task. This is because good governance, peace, stability, and security are necessary prerequisites for social and economic progress to take place in any society over a sustained period of time, and only a legitimate and effective state can provide the framework for this to happen.

Nigeria's definition of its cyber space aligns with international standards, but the proliferation of ICT should be an opportunity to realise the benefits of enjoying freedom of expression and association, right of access to information, and democracy and citizen participation in governance of Nigeria. The motivation for Nigeria's Cyber space security strategy, is that of its role as the fifth domain after air, land, sea, and space. It was tagged as a driving pillar for economic and social development but until the establishment of the Nigerian Communications Commission (NCC), Nigeria's journey in cyber space had been without a planned strategy, and with the growth in users with access, cyber crime grew at a proportional rate. From the initiatives made the government envisioned that Nigeria's cyber space would have a massive capacity to bridge gaps in mobility, commerce, innovations, education, poverty reduction, and economic empowerment but did not provide the environment or strategy to support it. To facilitate their cyber security capacity developed nations, build closer partnerships with bilateral and multilateral organizations to protect sector specific digital infrastructure and doing so enables them to strengthen their global networks.

Widespread poverty and poor economic growth indicate that the opportunities for socioeconomic development have not been widely harnessed by users of Nigeria's cyber space. Although general access continues to grow, it is not in itself actual utilisation and non-regulation has seen cyber abuse grow at a proportional rate. A core segment of Nigerian citizens and businesses remain excluded from the digital ecosystem because of limited access and non-availability of adequate devices. The state however intends to improve the current business climate, provide all citizens access to the digital economy by 2030 and create 100 million jobs. This task rests with the Nigerian Communications Commission and the newly constituted Federal Ministry of Communications and Digital Economy, of which both have stressed the importance of a conducive business environment and negative impact of an insurgency and corruption on the digital economy which increase the cost of business transactions and scare away foreign investors.

The newly published Digital Economy Policy and Strategy document has 8 pillars which aim to support socioeconomic development. Pillar #7 focuses on tying the development of the digital economy to indices of well-being in the lives of the ordinary citizens. The Digital Society and Emerging Technology pillar will map the development of the digital economy to the attainment of 7 of the Sustainable Development Goals (SDGs) that are most relevant to the digital economy, namely: (1) Poverty Eradication; (2) Good Health and Well-being; (3) Quality Education; (4) Decent Work and Economic Growth; (5) Industry, Innovation, and Infrastructure;

(6) Reducing Inequality; and (7) Sustainable Cities and Communities. Emerging technologies can enable the nation to attain these goals.

The National Cyber Security Strategy and National Cybersecurity Policy for Nigeria are managed by the Office of the National Security Adviser with the aim of mitigating the effects of cybercrime and improving safety and security of Nigerians. Consulting firms monitoring cyber crime have reported that cyber attacks will focus on Internet-of-Everything (IOE), personal devices and organisations in the non-financial sector. Cybercrime hinders government capacity to enhance socioeconomic initiatives and continues to damage the country's image and prevent interest from foreign direct investment.

Establishing the appropriate legal infrastructure is an integral component of a national cyber security strategy. United Nations call for the development of cyber crime legislation that is globally applicable and interoperable with existing national and regional legislative measures. This is essential when dealing with bilateral and multilateral organisations. The barriers to effective cyber security are rooted both in the technological composition of cyberspace and in the political, cultural, societal, and legal differences that hinder international cooperation in general.

With many state actors involved in cyber war, nations around the world recognize cyber security as a critical issue for public policy. Most governments including the Nigerian government comprehend the need for an effective cybersecurity strategy that supports social development.

7. Conclusion

Nigeria is trying to harness the benefits of a localised digital economy and has rolled out a strategy to enable it to do so by 2030. The strategy aligns with the 17 sustainable developmental goals of the United Nations whose member countries are expected to have attained by 2030. Nigeria like other developing countries is building up her local technological capabilities by increasing research and development expenditures accompanied by institutional reform and designing new policy making institutions. The transfer of technology from developed to developing countries is not an alternative to the development of local science. The effort of the Nigerian government to enhance social development as seen in its second Voluntary National Review (2020), the National Digital Economy Policy and Strategy 2020–2030: For a Digital Nigeria (2020) and the Nigerian Communications Commission, Strategic Management Plan (2020) are not accounted for in the National Cyber Security Strategy (2014). Nigeria therefore needs to develop a harmonised cyber security framework with necessary defence against cyber criminality and cyber warfare. Nigeria should continue to work with partner countries and other providers of social development to promote its civic space and counter negative narratives by highlighting the benefits of an open and enabled space for civil society, like the economy, delivering on the SDGs, tackling social issues and corruption.

8. Future Work

It is expected that the National Cyber Security Policy (2014a) and Cyber Security Strategy (2014b) used to undertake this study will be updated in the future to accommodate Nigeria's changing economy and growing population. Future work should include a revised study using any new or updated cyber security policy and strategy.

References

Aladenusi, T. 2020. Nigeria Cyber Security Outlook 2020: The Year of Shifts. Deloitte, Predictions. Available at: https://www2.deloitte.com/ng/en/pages/risk/articles/nigeria-cyber-security-outlook-2020.html. [Accessed 2 Sep. 2020].

Arroio, A. 2012. Governance of science, technology, and innovation programmes for development: is global financing getting it right? Institutions and Economics 4(2): 45–64. [online] Available at: http://ijie.um.edu.my/filebank/published_article/3942/Fulltext3.pdf [Accessed 3 Sep. 2020].

Bidemi, B. 2018. Cyberspace abuse and the proliferation of poverty in Nigeria: investigating the paradox of social-economic development. Africology: The Journal of Pan African Studies 11(8), June 2018. Available at: https://www.questia.com/library/journal/1P4-2071549197/cyberspace-abuse-and-the-proliferation-of-poverty [Accessed 2 Sep. 2020].

CSA. 2011. Cybersecurity Bill. Enacted by the National Assembly of the Federal Republic of Nigeria. [online] Available at: http://blogs.law.harvard.edu/mcash/files/2012/03/Nigeria-Cyber-Security-Bill-2011.pdf [Accessed 3 Sep. 2020].

Daskin, E. 2019. The Turkish cyber security strategy: structure, legislation, and challenges. The Journal of Intelligence and Cyber Security 2(1). Available at: https://www.academicapress.com/journal/v2-1/JICSVolume2Issue1_Daskin.pdf [Accessed 2 Sep. 2020].

Efthymiopoulos, M. P. 2019. A cyber-security framework for development, defence, and innovation at NATO. Journal of Innovation and Entrepreneurship 8: 12. Available at: https://doi.org/10.1186/s13731-019-0105-z [Accessed 2 Sep. 2020].

FMCDE. 2020. National Digital Economy Policy and Strategy 2020–2030: For a Digital Nigeria. [online] Available at: https://www.ncc.gov.ng/docman-main/industry-statistics/policies-reports/883-national-digital-economy-policy-and-strategy/file [Accessed 3 Sep. 2020].

Gelvanovska, N. 2013. Role of Multilateral organization in Cyber Security. Internet Governance Forum. [online] Available at: http://www.intgovforum.org/cms/wks2013/workshop_2013_status_list_view.php?xpsltipq_je=91 [Accessed 3 Sep. 2020].

Gercke, M. 2011. Understanding Cybercrime: A guide for developing countries. [online] Available at: http://www.itu.int/ITU-D/cyb/cybersecurity/docs/ITU_Guide_A5_12072011.pdf [Accessed 3 Sep. 2020].

Gercke, M. 2012. Understanding Cybercrime: Phenomena, Challenges and Legal Response. [online] Available at: http://www.itu.int/ITU-D/cyb/cybersecurity/docs/Cybercrime%20legislation%20EV6.pdf [Accessed 3 Sep. 2020].

Harknett, R. J. and Smeets, M. 2020. Cyber campaigns and strategic outcomes. Journal of Strategic Studies. pp. 1–34. Available at: https://www.tandfonline.com/doi/full/10.1080/01402390.2020.1732354 [Accessed 2 Sep. 2020].

Healey, J. 2019. The implications of persistent (and permanent) engagement in cyberspace. Journal of Cybersecurity 5(1): 1–15. Available at: https://academic.oup.com/cybersecurity/article/5/1/tyz008/5554878 [Accessed 2 Sep. 2020].

Ijeh, A., Preston, D., Imafidon, C. and Williams, G. 2009. Security strategy models (SSM). Proceedings of Advances in Computing and Technology. (AC&T) The School of Computing and Technology 4th Annual Conference University of East London, pp. 126–131. Available at: https://repository.uel.ac.uk/item/8608q [Accessed 2 Sep. 2020].

Ijeh, A. 2011. Geofencing as a Security Strategy Model. [Thesis] pp. 1–140. Available at: https://repository.uel.ac.uk/item/8608q [Accessed 2 Sep. 2020].

Levin, A., Goodrick, P. and Ilkina, D. 2012 Securing Cyberspace: A Comparative Review of Strategies Worldwide. Available at: https://www.ryerson.ca/tedrogersschool/privacy/documents/Ryerson_cyber_crime_final_report.pdf [Accessed 3 Sep. 2020].

Lin, H. and Zegart, A. 2017. Introduction to the special issue on strategic dimensions of offensive cyber operations. Journal of Cybersecurity 3(1): 1–5. March 2017. Available at: https://academic.oup.com/cybersecurity/article/3/1/1/3060285 [Accessed 2 Sep. 2020].

Mbanaso, U., Chukwudebe, G. and Atimati, E. 2015. Nigeria's evolving presence in cyberspace. The African Journal of Information and Communication Jan 2015, 15: 106–113. Available at: https://journals.co.za/content/afjic/2015/15/EJC189249 [Accessed 2 Sep. 2020].

NCC. 2020. Nigerian Communication Commission—Strategic Management Plan 2020–2024. [online] Available at: https://www.ncc.gov.ng/docman-main/industry-statistics/policies-reports/886-ncc-2020-2024-strategic-management-plan-aspire-2024/file [Accessed 2 Sep. 2020].

Ndulu, B. J., Chakraborti, L., Lijane, L., Ramachandran, V. and Wolgin, K. J. 2006. Challenges of African Growth: Opportunities, Constraints, and Strategic Directions. Washington, DC: World Bank. © World Bank. [online] Available at: https://openknowledge.worldbank.org/handle/10986/6656 [Accessed 2 Sep. 2020].

NMIS. 2016. Effects of Cyber Crime on Foreign Direct Investment and National Development [online] Available at: https://www.ncc.gov.ng/documents/735-nmis-effects-cybercrime-foreign-direct-investment/file [Accessed 2 Sep. 2020].

Obama, B. 2011. International Strategy for Cyberspace: Prosperity, Security, and Openness in a Networked World. https://obamawhitehouse.archives.gov/sites/default/files/rss_viewer/international_strategy_for_cyberspace.pdf [Accessed 3 Sep. 2020].

OECD. 2012. Cybersecurity policy making at a turning point: Analysing a new generation of national cybersecurity strategies for the Internet economy and non-governmental perspectives on a new generation of National Cybersecurity Strategies. Available at: https://www.oecd.org/sti/ieconomy/cybersecurity%20policy%20making.pdf [Accessed 2 Sep. 2020].

OECD. 2015. The Sustainable Development Goals: An overview of relevant OECD analysis, tools, and approaches. http://www.oecd.org/dac/The%20Sustainable%20Development%20Goals%20An%20overview%20of%20relevant%20OECD%20analysis.pdf [Accessed 2 Sep. 2020].

OECD. 2020. Digital transformation and the futures of civic space to 2030. OECD Development Policy Papers, No. 29, OECD Publishing, Paris, https://doi.org/10.1787/79b34d37-en.

Oloyede, F. and Elega, A. A. 2019 Exploring Hashtag Activism in Nigeria: A case of #Endsars Campaign. [online] Available at: Proceeding: 5th In Communication and Media Studies (CRPC 2018). https://crcp.emu.edu.tr/Documents/Books/CRCP%202018%20Proceeding%20Book%20-%20Approved%20One.pdf [Accessed 2 Sep. 2020].

ONSA. 2014a. National Cybersecurity Policy. Office of the National Security Adviser, Nigeria. [online] Available at: http://www.cybersecuritynigeria.org.ng/ncsf/index.php/downloadable-docs [Accessed 3 Sep. 2020].

ONSA. 2014b. National Cybersecurity Strategy. Office of the National Security Adviser, Nigeria. [online] Available at: https://www.cert.gov.ng/ngcert/resources/NATIONAL_CYBESECURITY_STRATEGY.pdf [Accessed 3 Sep. 2020].

ONSA. 2017. Action Plan for the Implementation of the National Cybersecurity Strategy. Office of the National Security Adviser, Nigeria. [online] Available at: https://www.cybertalknaija.com/wp-content/uploads/2019/06/draft-action-plan-ncss.pdf [Accessed 3 Sep. 2020].

Osho, O. and Onoja, A. D. 2015. National cyber security policy and strategy of nigeria: a qualitative analysis. International Journal of Cyber Criminology 9(1): 120–143. ISSN: 0973-5089-January–June 2015. [online] Available at: https://www.cybercrimejournal.com/Osho&Onoja2015vol9issue1.pdf [Accessed 2 Sep. 2020].

OSSAP. 2020. Nigeria Integration of the SDGs into National Development Planning. A Second Voluntary National Review Available at https://sustainabledevelopment.un.org/content/documents/26309VNR_2020_Nigeria_Report.pdf [Accessed 3 Sep. 2020].

Parmar, S. D. 2018. Cybersecurity in India: An evolving concern for national security. The Journal of Intelligence and Cyber Security 1(1). Available at: https://www.academicapress.com/journal/v1-1/Parmar_Cybersecurity-in-India.pdf [Accessed 2 Sep. 2020].

Sarbo, N. D. 2013. Re-Conceptualizing Regional Integration in Africa: The European Model and Africa's Priorities. [online] Available at: http://www.globaleconomicgovernance.org/sites/geg/files/Sarbo_GEG%20WP%202013_78.pdf [Accessed 3 Sep. 2020].

Senol, M. and Karacuha, R. 2020. Creating and implementing an effective and deterrent national cyber security strategy. Journal of Engineering, Article ID 5267564, 19 pages. Available at: https://www.hindawi.com/journals/je/2020/5267564/ [Accessed 2 Sep. 2020].

Targert, A. 2010. Cybersecurity Challenges in Developing Nations. [Thesis] pp. 1–157. Available at: https://kilthub.cmu.edu/articles/Cybersecurity_Challenges_in_Developing_Nations/6715520 [Accessed 2 Sep. 2020].

Weber, V. 2018. Linking cyber strategy with grand strategy: the case of the United States. Journal of Cyber Policy 3(2): 236–257. Available at: https://www.tandfonline.com/doi/full/10.1080/23738871.2018.1511741 [Accessed 2 Sep. 2020].

12

NATO's Current and Future Cyber-Defence Adaptability

Marios Panagiotis Efthymiopoulos

1. Introduction

The chapter's aim is to methodologically examine NATO's policy on cyber-security and its adaptability to current and emerging challenges. The chapter considers the latest strategic objective that was decided during the NATO London Summit by the end of 2019: To set up a new cyber-security operations centre in Mons Brussels (Cyber-Defence 2019) by 2023. The chapter evaluates and commends on NATOs current accomplishments. Examines achievements made to date while evaluates NATO's cyber-adaptability to current and emerging threats. The chapter is written at an important timeframe considering new and ongoing challenges raised during and in a post-Covid-19 Corona Virus pandemic, security environment. The chapter recommends measures based on strategic and tactical levels, so as to accomplish a complete cyber-security policy efficiency.

The chapter calls for an enhanced and continued cyber-security adaptability of NATO so as to continue meeting all and any challenges ahead. There is a new world order of cyberaffairs in 2020. 2020 is a year that is considered an 'eye-opener' for cyber-affairs, considering how fast we are now needed to move ahead into the virtual/digitized world. The Corona Virus Covid-19 global pandemic, needless to say, is a global human pandemic. It has nonetheless led us fast forward onto a pace that renders us completely dependent on the tools but also threats generated by the world wide web.

The chapter comments on NATOs' continued and diverse efforts (political legal and operational) to uphold clear targets towards a truly joined comprehensive security strategy at the level of cyber-defence. Cyber-Defence complements general defence

Associate Professor of International Security and Strategy, College of Security and Global Studies, American University in the Emirates.
Email: Marios.panagiotis@aue.ae

efforts as were decided during the adoption of the NATO strategic concept (NATO Strategic Concept 2010). In the year 2020, NATOs' predicament is to continue to hold a pragmatic operational approach, reflect real-time protection and defence methods between NATO members and its allies in also cyber-space.

Early on, we need to state that Cyber-defence or security, is not a traditional form of security policy or framework. It is a digital phenomenon that requires a constantly digitally enhanced interoperable framework and knowledge of operations (legal, political, military, operational). And NATO must do just that. It requires flexibility and holds unlimited, non-border like cyber-space to operate on.

NATOs' strategy is cyber-resilient. It does require operational efficacy and efficiency. It requires tactical agility, experiential resilience, at a virtual level. Cyber-defence and security is as referred to a "pledge" (Cyber-Defence 2019). And as we will explain below in fact its core policy idea dates back to the NATO Prague Summit of 2002 (NATO Prague Summit 2002). Cyber-defence policy is today a strategy. Reflecting protectionism and defence measures from any possible e-vulnerabilities at the digital world of cyber-space. Cyber-security is a multi-dimensional, virtual effort, to protect networks and infrastructure, software and hardware, 'wired' to the world of the internet that is used and operated by all civilian and non-civilian assets of the NATO member states.

In a more 'aggressive and ever adaptable' world with now an extensive use of the world wide web such as in the year 2020, vulnerabilities and malicious attacks have multiplied. Convergence on and about the internet of things and how to cope with them universally in a real-time strategy is thus required, legally and operationally both militarily and at a civilian cooperative level. Which means that NATO's cyber-security strategy may as it be at this time, can become one of the most important policies pillars for NATO. It may combine efforts and showcase how joined efficiency and cooperation takes place. An example on the way to a universal framework against cyber-attacks. NATOs' upcoming operational command would thus be one of the most important operational pillars of defence at NATO itself by the time of its operation in 2023.

It is quite evident that due to the increase levels of utilization of cyber-space in 2020, more malicious and hybrid attacks do already take place. Attacks have multiplied as said. It is also likely that while the pandemic continues beyond the normal time frame as was initially projected, our dependence on the internet will be greater. Which also means that attacks online will continue to take place and increase even more. Attackers will continue to exploit possible vulnerabilities that may come about. The world was not and is still not ready to a complete 100% dependency on the world wide web considering all possible universal defence and security measures that need to be taken into consideration. At this time we evidently distinguish fast-track national policies and strategies and services that come with, moving national strategies and policies into a format and operation in the digitization world. This means that we expect to have more and more 'smart' operations and methods of interaction to operate in cyber-space. While we become more expose to an unregulated internet, cyber-attacks are most likely to increase. These attacks are likely to be malicious in nature and will always be considered hybrid in their aims and objectives.

While NATO prepares its cyber-operational command, NATO is at the same time in need to (a) adapt to real-time threats as they currently emerge (b) showcase continued and enhanced operational agility (c) operationally short term and long-term tactical efficiency to secure, protect, create a sustainable and growing e-security military and civilian working environment. NATO is expected to innovate in and through the way that operations take place. While creating operational efficacy and efficiency; empirical knowledge is required so as to help adapt at a faster pace the socio-political e-environment that we have to live on.

Amazingly and simply put, 'trust' in a truly NATO cooperative security strategy is must amongst alliance members. If NATO allies wish to succeed future and emerging threats and if they wish for the alliance to continue to project agreement clarity. In 2020, while we proceed in battling the Covid-19 Corona virus, we are in effect looking for measures to (1) simplify daily operations, (2) enhance security operations both in a military and civilian cooperative frameworks, (3) understand the future of technology and cyber-based innovation. In turn, what is suggested is that NATOs' current strategic concept should make sure by leaders to continue to be applicable in the 'Internet of things' for purpose in this chapter I name it the "internet matrix". We should clearly understand the need for a clear and holistic, strategic convergence of the 4th industrial revolution with the 5th technological revolution that we can now term as the '5th Industrial/technological rising'.

The current chapter is part of the personal readings and empirical experiences of the author. The chapter blossomed throughout continued research and publications on the topic and subject of cyber-security as a strategy for security as a follow up since 2008. The author has an extensive experience on NATO policies from academic, research and professional experience levels. The work presented below is related with the specialty of the author with regards to NATOs' current and future threats and challenges. This chapter nonetheless, specializes on the strategy and operations of cyber-security and defence in an era of global pandemic and requests NATO to increase its cyber-adaptability considering the real-time threats that are ongoing and existential.

The current chapter has an added value. The empirical and working experience in various parts of the world has allowed the reader to conclude the strategic and operational objectives and aims on cyber-security and NATO. At this point, the attempt is to clarify the current and future options and opportunities on cyber-defence at NATO, considering that threats, vulnerabilities, malicious attacks of all hybrid levels will increase and the ongoing process to reach for a complete cyber operational capacity by 2023 through the cyber security command of NATO. The chapter assumes that the results of the global pandemic, will ultimately lead to more vulnerable e-security environment that will continue to be hybrid in nature. It is for this reason that the chapter requests for more security cohesion and cooperation, between all members states of NATO.

As a disclosure, I would like to stress, that the current chapter is in no way related with any government or private entity, institution or organization. It is not related with NATO as an organization rather its effort is concentrated on a scientific and academic level of research that is now being published and is for the reader to critically comment. The chapter is in no way funded by any institution or international organization, member or partner country or cooperative country or non-cooperative country to NATO. It is not associated with the current profession of the author at any level direct or indirect. Rather it is related with the academic and scientific personal research interests of the author over the last 12 years.

The opinions expressed in this chapter, reflect the authors' academic and scientific opinions only. They are based on the author's empirical experience. The chapter however is centred around secondary sources of information and follows both a deductive and inductive theoretical approach to the subject at hand. Any critical comments and parts of the chapter that will derive from its publication will be used as a source to recommend an upcoming publication in 2021, on the strategy and importance of cyber-security.[1]

This chapter is educative. It includes theoretical and practical elements as it examines the subject of concern from both an inductive and deductive approach. The chapter gives results and recommendations that can be used for practical purposes. This chapter is a 'good read' for both theory experts but also practitioners, in the field of security studies, science of cyber-security, war studies, social and political sciences, information analysis, intelligence studies and international relations, but also international institutions, organizations and research centres and universities, among others.

The current chapter follows a continued analysis and examination of various issues and variables and events to including May 2020. The chapter includes an extended discourse analysis that results to concrete recommendations. It comforts on the importance of cyber-security and NATO in 2020 and recommends ways towards a fast pace more universal operational capacity on cyber-security that is to serve towards the increasing cyber-demands for security and will reassure faster safety from various dimensional forms of digital vulnerabilities.

By the time of completion of this chapter (May 2020), swift changes continue to take place. The global Covid-19 pandemic has created for and in cyberspace vast, ample 'opportunities'. Ironically, liaised how to operate, do business and protect the world wide web, during and after this global pandemic. Cyber-space now offers a great deal of options related with new firmware among others, but also software tools. It also however increased malicious vulnerabilities. The global pandemic of Covid-19 corona virus, has made us all reflect from our own scientific and professional points of view on the operational and tactical protection mechanisms and methods that cyber-security should include both a personal and civilian level but also at military level namely of the NATO alliance.

2. NATOs' Cyber-Defence 'Story'

NATO's Cyber-defence 'story' backbone dates back to 2002, when NATO decided to strengthen and re-evaluate, its military capabilities including cyberspace. A new space would come along, where NATO would need to operate in, towards the near future. The aim was clear: to establish a clear security understanding at any emerging and future threats at the time, to include future cyber-attacks.

---

[1] The author is conducting an ongoing a research on and about cyber-security titled "Falkons' Maze on Cyber-Security". Expected date of publication is in 2021 contracted by Springer Nature USA.

The need for cyber-security was first acknowledged about 18 years ago at the Prague NATO Summit of 2002 (NATO Prague Summit 2002). NATO member states at the time, agreed that NATO cyber-policy was in fact needed. Infrastructure became more network centric, while infrastructure constantly needs to be renewed. Cyber-Defence and security became a steady and increasing necessity. Cyber-Defence became a defence policy in 2008 and consequently followed on in 2011. It needed however to be examined, analysed, jointly decided and policy adopted. Cyber-Defence is now ever adaptive; it is operational and reflective to current and future emerging threats. At all NATO summits, there is always an important referral to cyber-security itself.

Historically, the 2002 Prague Summit first marked NATO's tasking authority committee with regards to all activities that should be held in relations to Cyber-Defence. As technical achievements was delivered, so policy-makers delivered policy results on Cyber-Defence. That is why, Allied leaders during the Riga Summit of 2006 acknowledged the need to include these as is stated on its decisions at the Press Communiqué: (1) to protect NATO's operational information systems, and (2) to protect its allied countries from any e-, or in other words cyber-attacks by new forms and means developed by NATO's Allied Command Transformation (ACT) In Norfolk Virginia.

In the aftermath of the sudden cyber-attacks in Estonia in 2007, the informal Meeting of the Ministers of Defence in October 2007 of NATO, gave way and thus resulted to the inauguration of NATO's Centre for Excellence (COE) (NATO Informal Defence Ministers meeting 2007). This led to become the 'Allied Command Transformation on Cyber-Defence', named as Cooperative Cyber-Defence Centre of Excellence, CCDCOE (CCDCOE 2008). It was based, on the Concept and early understanding of cyber-resilience for NATO's future policies in countering challenges and threats, as was agreed by NATO's Military Committee.

18 years later, NATO's Cyber-policy has become a strategy, now a defence pillar of NATO. It was at the Wales Summit in 2014, that Cyber-defence became a core element of NATO's collective defence pillars (NATO Wales Summit 2014). By 2016, NATO allies recognized and reaffirmed cyber-space as the new space for military operations (NATO Cyber-Defence 2016). A new virtual area, which needed to be secured from virtual challenges and threats. Allies pledged to continue to enhance while network infrastructure with relations to internet cyber-defence and security with the creation of the CYOC Cyber-Security Operations Centre in Mons Brussels which will be fully functional by 2023. The idea is convergence at the level of cyber-security protection mechanisms and processes.

In 2020, cyber-security has become a priority for NATO. Both at military and civilian levels. Cyber-defence and security, is ever needed and ever tactical in the framework of operations. While the world becomes virtually more interconnected, NATO's cyber-security strategy, operational capabilities, constant preparedness and operational efficiency are evidently proven and constantly tested. Now a true challenge is for NATO to support civilian member's assets in the fight against cyber-threats and possible malicious attacks.

The recent outbreak of the global pandemic of the Corona Covid-19 virus, gave way to an increased use of current technological tools and software as well as increased internet use. This meant an increased flow of cyber-attacks including also in the civilian cyber-space; it meant increased vulnerabilities and attempts to measure attempts against it; threats coming from IOT attacks (Internet of Things) attacks. This added mere pressure to each government to step up on security measures: to increase the levels of secure networks and end to end lines and methods of communication, among others. And that is where NATOs' decision for a joined and unified form of cyber-defence falls into.

As of May 2020, Governments seek to operate methods of control against all possible current and new extended malicious e-vulnerabilities in cyber-space. NATO can support as a military organization the protective measures to be taken for internet protection systems, now. While is also considering strategies in a cyber-comprehensive cooperation framework for the future. NATO can jointly act as a collaborator and coordinator between members states and can support any level of cyber-protection against malicious attacks.

In 2020, as aforementioned, we evidently see a strong technological boost. All things change. And they change fast. Some may say, faster than one would anticipate. Smart systems and smart adaptiveness entails more today. While cyber threats and challenges are ever more evident. Attacks are more legally and criminally bonded, as attacks become more malicious and damaging. The pandemic Covid-19 Corona virus, has made possible a fast-forward pace of digital socio-political economic and military evolution. It aimed us towards an all-inclusive bundle of services through the 'matrix'; meaning the world of the internet. It was however a sudden 'virtual upgrade'; personal and professional 'internet upgrade'. Covid-19, has made the internet to maybe be the most important commodity and service at this time. It has made the internet look as the most optimal supply chain of information and services acquired in less than a millisecond/minute.

If the internet and its services provided through was not a necessity to date, it certainly is now. As foresaid, the bundle of services through the internet holds options, methods of work innovation and pleasure. Integration into the 'matrix of the internet' is a social move. It moves towards e-socialization and efficiency in doing business or providing social pleasures. However the internet does need regulation; it needs a world-wide synchronized international and national regulations, to be placed under the spectrum of a legal framework; operational national and international 'protective custody' as increasingly the internet can become hybrid in the nature of threats and vulnerabilities to be exposed.

Therefore, both a universal/global legal and operational management and collection protection mechanism needs to be put in place. New infrastructural capacities should be build. To offer capabilities on innovative software and hardware measures related to the world of the internet. The internet is a platform of change. It leads the way towards a 'digitized society'. Our world will now more than ever and in a fast pace, become digitized forever and ever again. As the Matrix will grow so will complexities and vulnerabilities.

The 'Matrix' system that we anticipate may meet our 'science fiction' we see, explore and describe over books and films or virtual games to date: with regards to the potential and threats accumulated through the use of the internet. We will see soon the creation of cyber-robotics and cyber-mechanics and engineering among others. We will see the merger between genetic engineering and robotics what we called in the 80s cyborgs.

High-level technological innovation and advancement will come forth. Knowledge transfer and creativity, robotics and genetic engineering combined with cloud computing and the next level of artificial intelligence among others, will lead the way in to the future of the 4th Industrial Revolution marking the start possibly of the 5th Industrial Revolution. In fact we will notice a convergence of the 5th Technological Revolution. The internet will therefore continue to be the 'space' where social, political, legal, economic and military modifications will take place leading the way in how and when and from where we conduct business, individually, collectively, institutionally and at all civilian and non-civilian government levels.

We are to see grave and sudden changes in the social community market: The way we conduct our business, do our shopping our schooling and education and we protect our health, among others. In all of its capacity we are to see, a world-wide total internet wired society. Yet with an unprecedented upgrade, while people try to find ways to contain the psychological phenomenon of social distancing that may cause more damage in the long-term socially than Covid-19 but will allow for new e-social methods to take place. What is certain to point is that we do not know the limitation of the internet uses and upgrades. We do not know the conditions, with which we will be handling and operating professionally and privately e-platforms; how will we work and with which capacity; what are the regulations and related applications or other software with regards to the internet of things and how to protect our own private network systems provided by our internet consumer provider.

The internet is getting more and more visible and operationally noticeable. Both in poor and rich countries. And easy led technology and infrastructure eases the way, especially for poor or underdeveloped countries to lead on the way and upscale growth in the long-term. Where education of and about the web and its ample opportunities will lead on the world through a new stage of e-innovation and reconstruction of societies that are considered to date developing. We have not witnessed before such a change. Now more than ever, 'high-tech' and 'Smart policies and strategies' will now become a most centralized norm of application and with it more security risks and vulnerabilities to come forth during and after installation of new infrastructure.

Dependency to the world of the internet, comes with a cost. An ever more vulnerable e-world is open to malicious attacks. Coming back to our main topic, NATO has and will have a great role to play in both the military and the civilian sectors, considering the aforementioned challenges while its need to secure the effectiveness and operational capability of its Cyber-strategy when applied.

NATO's current cyber-strategy and its operational capacity is evidently taking shape. NATO will have to speed up process, due to the Covid-19 virus. The objective still stands. To complete operational capacity by 2023, NATO may need to alter course and become earlier operational in its cyber-security operations centre in Mons, to a least a percentage of operations, if allies do jointly decide for it. NATO's cyber operational command has in the meantime plenty to coordinate, synchronize and gain access onto. To become even more jointly cooperative between allies, adaptive, coordinated and efficient. It needs in the meantime to counter, current and new, hybrid threat environments and vulnerabilities, while at the same time build upon non-vulnerable secure-based processes and installations that are and can be used jointly by military and civilian assets in the protection against cyber-attacks. While the world becomes more interconnected NATO is to secure its strategic planning for a secure Euro-Atlantic area also in the field of cyber-defence and cyber-security.

We may therefore see more resilience from a strategic point of view with regards to cyber-defence and agility and adaptable interoperability in joined cyber-operations and cooperation. We may see more synchronized, single orchestrated tactically and coordinated military and civilian strategy against e-threats and vulnerabilities of various kinds and dimensions, which will be needed to counter existing and future emerging threats. A cell of national and international cooperation solid in nature, legal aspects and operational military and political assets is requires, to protect the citizen, the country/member or partner country with respect to NATO.

3. Cyber-Security as a Strategic Discipline

"Cyber-security is a strategy of both preventive and/or pre-emptive action" (Efthymiopoulos 2019). If one can assess the efficiency and practicality of cyber-security, can scientifically define cyber-security as a 3 way pillar that (a) policy orients, (b) strategically defines and (c) methodologically applies on cyber space. 'Cyber-defence and cyber-security' main objective is to constantly counter all and any threats that come about, vulnerabilities and malicious or non-malicious attacks.

For strategic decision-makers, and as such related with this chapter, cyber-security is a policy orientation. Cyber-defence and cyber-security is a policy recommendation but a joint agreement and more so a necessity. It was decided by consensus from all NATO member-states for the 21st century to exist as a new pillar of security in its application. By 2020, and considering the corona virus, we are now becoming more interconnected hitherto also more vulnerable than ever before.

Cyber-security is a discipline of political, military and technical (IT), academic science and holds a great operational and professional value. Many have based their life's profession and work on cyber-affairs and among others security. Cyber-security is a discipline because is a framework of operational virtual importance, where among others true creativity, research, development and innovation play a predominant role and hold an impact to our technological and digital world.

Cyber-security is an interdisciplinary science of information technology. Yet, its nature and process, reflects and affects directly other disciplines. As such, it has become an interdisciplinary science. To include namely, political, sociological, economic, medical and other technological and business sciences specialties related with security levelled but also creativity and innovation industries.

Practically today, cyber-space has become a new space for engagement in a digital world which is unfortunately yet, not as reliable as one may think. Cyber-space is yet to be efficiently globally and universally regulated. But one can still be creative through the cyber-space, and practical. Practice and exercise e-market and e-commerce methods to expand market knowledge, innovate methods of trade and operate professions. One can surely exercise economic commercial and trade power and can also exercise government, civilian and military power projection.

Alas, where opportunities exist so do cyber-challenges. Cyber-vulnerabilities and malicious attacks are evident today. Malicious activity takes place in cyber-space and more so in times from the comfort of ones' virtual activity, method rather than physical.

4. Setting the Stage

Considering the constantly emerging hybrid cyber-threats in a current and post-Covid-19 environment of the year 2020 and beyond, cyber-space ought to be universally regulated and controlled. As cyber-space provides ample space to manoeuvre but also to create troublesome situations.

Cyber-security is whether we like it or not, one of the most lucrative sciences due to its ample practical effects seen in the market world. It is a bundle of elements for business creativity and operations. It includes tools, research innovation on and about technology software and hardware. It is a method and strategy of approach. Cyber-Security is attractive as the world wide web develops. Cyber-space is not evident and visible, where physical presence is not needed.

Cyber-affairs and in fact cyber-defence or security, is so deep rooted into our social structure that our democracies, our development methods and processes and our defence systems are constantly affected (Carayannis et al. 2018). Many great authors and scientists have a high level interest on the strengths, weaknesses, opportunities and treats (SWOT) of cyber-security and defence. Also on the business set up, educational set up operational efficiency (cost), enhanced opportunities and innovation in future technology that comes forth.

In an emphatically influential geo-dimensional strategic environment, that looks into the future through the prism of, more and more cyber-space utilization, a detailed, comprehensive and realistic universal cyber-security strategy is required. Covid-19 corona virus, simplified threats methods and assessments, accelerated processes of malicious and non-malicious vulnerabilities and increased the numbers of vulnerable locations.

Considering the aforementioned, NATO aims towards a complete tactical operation capacity by 2023, based on a cyber-strategic plan which offers the opportunity to move forward considering the new social, civilian and military realities with regards to cyber-space. Adaptability and interoperability of forces are now in need so as to enforce and accelerate technological innovation and entrepreneurship (Efthymiopoulos 2019).

The current chapter as previously mentioned is an ongoing research on the very subject with previous important and on the spot various publications amalgamated together in our 2014 book on Cyber-Development, Cyber-Democracy and Cyber-Defence (Carayannis et al. 2014). It aim was to bring forward key writers and specialists on the subject with the main aim convergence of policies and strategies with regards to cyber-space. Even more so, proceeded further with an increase in topics, subjects and authors making an ever growing handbook depository of ideas, knowledge and information on topics related with cyber-space (Carayannis et al. 2018).

Cyber threats and malicious attacks are real. They are seen as asymmetrical and hybrid in nature. Destruction can take place and can move to lethal casualties. The future of e-safety, lays at the global estimation of cooperation against specified or approximate threats that are due to Covid-19 required now more than ever, as we move along into a complete value set of dependency.

NATO forces and cooperative forces to NATO, need to be continuously agile and technologically advanced. They need to offer insights and innovate for their own national and supranational alliance level interest. Cyber-Space has no borders. And as such there are no limitation where any hostile can operate from.

Our world is today completely and utterly depended on cyberspace. Which however as said before is unforeseen with challenges and threats. We need unified methods of operations. We need a universal legal force to put boundaries and limit non-regulated cyber-space. We need cyber-forces and a command that is characterized with flexibility, adaptability, operational and strategic command structure, based on high technologically sophisticated information 'coming in', but also being used while in training or through active operations. NATO's 2023 operational cyber defence command is working towards this aim and reasoning.

On a theoretical scale, the current chapter, requests for a cyber-security strategic universal framework adoption with which NATO resilience, adaptability and interoperability strategy will lead the way for a clear operational and tactical framework in case of cyber-attacks and all other kinds of defence that may compromise the notion of security for all NATO members based on Article 5 and 4 of the NATO Washington Treaty (NATO Washington Treaty 1949).

Being thoughtful of the cyber-space realities of things in a post Covid-19 environment is by itself a natural innovation. Yet we need to move ahead into a smarter and more operationally efficient future with a clear universal and NATO structure to operate strategically based on legal and political Cyber-security commands and control, that is resilient in nature. 'Cyber-rules of engagement' should not be complex in the 'matrix'. But only adaptive as convergence of societal structures continues to take place in a faster pace than ever before.

5. Practicality in Cyber-Strategy

By 2009, I had published my first scientific/academic cyber-article. It was published, not long after the Cyber-attacks in Estonia (Efthymiopoulos 2009). What made me interested in the subject was the style of the cyber-attack. It brought the country at a standstill with a push of a button. It astonished the world. At the time, NATOs new 21st century Strategic Concept identity and policies, would yet to be completed and announced. NATO's New Strategic Concept would only come about by 2010. Once member states of NATO would agree to it, by consensus. Cyber-defence or security would merely be a possibility, an action plan, a method and a policy, but would not be at the time considered a strategic defence pillar and an absolute necessity.

In contrast to NATOs action plan, my scientific opinion differed. And I made it sure to publish my position in this matter. It was published far earlier than the Strategic Concept: From as early as 2008, I had argued that we should expect that "future war-like operations to be held in a far more complicated level (cyber and technological way)" (Efthymiopoulos 2009). Which in fact would require NATO to look at the matter from a holistic, strategic point of view marking possibly cyber-defence or security to become a defence pillar NATO.

The requirement to hold cyber-defence as a pillar, as a strategy was nevertheless there. The attacks on Estonia in 2007, evidently shown why it should be a central pillar of defence. Now the only reason would be why one would concentrate into making cyber-security a strategic defence pillar. One would need a reason to concentrate on cyber-security. In turn, why would one believe that cyber-operations would increase? 12 years later, by 2020, it is evident why.

The market in 2020, is more converged for use in cyber-space than ever before. And that includes both civilian and military assets, cyber commodities and services amongst others. NATO is ever needed politically (in protecting the civilian infrastructure and militarily). NATOs cyber security strategy requires the Alliance to enhance its cyber-agility in its operational field, to continue to hold interoperable abilities of its forces and to be adaptable to all technological advances.

NATOs' infrastructure and operational command is to become completely operational, by 2023. Cyber-Defence (2019) requires NATO to work in both civilian and military capacities as cyber-space does not limit itself to anything. Therefore concrete civilian-military-government cooperation would be required to tackle current and future threats. This entails NATO to hold state of the art interoperable military and political infrastructure preparedness forces (human capital) and to hold operational capacity and capability to lead on fights against all and any potential military and political/civilian threats through cyber-attacks. Considering the advances of cyber-technology in the years to come, NATO needs to continue to be adaptable. To become ever more e-flexible and use agile operational methods for the protection of its member states individually and collectively as per NATOs Washington Treaty assures.

The attacks in Estonia in 2007, seemed to be a 'technological wake-up call'. Yet, at the time seemed not to be enough to announce the creation of NATOs' cyber-security pillar for defence. It did however lead to the creation to the Excellence Centre of CCDCOE in Tallinn, Estonia (CCDCOE 2008). The only thing that a cyber-attack did in reality is to accelerate defence systems, help form cyber-defence companies while also transform the way we do business with more enhanced uses of cyber-space, namely in the world of e-governance and in specialized frameworks cyber-governance. E-commerce and providence of software for services at all levels was blossoming at the time. A strategic pillar however was lacking still. The events in Estonia would eventually boost technology agility, innovation research and development in all sectors not only the military and defence sectors, which would lead us to today's abilities and current outcomes, yet without a concrete operational and universal legal level of cyber-protection mechanisms and tools.

It had to be a global health pandemic in 2020, to make things become ever changing: among them, the reason and concentration on the importance and uses of the world wide web and in turn the importance to protect and regulate cyber-space while we increase our utilization of it. The pandemic made it abundantly clear that without an extensive use of the web, the world could and would come onto a real market standstill. It made it entirely clear that the Internet and its services provided can only help us operate aiming to the future. Aiming virtually in an environment, where however solitude is steadily becoming its main characteristic, the use of the web would increase. With it also vulnerabilities and cyber-threats.

I presume most of us, never considered how unlimited the world wide web is. The world wide web has become in fact in a short period of time, the most precious commodity. It links us all. And this is a true global change; a global simultaneous technological and web-based innovation. By May 2020 (at the time of the chapters' writing), we evidently see a convergence of our social structure, our work and all surrounding services and market economies through the world wide web. What we already do, or permit me to say, did not do, through the internet, is no longer a choice but is a must, that must go through the internet.

Nonetheless to date, many countries are yet to boost efforts, to move ahead into the world of cyber-space and although opportunity is there. By 2020, it is now more evident than ever before, that the internet has become a central pillar of our system of our society. With which we cannot live without. In 2020, the importance and utilization of opportunities granted of and from the use of the internet is important, as ever before. For without it, our economies and our society cannot be sustained or continue to grow. We are as much as interconnected as ever before. And therefore we should proceed to an extended version of global digitization formulation.

Needless to say, while we move along into the world of cyber-space, we do also become more depended and at the same time vulnerable. We are depended from the tools, methods and actions of the internet. We are now processing new ways, seen in the abilities of cloud computing, artificial intelligence and block-chain management among others. Tools and elements with which the use and utility of the internet and cyber-space is projected and enhanced. As without the use of the internet we would not know what currently takes place in the world in less than a minute, we would not be able to share information and we would not be able to reach to each other in any place over the planet in less than a second away.

It therefore so ironically happens that Estonia was in fact a great 'eye opener'. The effects of Estonia should have been understood at a 'strategic level' and should have been seen as a strategic challenge for the future for NATO in its complete formation and organization at the time. Cyber-security should have become back then, a strategic objective; a pillar of defence for NATO. It would however only be years later that cyber-security would become a central policy and today to expect a full operational capacity as cyber-security becomes a command centre in 2023. All countries, namely NATO member countries should have had to become cyber-interoperable, smart and achieve a strategic conceptualization and application of all kinds of uses against possible current and future cyber-security attacks a decade ago.

In contrast yet again, as all future like-minded person and younger at the time, I considered that cyber-space would become the new ground of strategic competence and therefore future or at least, the spot for a continuously emerging competition. But again, I would not see the reason why, expect the element of technological vulnerability that is attractive to hackers. Why one would implement a stronger attack. In the year 2020, however, things are so ever different. The Covid-19 Corona virus pandemic made utterly noticeable and possible for all systems and our global society to move online. A move that is swift and marks our daily lives as we have now moved to the virtual world of the web, almost in its totality.

6. NATOs' Strategic Resilience and Operational Efficiency in Cyber-Space

Strategic resilience is required in every pillar of NATOs strategic and operational defence. And more so, towards its cyber-security strategic planning and operations. Resilience is all about efficient dedication to the cause. It requires flexibility and adaptability to the current and future operational environment while challenges increase.

NATOs' vigilance and resilience in security affairs, defines strategic plans. It allows for re-assessment of risks that allow member states to think entrepreneurial and innovative. To propose methods for negotiation and adaptation by consensus. It makes NATO more adaptable onto the future of security affairs.

NATO is becoming more and more cyber-based. So much, that future pillars of NATO including the method of negotiations, and enlargement among others of NATO can and could be affected. Much work will be able to be completed remotely. Military and civilian operations will be handled in a more flexible but still secure operational environment, marking a cyber-security command operations the most important pillar for e-security working and operating cyber-space environment.

Resilience on future security affairs will render NATO easily adaptable to the new and future emerging threats, so far as the strategic objective are clear. However, NATOs adaptation process should have a completion date. It should conform to being prepared for all kinds of cyber operational defence measures.

In 2016, strategic report of the Atlantic Council of the USA referred to NATOs smart defence and strategic resilience a 'stability generation' policy (Kramer et al. 2016), adding that NATO's collective defence itself should be re-strategized. In 2020, we still assume that NATOs' strategic policy vis a vis cyber-defence among others, should be adaptable to the constantly ever more increasing needs in a post pandemic 2020 environment. It is recommended that NATO ensures technological secure and agile operational environment, in a period of grave challenges and emerging threats from remote areas in the world, yet also could take place from within NATO's members and cyber-space.

7. NATOs' Current State of Cyber-Affairs

"Future war-like operations will be held in a far more complicated level of military operations" (Efthymiopoulos 2009). Current military operational and tactical needs, considering the asymmetrical and multi-dimensional environment, require good and agile capacities and capacity building. Joined forces themselves, require proper command and operations. They require agility but also resilience into the cause.

We live in an age "in which more and more people have access to highly sophisticated technologies and almost every social, economic or military asset has become 'securitized' or vulnerable to disruption—whether temporary or more lasting—from an outside attacker or even an inside source...In a globalized but also more confrontational and complex world, resilience will remain an ongoing concern for Allies, requiring constant adaptation as new vulnerabilities and threats emerge (Efthymiopoulos 2009)".

By mid-2020, operations are conducted within the complexity of what was initially termed as 'matrix environment'. One that requires efficiency, efficacy and ability to operate in cyber-space. The use of technology necessitates, accuracy and efficiency so as to hold success in operational defence. Interoperability of forces require constant technological adaption to the operational digital environment considering always current and emerging threats as they arrive.

When NATO leaders first considered cyber-security as a policy, questions were raised on how to find a smart way and operational way to use technology for its benefit both operationally and strategically in a fast and technologically advancing world.

With the complete operational preparedness of the cyber security command in 2023, NATO forces will be fully committed to cyber-operational capacity. In the meantime, NATO is required to counter threats and challenges under the operational rules of engagement; in various possible cyber-dimensions. Counter symmetrical and asymmetrical, attacks, threats or challenges which would fall under article 4 and 5 of the Washington Treaty on its rules and conditions of engagement (NATO Treaty 1949).

Since the adoption of the NATO Cyber-Defence policy (NATO 2011), NATO is constantly training its forces on Cyber-defence. NATO is to be fully committed to a joint operational structure as foretold by 2023. Training can be achieved through national, bilateral even multilateral levels of NATO, through the association of member states, but also through the level of Centres of Excellence, such as the NATO Cooperative Cyber Defence Centre of Excellence CCDCOE "a multinational and interdisciplinary cyber defence hub" (CCDCOE 2008). By 2023, NATO is expected to be completely committed to 'defence' in cyber-space. To be enabled to counter by consensus decision of the 30 as of today NATO members, multiple and multileveled dimensions of cyber-attacks. Yet, it also holds an open option if necessary, to conduct counter-offensives to prevent further escalation of cyber or military actions (Hughes 2009).

NATO Missions, "will continue to require agile and interoperable, well-trained and well-led military forces" (Hughes 2009). This new technological and operational environment through cyber-defence, provides NATO with a new level of technological possibilities; new tools for use against possible threats but also protective 'cyber-objectives'.

August 13th 2019 is an important date. To what was aforesaid, Allies have taken a clear policy decision. They created a new operational reality. A mission, of strategic value and orientation (Cyber-Defence 2019). Ongoing and constant digital and electronic operational transformation through its cyber-resilience strategy will enable to build on its future capacity. NATO will in turn meet its political excellence related with future and emerging challenges.

NATO is aiming for well-operated well-coordinated missions in cooperation with and/or participation with other international organizations, when prompted to react on international threats or challenges in cyberspace. NATO's cyber-operational command of 2023, is expected to show case NATOs ability to be a security provider, delivering an 'online' security protection initiative against all possibly known threats.

If NATOs' cyber-defence capabilities are efficient, then we can surely talk about a smart and resilient way of the future, 'towards a framed operational goal', reaching to what I called it some 8 years ago Smart Defence:[2] a policy framework for tactical advice and operational defence, used for among others to brand the need for a cyber-defence policy.

NATO's Cyber-resilience, adopted during the Warsaw Summit in July 2016 has been reflective ever since, to the July NATO Brussels summit of 2018 (NATO Brussels Summit 2018), and also during the NATO London Declaration of 2019 (NATO London Summit 2019). What is clearly implied, is that NATO is expected to take continued actions through standardized procedures for operational effectiveness, innovation openness and adaptation through its technological agencies, to reach full operational capacity by 2023.

NATO military forces should therefore reach to appropriate operational and tactical levels, so as to operate in and around "article and non-article 5 operations" (Sendmeyer 2010) meaning not only defensive-clause operations but also in counter-offensive operations. Cyber-protection and cyber-security methods are needed.

NATO Cyber-Defence policy, will be required to constantly transform, as threats emerge. Technology will continue to progress. While a world of insecurity continues to emerge. Estonia's cyber-attacks was only the beginning at the time. Since then many attacks and threats took place all over cyber-space. A strong smart cyber-defence 'umbrella' is therefore needed. And NATO can provide for such a military and civilian if needed capacity to operate in cyber-space. Its operational centre will hold agility, adaptability and resilience to all future emerging challenges and threats, to be achieved at a constant pace.

8. Cyber-Security Adaptability and Liability at NATO

Considering current NATO's strategic decisions on its cyber-command and operations, one needs to stress that cyber-space is unlimited. And while NATO needs to operate within the legal framework as adopted by the Washington Treaty of 1949 based on article 4 and article 5 operations, cyber-space is yet to be universally regulated. And this is the job of another organization to complete. Namely the United Nations. While a universal regulation takes place, NATOs' cyber-security liability needs to be enabled to meet both current and future challenges ahead. To become as foresaid adaptable to the realities of cyber-space today and into the future, while agility, flexibility and operational status characterizes its various dimensional operational environments.

As such, we may stress that while get onto a universal cyber-space agreement and constitution, NATO's role in cyber-space in the meantime, could become expeditionary and pre-emptive, not defence-led solely. It could be pro-active. Not solely reactive. It could operate in an environment that should be in the meantime, universally accepted and regulated, presumably through the Security Council and the

---

[2] NATO Watch, organized its own "Shadow Summit of NATO's Washington Summit of 2012", http://www.natowatch.org/node/676 on May 14–15, 2012 at The Elliott School of International Affairs, The George Washington University Washington, DC. In it I presented a first idea on what is Smart Defence and what it means for NATO. For more information, you can visit USAs' Cspan. See a recorded the speech on NATO here: http://www.c-spanvideo.org/mariosefthymiopoulos.

General Assembly first of the United Nations. Only then would, NATO be enabled to overview operations and limitations to what constitutes real cyber-defence in action.

NATOs' role in this is clear: as a military organization, NATO is a force projector, force planner, force multiplier, force initiator and force applicator. These operational projections reflect NATO strategic ethics of safeguarding and securing our cyber-space and environment (Efthymiopoulos 2019).

Cyber-vulnerabilities and threats considering multidimensional challenges require NATO to be truly, strategically and operationally agile. It requires NATO to be adaptable to conditions unforeseen.

Considering technological advancements and considering the challenges that are laying ahead of us in a post Covid-19 Corona virus pandemic world, we are yet to acquaint ourselves, our institutions, governments and international organizations with true phenomena of a new, yet networked global governance methodology and e-society. In this borderless society, where, electric grids, information or installations failures may have in the past solely affect a country, now affect a region and possibly a larger area. Our abilities are limitless to point out challenges and face them. We also have the ability to innovate through methodological approaches and security cooperation utilizing the constant upgrade of technology. However, when decisions come to being this may not be easy.

In a new virtual world of things, where the internet has managed to innovate, eliminate, distances and borders but also time, NATO should be set to comply with the new 'global rules and standards of operational business-minded and political efficiency'. It should create agile and limitless policies, security basic and specialized military and civilian installation if NATO is to continue to be a crisis management international security organization.

9. Analysing and Associating Cyber-Resilience with NATO's 'Smart-Defence': "Engagement through Policy Adaptation"

Many steps have been taken towards a resilient framework on cyber-space. Yet, overall NATO lacks still its 'smart defence' capabilities. An overall strategic reorientation process for a truly smart defence for the Alliance and its future capabilities is required. In a 'smart world' one should decide how decisions should be taken; with which methods of communication and approach. Possibly this would mean an entirely new strategic plan of operations, yet not a renewed strategic concept for the Alliance. It would be based on the notion of technological agility and future simplification in utilization of high-tech tools. In a post pandemic virus environment this could well may be considered as an early assessment on and about the future daily operational and managerial work at NATO.

To date, fiscal austerity was the obstacle for NATO member states to invest in overall smart defence of the NATO alliance, according to the Chicago Council on Global Affairs (Chicago Council of Global Affairs 2012). Strategically, the Atlantic Council, further had stressed that "…The Alliance, given its new strategic landscape, currently finds itself in, requires a new strategy. NATO's current three core tasks— collective defence, crisis management, and cooperative security—are "tasks" but not strategies—they do not identity the full spectrum of ends, ways, and means, and therefore do not tell the Alliance and its members either what to do or the risks involved. NATO has been working diligently but without great clarity or common agreement as to its end goals (Kramer et al. 2016)".

"Defence capacity building for the 20th century requires a modern way of thinking. It is about encouraging cooperative defence at the level of expected outcomes considering global but also regional risk assessments. NATO is still to enhance but also maintaining military capacities and military capabilities" (Efthymiopoulos 2019).

NATO force command, technology and methodological approach in military elements and standards cannot be or remain static. They need to technologically advance, progress methodologically and innovate; accommodate for the increasing need for multi-dimensional ways of security and defence. NATO needs to have interoperable, capable and well equipped technologically agile forces considering innovation and thinking entrepreneurial in a period of technological cooperative security.

Throughout the attempt to achieve a truly cooperative defence, 'smart defence' stands out as a policy option. Based on renewing operational and tactical effectiveness; an innovation and business led orientation for political, tactical and future operational coordination of the Alliance. It is all about specialization and interoperability of forces mainly through technological agility. By 2020, in a period of much needed for strategic and tactical resilience, smart defence stands out as a request for geo-political capability and capacity building; so as to implement operational preparedness and effectiveness; reflective in operations both on a regional and global scale of operations including to operate in cyber-space.

Smart defence is still NATO's priority policy. But this is not yet evident. It does allow for defence entrepreneurial thinking and application, so far as cyber-security is extended. Constant changes in strategy and policy do request efficient leadership and management skills to operate. And so, should NATO's cyber-resilience strategy to operate in a complete capacity by 2023.

Smart defence is prioritized as a method of innovative approach and more so related to innovative approached with an extensive use to technology statecraft. It will allow for NATO forces to enhance the command and structure of operations, through the following steps: (1) Sound strategic structuring and planning for future that is not there just yet; (2) Good operational coordination in exercises and in the field, (3) A new strategy on specialization of force structure, command and operations based on sound technological utility and agility (4) Achieving collective defence, through collective efforts, (5) Sound burden-sharing (6) technological creativity, development and advancements, considering emerging threats and challenges such as in cyber-space.

All 30 member states need to move forward towards the extra mile; to negotiate or mitigate current state of affairs and allow for innovation and forecast the future of security affairs. NATO should push for renewed strategic reports to come about on future challenges and threats. In the meantime, member states should elaborate more, and framework on how to change daily civilian and military day to day operations, strategizing the future. Elaborate and concentrate more on the digital transformation of the Alliance's economic, political, military and management innovation and efficacy of administrative efficiency in a sound cyber-security environment.

The framework policy of 'smart defense', would in turn give a boost to the cyber-defence command. It would allow for consultations to take place and for the command to become more operationally visible on a day to day operations, not only threats. While transformation towards the future continues to comes about. Eventually, a digital transformation overall of NATO, would render cheaper the cost for the total sharing of burden by member states; while attract more innovation while technology would actually in the long-term minimize costs.

At a time of a global pandemic virus, while also newly austerity measures to take place, we are expected to see political and military changes. Emerging challenges (non-military) within and outside (global trade wars and emerging military threats), the Euro-Atlantic area. Countries of NATO, are yet to realise how a pragmatic and realistic forecasting takes place, through smart and innovative 'budget for daily' and long-term management and operations including operations being conducted through a secure cyber-space.

While smart defence lowers overall long-term cost, burden sharing becomes more viable as an option. In a digital world there can be lower levels of fiscal sharing, more optimal long-term results, better production and feasibility in assuring security in the networked landscape of NATO. The cost will be equally associated with the value of services provided that operational services such as the new cyber-security command will reflect the needs of strategic management and planning of all 30 member states.

While, national and collective defence remains at the forefront of interests of states, a new 'rapprochement' is needed between member states as threats are now borderless.

Cyber-defence, is a strategy. But is also a core policy leading to smart defence itself. It works as a 'decree of specialization', which now requires adaptation to the current state of affairs in 2020. Cyber-defence policy must and should always be provided as a methodological tool for operational success of NATO and operational daily work at NATO. It should also be created to face current and emerging and lasting threats. Cyber-defence can and should always be a tool for a joint framework of cooperation, regionally and globally.

As smart defence is being upgraded and developed, Cyber-defence "...not a conception but a real-politic issue...(Kramer et al. 2016)", should remain an element of specialization policy, a key for concrete strategic engagement of all resilient member states. It will emerge to become a policy of innovative unity among states (political) yet also business continuity (strategic orientation) about the future of NATO (The entrepreneurial and managerial side of things).

NATO's strategic approach post Warsaw, Brussels and London summits, is estimated to reflect a much needed realistic plan of operations and engagement in the field of cyber-security and defence. NATO should continue to be a collective to be a force projector and force protector. It should not limit its role and actions but should allow and seek out enlarged cooperation tailored to the global and regional needs to counter the existing challenges or emerging challenges, considering that as aforementioned challenges are now borderless.

Cyber-defence and technological progress within NATO, can therefore be seen as the core of collaborative smart defence. Smart Defence is to be realized in a post 2023 operational framework and standards while cyber-security holds a complete clear picture of operational command, as things stand as of today.

With challenges raised by cyber-dimensions namely darknet, cyber-defence, as a strategy in security affairs becomes a necessity. An absolute importance in the Alliances' business continuity, innovation, legal, political and economic framework. NATO needs for its viable future, to become operational. From then on, define a solid high-tech led future in security policy, operation, orientation, adaptability in the how to conduct military and civilian business and operations through cyber-space.

Innovative changes through technology agility and development will simply put pressure to NATO to change. To reflect market needs and security concerns; for NATO to meet the 'smartest and easiest way' to operate at a time of financially and socially emerging markets, where non-member states require individual or tailored cooperation and less fiscal implications and human resources with NATO. It will facilitate NATOs expeditionary role for force projector, trainer and crisis management operator, as an "…active leader in peace and security (NATO 2016)" through innovation and methodological approach of entrepreneurship.

10. NATO's Cyber-Defence Tendencies in 2020

It was NATO's Military Committee's decision to adopt a 'Cyber-Defence Concept' (Kramer et al. 2016). It is also the Military Committee's aim in 2020 to continue delivering business continuity and military resilience in 2020 and more so on and about cyber-space in conjunction with other Fusion aspects, to include CIS (communication and information systems) and technical aspects such as the NATO Communication and Information Agency -NCIA- (NATO NCIA), the NATO Systems Group -NCISG- (NATO NCISG) among them.

NATO is a provider of collective defence. And as a collective organization in a globalised and currently unsafe e-world, the Alliance needs to be constantly agile, adaptive and flexible to new and emerging challenges. In an environment of complete global insecurity, the Alliance' delivers new policy results. Taking into perspective new forms of asymmetrical threats, such as cyber-attacks.

The implementation of NATO's Cyber-Defence strategy is considered as a most important decision and therefore security pillar of NATO. The 'Concept of Cyber-Defence' is seen to this day as an added value to the strategic concept of NATO.

NATO's cyber-strategy, policy and activity is 'encouraged' by Allies. The aim is to adapt the alliance to the new strategic and security environment that as we now know is "hybrid". To engage as many as possible governments, industry related market companies and individuals. In accordance to its best practice policy, NATO considers that its 'operational forum' can and should be considered as the best joint operational co-operation between states and market, as to also avoid duplication of efforts and use the necessary global knowledge to achieve interoperability of force action and command also in cyber-space.

Practically, NATO had adopted 'phases of practical activity and cooperation' on the road to a complete operational readiness to cyber-security: The initial phase included a NATO Computer Incident Response Capability (NCIRC). It was established as 'interim operating capability' for NATO to build up on both security risk and manage the element of cyber-threats. Its second phase involved an ever more realistic and pragmatic perspective that required the co-ordination of all initial 'offering' states to the attempt to establish a Cyber-Centre (under the NATO agreement between states of a voluntary national contribution – VNC), in bringing the NCIRC to a full operational capability (NATO NCIA). And this is where things stand as of today. The CYOC is expected to be fully operational by 2023.

11. NATO Adaptation to Cyber-Security

By 2020, there is a clear need for better awareness, readiness and adaptation to cyber-security and its importance in a swiftly changing world. Allies, must decide for a robust long-term planning innovative and entrepreneurial strategy for current and future operations of NATO including at the level of Cyber-security. Keeping in mind the need for strong success in field operations, including success in and at a multi-dimensional level of operations against all emerging threats while making operations to be cost efficient with minimum human casualty numbers.

NATO increasingly recognizes that organized cyber-attacks seek to take advantage of 'gaps' in the 'social system and the market matrix' and more so during a covid-19 and post virus era. Therefore, it should be a request from member states to examine the increasing need for co-ordination of human factors related to the issues of electronic warfare, operational network, intelligence and Cyber-Defence, whether for training, scientific exchange and or operations. And presumably so, all training will take place, as was decided in the London summit to take place at the premises of the CCDCOE in Tallinn Estonia.

NATO is currently using people involved physically through, e-security, IT engineers, researchers and military officers dealing with network operations and operational centres as well as professional and academics giving way to a larger discussion on the future of cyber-security. It is the assumption that during this swift period of change within 2020 and beyond, specialists in the field on both a strategic and tactical levels, should be systematically involved at organized levels of research, sharing, discussion and exhibition of outcomes, which will in turn enrich the abilities, capabilities and capacities of rendering current smart-defence and cyber-defence as a key and successful resilient and collaborative defence policy to NATO.

12. Recommendations and Proposals

NATO's level of ambition in cyber-defence should be considered for the future. A forecast report should be drafted. A future strategy as well. A much needed, resilient policy is needed for operational efficiency post 2023 is needed for the domain of NATO's cyber-space and Cyber-Defence. It should be approached from the perspective of military and civilian innovation, inclusion of operations with other organizations and civilian entities with non-military as well businesses. This should in turn reflect parts of the cyber-security agenda in the next NATO summit. Specialized policy against hybrid threats should be adopted. A specialized commitment of Allies to share information and simplify procedures for cooperation with cyber-companies in electronic warfare should increase.

NATO should and could do more, on a strategic level by:

1) Sharing concrete information on status of security affairs on cyber-defence and cyber-security within and among member states but also with non-NATO members.

2) NATO should enhance global cooperation with non-member states in the field of electronic security and safety, as there is an increasing of cooperation level with external members from around the globe.

3) During the following summit meeting of NATO, Allies should agree on forecasting command methods of operations and emerging threats of the future.

4) NATO should reach out for interoperability levels for NATO forces for 2023. Where smart defence stand out. Where operational and fiscal standards that are long-term viable, reflecting the efficiency and operations through cyber-platforms.

5) A joined NATO and non-NATO yet allied co-operation at the level of electronic-warfare prevention, detection and reaction to attacks towards member allied states is required.

6) Legally, a universal cyber-understanding of what constitutes, a crime, should in the meantime be achieved. NATO-UN cooperation framework could be the platform of request to examine the universality of what and how cyber-defence can be achieved and how offenders (physical or virtual) can be stopped.

It is crucial for NATO to achieve cyber-interoperability of force command and structures through a methodological and innovative application.

Tactically, NATO needs to do the following:

1) Adapt to reflective hybrid threats in a cyber-environment.

2) Assess future warfare operations through the cyber-space environment.

3) A future foresight agency is required to enable unlimited procedures and reports on not only emerging threats but also future combination of threats including to cyber-space.

4) NATO should allow for alliance progress through resilience on all operational levels which involve the creation of interoperable cybernetic command structure and technologically agile cyber-military forces for all levels of 'analogical and digital' engagement of forces in electronic warfare. These should be flexible, reliable and be enabled to operate from remote areas.

13. Conclusion

This chapter examined NATO's policy on cyber-security and its adaptability to the emerging challenges in 2020. The chapter recommended measures based on strategic and tactical levels, so as to accomplish a complete cyber-security policy efficiency by the time of its cyber-security command operations centre in 2023.

The Corona Virus Covid-19 global human pandemic has led our society fast forward onto a pace that renders us completely dependent on the tools but also threats generated by the world wide web. In this new world order, cyber-affairs are an 'eye-opener'. While we integrate to a new matrix in operating deeper through cyber-space, we need to continue to bid on operational and tactical agility, adaptability and flexibility. We need to go beyond traditional methods of operations and with it future operations. More so in the field of cyber-defence and security, which constitutes one of NATO's defence pillars.

NATOs' predicament is in fact to continue to hold a pragmatic operational approach, reflect real-time protection and defence methods between NATO members and its allies in as well cyber-space, at a time of change in geostrategic and geopolitical affairs. Cyber-defence is a key strategy for NATO. In 2020 it is a key priority. It is innovative. Yet it does require good understand of future management skills and operational efficiency when networked centric, within the framework of a cyber-operational NATO of 2023.

This chapter evidently demonstrated the necessity and need of military cyber-defence policy. The chapter analysed the policy of smart-defence in its cyber-security action framework. It provided the reader with an updated information up to May 2020, on NATOs' cyber-defence strategy and policy. It projected proposals and expectations for a resilient cyber-strategy in view of a new dawn, in a post 2023 cyber-operational year. The chapter commended on NATOs' current cyber-operational efforts. The chapter has set proposals for future consideration on effective and enhanced cyber-management, considering that our world in a post Covid-19 global pandemic will be more interconnected than ever before. Cyber-defence at NATO is expected to become an even more important pillar at NATO. It will ultimately reflect all future operations and defences on and against any kind of electronic malware attacks.

References

Carayannis, E., Campbell, D. and Efthymiopoulos, M. P. (eds.). 2014. Cyber-Development, Cyber-Democracy and Cyber-Defense. Springer. New York, USA.

Carayannis, E., Campbell, D. and Efthymiopoulos, M. P. (eds.). 2018. Handbook of Cyber-Development, Cyber-Democracy and Cyber-Defense. Springer. New York, USA.

Efthymiopoulos, M. P. 2009. NATO's security operations in electronic warfare: the policy of cyber-defence and the alliance new strategic concept. Journal of Information Warfare 8: 3.

Efthymiopoulos, M. P. 2019. A cyber-security framework for development, defense and innovation at NATO. Journal of Innovation and Entrepreneurship (Springer) 8(12): 26.

Global Affairs, Council Chicago. Conference: Smart Defence and the future of NATO. Smart Defence and the future of NATO. March 28–30, 2012. Chicago: Chicago Council of Global Affairs.

Hughes, Rex. B. 2009. NATO and Cyber-Defence: Mission Accomplished? US Army War College N1: 4. Carlisle. USA.

Kramer, Fraklin D., Binnendijk Hans and Hamilton Daniel S. 2015. NATO's New Strategy: Stability Generation. Atlantic Council of the USA; Brent Scowcroft Centre on International Security. Washington DC, USA https://www.atlanticcouncil.org/wp-content/uploads/2015/09/NATOs_new_strategy_web.pdf.

NATO. 2016. NATO Operations and Missions: Past and Present. Accessed May 5, 2020. http://www.nato.int/cps/en/natohq/topics_52060.htm.

NATO. 2019. NATO's role in cyber-space. 12 February. Accessed May 20, 2020. https://www.nato.int/docu/review/articles/2019/02/12/natos-role-in-cyberspace/index.html.

NATO London Summit. 2019. 4 December. Accessed May 20, 2020. https://www.nato.int/cps/en/natohq/official_texts_171584.htm.

NATO Brussels Summit. 2018. NATO. 18 August. Accessed May 3, 2020. https://www.nato.int/cps/en/natohq/official_texts_156624.htm.

NATO NCIA Agency. 2016. Accessed May 24, 2020. https://www.ncia.nato.int.

NATO Cyber-Defence. 2011. NATO Cyber-Defence Policy. Accessed May 20, 2020. http://www.nato.int/cps/en/natolive/topics_78710.htm.

NATO Cyber-Defence. 2016. NATO Cyber-Defence Fact sheet. July. Accessed May 4, 2020. https://www.nato.int/nato_static_fl2014/assets/pdf/pdf_2016_07/20160627_1607-factsheet-cyber-defenceeng.pdf.

NATO Summit Wales. 2014. NATO Wales Summit. 4 September. Accessed May 5, 2020. http://www.nato.int/cps/en/natohq/events_112136.htm.

NATO Strategic Concept. 2010. NATO. June. Accessed May 01, 2020. https://www.nato.int/strategic-concept/index.html.

NATO CCDCOE. 2008. CCDCOE. Accessed May 20, 2020. https://www.ccdcoe.org/.

NATO Informal Defence Ministers Meeting. 2007. NATO. Accessed May 24, 2020. http://www.nato.int/docu/comm/2007/0710-noordwijk/0710-mod.htm.

NATO NCISG, NATO NATO Communication and Information Systems Group. Accessed May 24, 2020. https://ncisg.nato.int

NATO Prague Summit. 2002. NATO Prague Summit. Accessed May 01, 2020. http://www.nato.inr/docu/comm/2002/0211-prague/.

NATO Washington Treaty. 1949. NATO. Accessed May 5, 2020. https://www.nato.int/cps/en/natolive/official_texts_17120.htm.

Sendmeyer, M. S. A. 2010. NATO Strategy and NATO Out of Area Operations. School of Advanced Military Studies; US Army Command & General Staff College. August. Accessed May 20, 2020. Fort Levenworth. http://www.hsdl.org/?view&did=713508.

Index

For Product Safety Concerns and Information please contact our EU
representative GPSR@taylorandfrancis.com
Taylor & Francis Verlag GmbH, Kaufingerstraße 24, 80331 München, Germany

www.ingramcontent.com/pod-product-compliance
Ingram Content Group UK Ltd.
Pitfield, Milton Keynes, MK11 3LW, UK
UKHW021003180425
457613UK00019B/789